DOWN THE SANTA FE TRAIL
AND INTO MEXICO

SUSAN SHELBY MAGOFFIN, IN 1845

From a daguerreotype.

DOWN THE SANTA FE TRAIL

AND INTO MEXICO

The Diary of
Susan Shelby Magoffin
1846-1847

EDITED BY
STELLA M. DRUMM
With a foreword by Howard R. Lamar

YALE UNIVERSITY PRESS
NEW HAVEN & LONDON

To

JANE TAYLOR

The Gentle Daughter of
Susan Shelby Magoffin

CONTENTS

ILLUSTRATIONS

A map showing the route of the expedition will be found overleaf, facing the Foreword.

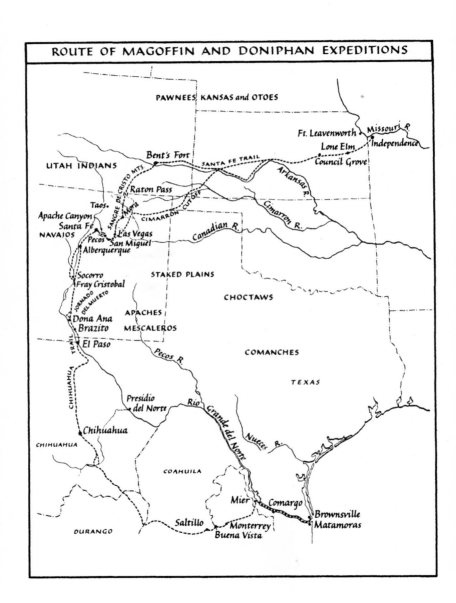

ROUTE OF MAGOFFIN AND DONIPHAN EXPEDITIONS

FOREWORD

by Howard R. Lamar

EARLY in June, 1846, Susan Shelby Magoffin, a pert, observant young lady of wealth and fashion set out from Independence, Missouri, on one of the most memorable frontier journeys ever made by an American woman. With her husband, Samuel Magoffin, a veteran Santa Fe trader, she was to cross the plains and mountains to the New Mexican capital, travel along the Rio Grande to El Paso del Norte, and then turn south into Chihuahua for a stay of several months. When she rejoined her family in Kentucky some fifteen months later she had a remarkable story to tell, for in all likelihood she was the first American white woman ever to go over the rude trail of the Santa Fe traders.

What made Susan Magoffin's trip historically significant as well as colorful and exciting, was not simply that she kept an excellent daily record of her experiences in the form of a journal, but that she traveled at a crucial time in the history of the trans-Mississippi West. As a member of her husband's large merchant caravan she was to see the Santa Fe trail in one of its busiest years of trade, a year when American goods valued at well over a million dollars were laboriously hauled more than a thousand miles into the northern provinces of Mexico.[1] But more im-

1. Max Moorhead, *New Mexico's Royal Road, Trade and Travel on the Chihuahua Trail* (Norman, Okla., 1958), p. 156, estimates that the value of goods in 1846 was well over a million dollars.

portant, it was Susan's luck to go west in "the year of decision," when American expansionist sentiment, guided by James K. Polk, resulted in the Mexican War and the eventual annexation of lands which would nearly double the size of the United States.

Mrs. Magoffin's encounters with the workings of Manifest Destiny were far from casual. Her husband's oldest brother, James Wiley Magoffin, another Santa Fe merchant, was also a government agent entrusted by President Polk with the task of preparing the way for a peaceful American occupation of New Mexico in 1846. James Magoffin's successful negotiations with General Manuel Armijo, governor of New Mexico, enabled Susan and her husband to enter Santa Fe only two weeks after General Stephen Watts Kearny had occupied that city. After being a keenly interested eyewitness to the New Mexican conquest, the couple followed the intrepid Colonel Alexander W. Doniphan and his Missouri Volunteers further down the trail into Chihuahua. There they sojourned in a troubled atmosphere of uncertainty, proud one moment of the exploits of Taylor, Wool, and Doniphan, and terrified the next of being murdered by an anti-American uprising. No disaster befell them, and in the early fall of 1847 they returned by vessel to the United States.

The circumstances which prompted Susan Magoffin to keep a journal of her travels were almost as romantic as the trip itself. She was only eighteen years old in 1846 and had been married to Samuel less than eight months at the time of the journey, so that it was, in part, an extended honeymoon safari. Although Magoffin was Susan's senior by some twenty-seven years, she was hopelessly in love with the tall, big-boned Kentuckian, and intrigued by his seemingly romantic and hazardous career as a frontier merchant. Ever since their marriage Susan had kept a journal of her travels and experiences. An initial honeymoon trip of six months to New York and Philadelphia filled an entire volume. On her western trek she began and completed a second notebook some eight and a half inches wide and ten inches long, which was partially bound in three-quarter calf. After about forty-nine pages of copied and original poems —mostly sentimental or concerned with love—the western diary proper starts: a neat, legible account some 206 pages in length, entitled "Travels in Mexico Commencing June, 1846. El Diario de Dona Susanita Magoffin." [2]

The account itself is full of personal items, and is given to many hero-worshiping references to *mi alma,* Susan's affectionate phrase for her husband. But even a superficial reading of this western volume reveals the extremely valuable historical material it contains about the Santa Fe trade in its heyday, Mexican life and customs, Kearny's conquest of New Mexico, and the progress of the Mexican War in the border provinces. As the original editor of the diary aptly commented: "In her simple and gentle way the young lady deftly raised the curtain from before characters

2. The original diary remains in the private possession of the heirs of the late Stella M. Drumm.

and events of great importance in American history." [3]

Unfortunately for the historian, Mrs. Magoffin's first-hand account remained securely hidden from public view until the late Stella M. Drumm, librarian of the Missouri Historical Society, persuaded Susan's daughter, Mrs. Jane Taylor, to permit its publication by the Yale University Press in 1926. Although many scholars of the American Southwest immediately recognized the great value of the journal, the volume attracted little attention at the time of publication. It was ignored by the *New York Times,* and a review did not appear in a single major historical journal until the *Hispanic American Historical Review* gave it a very favorable notice in 1928.[4] Since then, however, it has become both a standard and a distinguished item of Southwestern bibliography.

While it will never outrank Dr. Josiah Gregg's classic story of the Santa Fe trade in his *Commerce of the Prairies,*[5] Mrs. Magoffin's account deserves equal recognition with the letters of James and Robert Aull and the papers of James J. Webb.[6] Her

3. Stella M. Drumm, ed., *Down the Santa Fe Trail and into Mexico, 1846–1847* (New Haven, 1926), p. xi. Bernard De Voto, in *The Year of Decision, 1846* (Boston, 1961), p. 525, called it a "prime source."

4. James Alexander Robinson in the *Hispanic American Historical Review, 8* (1928), 114–16.

5. Josiah Gregg, *Commerce of the Prairies* (2 vols. New York, 1844).

6. Ralph P. Bieber, ed., "Letters of James and Robert Aull," *Missouri Historical Society Collections, 5* (St. Louis, 1927–28), 267–327. Idem, "The Papers of James J. Webb, Santa Fe

accurate and detailed descriptions of life and customs
are certainly as good as those found in Lewis Gar-
rard's *Wah-To-Yah and the Taos Trail* or F. A.
Wizlizenus' *A Tour to Northern Mexico, 1846–47*.[7]
Her coverage of the northern reaches of the Mexican
War is a useful supplement to the on-the-march ver-
sions by George R. Gibson, Frank S. A. Edwards,
John Taylor Hughes, and Philip St. George Cooke.[8]
Finally, Mrs. Magoffin's journal is far more per-
ceptive and detailed than Thomas J. Farnham's and
George F. Ruxton's superficial and often snobbish
writings about the Mexican borderlands.[9]

Trader, 1844–1861," *Washington University Studies*, 11 (St.
Louis, 1924), 255–305. James Josiah Webb, *Adventures in the
Santa Fe Trade, 1844–47*, ed. Bieber (Glendale, Calif., 1931).
Matthew C. Field, *Matt Field on the Santa Fe Trail*, ed. John E.
Sunder (Norman, Okla., 1960). Archer B. Hulbert, ed., *South-
west on the Turquoise Trail: The First Diaries on the Road to
Santa Fe* (Denver, 1930).

7. Lewis H. Garrard, *Wah-To-Yah and the Taos Trail* (Cincinnati, 1850). F. A. Wislizenus, *Memoir of a Tour to Northern
Mexico, 1846–47* (Washington, 1848).

8. George R. Gibson, *Journey of a Soldier under Doniphan
and Kearney, 1846–1847*, ed. Bieber (Glendale, Calif., 1935).
Frank S. A. Edwards, *A Campaign in New Mexico with Colonel
Doniphan* (Philadelphia, 1847). John Taylor Hughes, *Doni-
phan's Expedition* (Cincinnati, 1848). Philip St. George Cooke,
The Conquest of New Mexico and California (New York, 1878).
W. E. Connelley, *Doniphan's Expedition* (Topeka, 1907). See
also Ralph P. Bieber, ed., *Marching with the Army of the West:
The Journals of Abraham R. Johnston, 1846; Marcellus Ball Ed-
wards, 1846–47; and Philip Good Ferguson, 1847–48* (Glendale,
Calif., 1936).

9. Thomas Jefferson Farnham, *Mexico: Its Geography, People*

Down the Santa Fe Trail, which is here being re-printed for the first time since 1926, needs surprisingly little explanation and amplification, except to identify its charming young writer more properly and to clarify the relation of the Magoffin brothers to the Santa Fe trade. It may be useful also to re-examine the controversial role played by Susan's unusual brother-in-law, James Wiley Magoffin, in bringing about the peaceful American occupation of New Mexico.

Commentators have frequently characterized both Mrs. Magoffin and her diary as "girlish," "naïve," and "charming"; yet it is also apparent that she was an intelligent, observant, and tolerant person with a genuinely inquisitive nature. Far from being the average American girl of her time, Susan Shelby had been born into one of the first as well as one of the wealthiest families of Kentucky. From her birth on July 30, 1827, at Arcadia, her father's estate near Danville, she moved in an atmosphere of ease and comfort;[10] and as befitted the daughter of Isaac Shelby, Jr., she was educated by private tutors. She soon learned, too, that her family had more than its share of prominent men, public heroes, and vigorous pioneers. The aunt

---

and Institutions (New York, 1846); George F. A. Ruxton, *Adventures in Mexico and the Rocky Mountains* (New York, 1847).

10. The biographical data concerning Mrs. Magoffin was originally compiled by Miss Drumm for her introduction to *Down the Santa Fe Trail* (1926), pp. xxi–xxiii. The Filson Club reports that details and letters of Susan's parents—Isaac Shelby, Jr., and Maria Boswell Warren—are lacking. See, nevertheless, Cass K. Shelby, *A Report on the First Three Generations of the Shelby Family in the United States* (privately printed, 1927).

for whom she was named was married to Dr. Ephraim McDowell, one of the most famous surgeons in the pre-Civil War period.[11] Susan's great-grandfather, Evan Shelby (1719–94), had been a distinguished soldier and pioneer who, after helping build Braddock's Road across the Pennsylvania wilderness in 1755, had gone into the Great Lakes fur trade and later participated in Lord Dunmore's War.[12] Not content with these exploits, Shelby migrated south to become one of the pioneers of Tennessee and an able Indian fighter and treaty-maker. Susan's grandfather, Isaac Shelby (1750–1826), whose estate, Traveler's Rest, adjoined that of Arcadia, had a similarly outstanding frontier record.[13] He had furnished the boats for George Rogers Clark's Illinois campaign during the American Revolution and had himself aided in driving the British from South Carolina. After earning a hero's reputation at the Battle of King's Mountain and serving as the strategist for the Revolutionary forces at the battle of Cowpens, South Carolina, Isaac turned from military to public life in frontier Kentucky. There he helped frame the first state constitution and was elected the first governor of Kentucky in 1792. During the War of 1812 he participated in the Battle of the Thames. When he died at his home in 1826, he was considered so famous an American that public funeral orations were delivered lamenting the almost simultaneous

11. See below, p. 203 n.

12. "Evan Shelby" in *Dictionary of American Biography* (1935), *17*, 59–60.

13. *DAB, 17,* 60–62.

passing of three great men: John Adams, Thomas Jefferson, and Isaac Shelby.[14]

Among the people who visited the Shelby household at Arcadia were the sons of another successful Kentucky pioneer, Beriah Magoffin, an Irish immigrant who had settled in Harrodsburg in the 1790s. After his marriage to Jane McAfee, member of still another pioneer family, Beriah became the father of ten children. One of the sons, Beriah, Jr., married Susan Shelby's elder sister, Anna, in 1840. Five years later, Samuel, another Magoffin, wooed and won young Susan on November 25, 1845.[15]

Given her background, her training, and her marriage to a Santa Fe trader, it is not unlikely that Susan felt she was capable of being a pioneer herself. On the eve of her departure from Independence she began her diary somewhat histrionically with the words: "My journal tells a story tonight different from what it has ever done before. The curtain rises now with a new scene." Later, on more than one occasion after a rough experience in a prairie storm or from an Indian scare, she compared herself favorably with the Oregon pioneer woman or made a reference to her own pioneering grandmother, Susannah Hart Shelby.[16] And when she reached Santa Fe in August 1846, she boasted:

I have entered the city in a year that will always be remembered by my countrymen; and under the "Star-spangled banner" too, the first American lady, who has

14. Ibid., p. 62.
15. *DAB, 12*, 199 ff. Samuel was born March 31, 1801.
16. Ibid., *17*, 60–62.

come under such auspices, and some of our company seem disposed to make me the first under any circumstances that ever crossed the Plains. [pp. 102–03]

It is also apparent that while Susan did not contemplate publication, she did write with a certain self-consciousness that her words might one day be read aloud to her family. Thus for a time at least she wrote with a model in mind: Gregg's famous *Commerce of the Prairies,* a copy of which she not only owned but appears to have learned by heart. Until she and her husband reached Bent's Fort, in fact, the diary clearly resembles Gregg's chapters dealing with life on the trail, the major difference being that Mrs. Magoffin traveled in what was, for the Santa Fe Trail, extraordinary luxury. In addition to a small tent house, a private carriage, books, and notions, her indulgent husband provided her with a maid, a driver, and at least two servant boys. Well she could explain at one point: "It is the life of a wandering princess, mine."

Mrs. Magoffin's accurate observations of life on the trail, her faithful record of the names of persons met, miles traveled, and general information about the countryside, owed much to the fact that her husband's family had been in the Santa Fe trade for over fifteen years. The Magoffin interest in Mexico began when James Wiley, the eldest son of Beriah senior, took a vessel of merchandise to Mexico from New Orleans prior to 1825. Despite a shipwreck in Matagorda Bay, he made his way as a trader to Saltillo. There a brief taste of Mexican life and the economic possibilities of the border provinces awakened his interest in the newly burgeoning Santa Fe trade.[17] He had entered the West's newest and most romantic business by 1825—within three years after Captain William Becknell had returned from a Plains trading expedition to the Rio Grande to report a fantastic success at bartering with the New Mexicans in Santa Fe. Becknell's report, and the information that the new nation of Mexico had abandoned the restrictive Spanish mercantile system and would open her borders to foreign merchants, led scores of Missouri traders to retrace Becknell's steps and initiate a flourishing business with the northern provinces of Mexico.[18]

A statistical account of the great value of the trade by the merchant Augustus Storrs in 1824 induced Thomas Hart Benton, then a young Missouri senator, to persuade the government to mark the trail in 1825 and to provide military escort in 1829, when Indian attack endangered the caravans.[19] As merchant after merchant returned to the outfitting towns of Franklin and Independence laden with silver coin or furs and driving herds of Mexican mules before them, the lure of profits became so great that by 1828 Samuel

17. *DAB*, *12*, 200–01. Connelley, *Doniphan's Expedition*, p. 196. Moorhead, *Royal Road*, pp. 83–84 n. El Paso *Times*, November 4, 1948. See also Shirley Seifert's introduction to her novel *The Turquoise Trail* (1950). The Magoffin family papers and letters remain, as Miss Seifert indicates, in the possession of descendants, General and Mrs. W. J. Glasgow, of El Paso, Texas.

18. For the origins of American interest in the Santa Fe trade see Moorhead, *Royal Road*, pp. 55 ff.

19. Ibid., pp. 67 ff.

Magoffin appears to have joined James in the trade. Eventually a third brother, William, also entered the business.[20]

Not only did the Magoffins prosper; they became known throughout northern Mexico. Their travels at one point took James all the way to Mexico City. Far from confining their trade to Santa Fe, they established stores in Chihuahua and Saltillo, where they found other American merchants, such as Dr. Henry Connelly, Edward J. Glasgow, Samuel Owens, James White, and William S. Messervy. With a tolerance rare for most Americans, who consistently deprecated Spanish culture and religion, the Magoffins grew to like the Mexican people, became fluent in Spanish, and spent more and more time in Mexico itself. Of the brothers—all of whom were notably able, lively, and extremely energetic—it was evident that James was the most popular and attractive to the Mexicans. Naturally convivial, full of Irish wit and drollery, a master story-teller, and a lavish dispenser of hospitality and drinks, he soon became "Don Santiago" to nearly every person of note in the Mexican border provinces. In 1830 James further entrenched himself in the economic and social life of the northern provinces by marrying Dona Maria Gertrudes Valdez de Beremende, who came from a prominent Chihuahua family. Her brother, Gabriel Valdez, was also a Mexican trader on the Santa Fe Trail, and

20. Authorities are vague as to the exact year of Samuel's entry into the Santa Fe trade. Most say it was before 1840; Moorhead says it was prior to 1830. Moorhead, *Royal Road*, p. 156; El Paso *Herald-Post*, November 4, 1948.

her cousin, Manuel Armijo, was a rich, self-made merchant from Albuquerque who was soon to be governor of New Mexico.[21]

Such high level connections made James Magoffin a valuable man for both Americans and Mexicans to know. It is not surprising to find that the federal government appointed him the first United States consul at Saltillo in 1828, and at various times between 1830 and 1846 persuaded him to serve as United States Commercial Agent in Chihuahua and Durango.[22] Among Mexicans, the Magoffins' high standing was evidenced by the fact that only one year after the ill-fated Texan expedition against Santa Fe in 1841— an effort which created a real fear of all Americans —Samuel Magoffin's wagons were entrusted with carrying the annual payroll for the Santa Fe garrison.[23]

James Magoffin's personal success was symbolic of the subtle but significant and far-reaching impact of things American in the border provinces. As Max Moorhead has recently suggested in his excellent study of the Santa Fe–Chihuahua trade, the goods brought in by American merchants like the Magoffins had not only "raised the standard of living of the New Mexicans" but made them so dependent upon the

21. *DAB*, pp. 200–01; El Paso *Herald-Post*, November 4, 1948.

22. Moorhead, *Royal Road*, pp. 84 n., 141 n.; *DAB*, 12, 200–01.

23. Moorhead, *Royal Road*, p. 198. See also George W. Kendall, *Narrative of the Texas Santa Fe Expedition, 1841* (New York, 1850), *1*, 329, for an account of Samuel's efforts to help the imprisoned Texans.

cheaper American wares that it turned the long-stand-
ing economic orientation of New Mexico away from
Chihuahua and Mexico toward Missouri and the
United States. With James and Samuel Magoffin
had come books, fashions, drugs, a printing press,
American wagons, and, most important, new ideas
and new horizons. The trade even turned the "ricos"
of New Mexico into mercantile as well as feudal
lords.[24] Like the Phoenician traders of old, the Santa
Fe traders had broken the cake of custom, caused two
distinct peoples and cultures to blunder into contact,
and had prepared the way for political as well as
economic conquest of Spain's northernmost provinces.

Having made a sizable fortune as a merchant-
trader by 1844, James decided to return to Missouri.
He established himself and his family near Independence, only to lose his wife by death a year later.
Whether James had originally intended abandoning
the trade is not clear, but it was obvious that he was
still very much in business when he arrived in Missouri on May 25, 1846, from Chihuahua with wagons
that carried a purse of $40,000.[25] The elder Magoffin
returned at a crucial moment in the often stormy
history of Mexican-American relations. When the
American Congress annexed the former but now independent Mexican state of Texas in 1849, Mexico
had severed relations with the United States. The
failure to negotiate a settlement of differences was
climaxed by a shooting war the next spring, after
General Zachary Taylor moved troops into the dis-

24. Moorhead, *Royal Road*, pp. 192, 194, and passim.
25. *DAB, 12*, 200–01.

puted area between the Nueces and the Rio Grande rivers and claimed that the latter stream was the proper border of Texas. After an encounter between Taylor's men and Mexican troops, President Polk declared on May 11 that war "by act of Mexico" existed. Two days later, Congress formally voted a state of hostilities.

Although the prospect of a conflict with Mexico was immensely popular with Missourians and with the entire population of the lower Mississippi Valley, it promised to affect the fortunes of the Santa Fe traders, many of whom were already on the trail by the time Congress had declared war. Not only did the conflict threaten to close the market, but the traders stood in danger of arrest and of losing their goods by confiscation. Thus while President Polk seemingly pursued a vigorous military policy to conquer and reduce Mexico, he also prayed for a small localized war which would avoid bloodshed in New Mexico, Chihuahua, and, if possible, the more distant province of California. At the same time he felt a small war would prevent the growth of "military reputations dangerous for the Presidency."

No one was more in agreement with this "small war" policy than Missouri's Senator Thomas H. Benton, one of Polk's chief advisers. It was Benton's fervent hope to avoid any interference in the New Mexican part of the trade through the twin devices of a peaceful occupation and a full assurance that all the rights and privileges of the local Mexican citizens would continue to be respected.[26] To implement such

26. Benton, *Thirty Years' View* (New York, 1854), 2, 680.

a policy, Polk and Benton first sent Colonel George Howard to warn the traders already on the road that war existed and to wait until American troops could precede them into Mexico. Howard then went on to Taos and other border towns to create a favorable sentiment toward Americans.[27] Orders were also given to stop any trains which might be carrying military supplies for the enemy. While these initial precautionary measures were being taken, Polk had appointed Colonel Stephen Watts Kearny, an army official long familiar with the Santa Fe Trail, to take some 1600 regular and volunteer troops rather grandly titled "The Army of the West" and carry out a bloodless occupation of New Mexico, Chihuahua and California.[28]

The great care Polk and Benton took to prevent fighting was indicated both by the orders to Kearny and by the fact that the President invited the Catholic bishops of New York and St. Louis to the White House to ask their advice about the best means of placating the priests in New Mexico. Polk in particular was convinced—and correctly so—that the priests occupied such a dominant position in the lives and government of all Mexico that without their coopera-

27. Milo M. Quaife, *The Diary of James K. Polk during His Presidency, 1845 to 1849* (Chicago, 1910), 396. See also Secretary of War William L. Marcy to S. W. Kearny, *1*, June 3, 1846, in House Executive Doc. 19, 29th Cong., 2d Sess., *3*, 5 ff.

28. Quaife, p. 403. William A. Keleher, *Turmoil in New Mexico, 1846–1868* (Santa Fe, 1952), pp. 3–140, treats Kearny and the Army of the West in detail. A major part of De Voto's *Year of Decision, 1846* covers the same ground.

tion peaceful conquest of the border provinces could not possibly be accomplished.[29] While the bishops promised to do all in their power to aid Polk, the President was still dissatisfied. What he wanted, Benton later reported, was a person of good character, preferably of the Roman religion and well known to the Mexicans, to precede the Army. At this point Senator Benton himself remembered James Magoffin, whom he had met in 1845. He wrote the trader to come to Washington posthaste. On June 15 Benton brought Magoffin to the White House with the proposal that the experienced trader with his Mexican connections might be the ideal man to pave the way for the Army. In this first interview and a second one on June 17, 1846, Magoffin appears to have impressed the President so favorably that the latter wrote: "he is a very intelligent man and gave me much valuable information." [30] As a result of the meetings Polk directed Secretary of War Marcy to instruct General Kearny to use Magoffin's services as part of his strategy.[31]

From this point on, James Magoffin's life became a series of intrigues and high adventure. He had rushed to Washington in great haste upon the summons of Benton; now he rushed back to Missouri in order to set out across the plains in a buckboard in a race against time to catch Kearny. Both the caravan in

29. Eugene I. McCormac, *James K. Polk: A Political Biography* (Berkeley, 1922), p. 421. Polk, *The Diary of a President, 1845–1849,* ed. Allan Nevins (New York, 1929), pp. 107 ff. Quaife, pp. 408–11.

30. Quaife, p. 474. Benton, *Thirty Years' View*, pp. 682–84.

31. See Appendix, p. 363.

which Susan and Samuel traveled and the main body
of Kearny's Army of the West were so far ahead of
James, however, that the brothers and the General
did not meet until they all arrived at Bent's Fort on
July 26.[32] There, after consultation, Kearny appears
to have fallen in with Magoffin's plans, for on August
1 he detailed Captain Philip St. George Cook to take
twelve men to accompany Magoffin to Santa Fe under a flag of truce and to negotiate with the Governor,
General Manuel Armijo.[33] When the small party
arrived in the enemy capital twelve days later, Magoffin acted as if he were merely a merchant riding under
Cooke's protection. But long after the guards and
officials had gone to bed and left the Palace of the
Governors in darkness, Magoffin brought Armijo,
who was his cousin by marriage, to Cooke's chambers
for secret conferences. They also held talks with
Armijo's second in command, the able, hot-headed,
patriotic Diego Archuleta. Exactly what arrangements were made between these men remains historical speculation. But it does appear that Magoffin first
persuaded the already doubting Armijo not to resist
Kearny, a decision which may or may not have been
influenced by bribing the avaricious governor. Since
Armijo's rule of New Mexico was notably harsh,

32. Again there is some confusion as to the precise time of
meeting. Keleher in *Turmoil in New Mexico*, p. 6, says July 26;
David Lavender in *Bent's Fort* (New York, 1954), p. 259, im-
plies it was July 31; Mrs. Magoffin fails to mention James' arrival at the Fort, but James himself in a report to Secretary of
War Marcy says July 26: Executive Doc. 41, 30th Cong. 1st
Sess., 1848.

33. Keleher, *Turmoil in New Mexico*, p. 18.

arbitrary, and unpopular, it is quite likely that the governor so feared an internal uprising against his own regime when American troops appeared that he deemed flight the better part of valor.[34]

Young Diego Archuleta, already in command of several thousand impatient troops who had gathered in Santa Fe along with many provincial priests and leaders to resist the Americans, proved more difficult to persuade. But Archuleta's own opposition seems to have collapsed when Magoffin—with what authority is not clear—assured the commander that Kearny was only interested in occupying New Mexico up to the east bank of the Rio Grande, and that the ambitious Archuleta might seize the western half himself and become its governor.[35]

What followed is well-known history. At the approach of the American troops Armijo fled into Mexico with a few regular soldiers while Archuleta finally agreed to disband the New Mexican volunteers. Late in the afternoon of August 18, Kearny after having marched over Raton Pass and occupied

34. For a sketch of Armijo see below, p. 96 n.; and Keleher, *Turmoil in New Mexico,* p. 19. Earlier accounts by Americans were extremely prejudiced against Armijo for his role in the Texan Santa Fe Expedition and his prohibitive customs duties on American goods so that little more than caricature emerges. While there is no doubt that Armijo was a venal official, it is also clear that he was a man of intelligence and ability and possessed feelings of patriotism. The details of Armijo's career are colorfully dramatized in Elliott Arnold's historical novel, *The Time of the Gringo* (New York, 1953).

35. Keleher, *Turmoil in New Mexico,* p. 33. Appendix, pp. 264–65.

Las Vegas and San Miguel some days before, came through Apache Pass and entered Santa Fe. There a nervous acting governor, Juan Bautista Vigil y Alarid, turned over the province to the General, and the Stars and Stripes were raised in the dusty plaza. As couriers with proclamations rode out to every village along the Rio Grande to urge peaceful acceptance of the new order, many people congratulated Magoffin and Dr. Henry Connelly—another Santa Fe merchant who appears to have been privy to the negotiations with Armijo—for effecting the bloodless conquest.[36] Magoffin himself wrote Secretary of War Marcy a detailed report of the peaceful occupation on August 26.[37]

Then on September 1, a day after Susan and Samuel arrived in Santa Fe to be welcomed by James with an oyster and champagne supper, the latter was on his way to Chihuahua, apparently to pave the way for General John Ellis Wool's peaceful conquest of that province. Magoffin's great haste strongly suggests that this was his sole purpose in rushing ahead of both the traders and the American troops under Colonel Doniphan, who had been detached from Kearny's command and ordered south to join Wool. This time, however, Magoffin's plans went awry. Near El Paso del Norte he was arrested by Mexican

36. For a sketch of Connelly, see below pp. 104–05 n.; the occupation is covered in great detail by Ralph E. Twitchell, *The Leading Facts of New Mexican History* (Cedar Rapids, Iowa, 1912), *2*, 199 ff., as well as in Keleher and De Voto.

37. James W. Magoffin to Secretary of War William L. Marcy, Executive Doc. 41, 30th Cong. 1st Sess., 1848.

authorities and taken as a prisoner to Chihuahua. When Doniphan's troops came near that city, he was then sent to Durango. There one of the hair-raising adventures which characterized his life took place when Henry Connelly was captured bearing a letter from Kearny to Magoffin in which the General praised the merchant for his aid in taking New Mexico. This letter contained sufficient evidence for the Mexican officials to shoot Magoffin. Instead, the Mexican officer in charge of Magoffin had become so fond of his convivial and extraordinarily hospitable prisoner— Magoffin later boasted that he had expended 2900 bottles of champagne on his captors—that he handed Magoffin the letter upopened with the remark that if it was unimportant just to pitch it into the fire. Upon seeing its contents Magoffin hastily burned the message and the nearly fatal incident was closed.[38] Nevertheless, it was several months before Magoffin, through more bribery and champagne, managed to get free of his jailors and to return to El Paso and American protection.

Naturally, Susan Magoffin's dairy is of use in throwing light on her brother-in-law's often mysterious movements and the reasons and circumstances of his arrest. Since James' later claim that "bloodless

38. Magoffin's life is so full of extraordinary events it is difficult to separate unusual fact from exaggeration or myth. In one version of the above story, for example, the officer who saved Magoffin's life by ignoring the letter is identified as Armijo. But the most recent scholar to treat the episode finds only indirect authority for such a coincidence: Moorhead, *Royal Road*, pp. 174–75 and 175 n.

possession of New Mexico was what President Polk
wished; it was obtained through my means" was considered a mere unsubstantiated boast, Mrs. Magoffin's diary, as well as Senator Benton's *Thirty Years'
View*, suggest that the accomplishment was quite true
if somewhat overstated.[39] With Kearny's unexpected
death in 1849 and Armijo's natural reluctance to
talk, it is true that little documentary evidence can
be produced. It is significant, however, that Magoffin
presented a $50,000 claim to the government for serv-
ices rendered in 1846 and 1847. Among the rather
dramatic items which Magoffin listed as deserving of
compensation were: "Nine months' imprisonment in
Chihuahua and Durango (can't be estimated)." It is
also significant that despite the War Department's
complaints that Magoffin's claims were vague, it paid
him $30,000.[40]

Even had Magoffin's claim been denied, his career
as both a trader and a war diplomat dramatically reveals the tremendous importance of the American
merchant in the economy and political fortunes of
New Mexico by 1846 and goes a long way to explain-
ing its peaceful conquest. Other merchants with secret
government orders or consular status were busy in
California trying to do the same thing that Magoffin did in Santa Fe. The key importance of such
men continued to be recognized after the conquest,

39. Benton, *Thirty Years' View*, *2*, 684. Keleher, *Turmoil in
New Mexico*, pp. 32–34.

40. Keleher, pp. 34–35. Documentary evidence to support
Magoffin's claims was first discovered and printed in Connelley,
Doniphan's Expedition, pp. 183, 196, 587.

for nearly every New Mexican government official, whether Mexican or American, appointed by General Kearny turned out to be a merchant. The first "delegate" to Congress from New Mexico was William S. Messervy, an old colleague of Magoffin's in Chihuahua. Quite unexpectedly the Santa Fe trader turned out to be the nearest thing Washington could muster in the way of a temporary colonial civil service to run the latest American acquisition. And as Max Moorhead has observed, leading Mexicans already respected the American merchant and admired the way he dealt with Indians. Certainly the royal treatment given Susan and Samuel wherever they traveled, as well as their reception by the first families of New Mexico and Chihuahua, indicates that this was so. Simply by recording the great number of contacts with leading natives of the border provinces Mrs. Magoffin demonstrated why the Santa Fe trader was so important diplomatically and politically and why he was to dominate the government of New Mexico long after the conquest of 1846.

Quite apart from its worth as a trail journal, a Mexican war account and an insight into the political as well as economic role of the American borderlands merchant, Mrs. Magoffin's journal has a final merit as social history. Upon her arrival at Bent's Fort she was quick to note the habits of the native wives of the traders; with unusual frankness she compared the conditions under which her own baby and that of an Indian woman in the room below had been born. Later in New Mexico and at El Paso she explained with accuracy the food, dress, social habits, and routine of a normal day. The physical layout of houses and the decor of their interiors never escaped her attention. As one review noted: "The Diary bristles with good descriptions both of country and of people, and she throws many interesting sidelights on the Mexican people and their social status."[41] With unusual tolerance she made friends with peon women, helped her husband in his store, and good-naturedly haggled in the Santa Fe market for vegetables. Determined to understand everything, she faithfully mastered Spanish just as she had soon mastered the lingo of the Santa Fe Trail.[42] From the names and descriptions of prominent Spanish-Mexicans that she mentions, one can almost reconstruct the social register of pre-American New Mexico. On the other hand, she gave equal space to Santa Fe's most celebrated demimonde, Gertrudes Barcelo, an extraordinary monte player and madam who befriended the Americans.[43] Finally, her frank descriptions of the character of scores of American army officers is revealing. Her comments about Zachary Taylor go far to confirm that "Old Rough and Ready" was certainly just that in his attire. Her favorable impressions of General Kearny help counter the prejudiced versions of that officer's nature given out by Frémont and Benton.

Susan appears to have lost some interest in her

41. *Hispanic American Historical Review, 8* (1928), 114–16.

42. R. L. Duffus, *The Santa Fe Trail* (New York, 1930), p. 151.

43. Gertrudes Barcelo is credited with warning the Americans of the Revolt of 1846–47, in which Governor Charles Bent lost his life. Her extraordinary career has been fictionalized in Ruth

journal after her stay in Santa Fe. The uncomfortable trip down the Rio Grande and across the Jornado del Muerto was halted by so many rumors of American military defeat that Susan and Samuel became chiefly concerned for their own safety and for the fate of James Magoffin, whose death more than once was reported to them. During this time they were also plagued by bad health and bothered by the serious illness of her younger brother-in-law, William, whose caravans had joined the other Magoffin wagon trains below Santa Fe. Susan's own fears became so overwhelming, in fact, that she took refuge in prayer and an awakened religious feeling. Even so, she managed to describe life in El Paso, Chihuahua City, and Saltillo and to report second hand the daily rumors about the movements of Wool and Taylor as well as of the colorful exploits of Colonel Doniphan.

Mrs. Magoffin ended her journal on September 8, 1847, on a note of anticlimax, for it stops before she suffered a siege of yellow fever at Matamoras during which she gave birth to a son. Unfortunately the child died soon afterward. Taking a vessel from the Mexican coast to New Orleans, she returned to Kentucky, to live in Lexington. In 1852, however, she and Samuel moved to Barrett's Station near Kirkwood, Missouri, where he acquired a sizable estate. Unhappily the rigors of her Mexican trip appear to have ruined Mrs. Magoffin's health, for though her third child, Jane, was born in 1851 without mishap, Susan herself died in 1855 soon after another daughter,

---

Laughlin's *The Wind Leaves No Shadow* (Caldwell, Idaho, 1948).

named after herself, arrived. She was buried in Belle-fontaine Cemetery in St. Louis.

Just as 1847 was a turning point in Susan's life, so it was in Samuel's, for after his return he abandoned the Santa Fè trade to deal in real estate in St. Louis County. After Susan's untimely death he married one of her cousins, who was also named Susan Shelby. Some of the first Susan's ardent concern for religion appears to have affected Samuel in these later years, for he became an elder in the Presbyterian Church. His death came in 1888.[44]

Samuel's withdrawal from the Santa Fe trade did not halt the important role which James Magoffin continued to play in the annals of the American Southwest. After his release from prison he settled on the American side of the Rio Grande at El Paso del Norte, where he soon turned his home and store-houses into the thriving settlement of Magoffinsville. His lavish hospitality, punctuated by frequent balls, made his home the rendezvous of hundreds of travelers over the next score of years. In 1851 John Russell Bartlett made the Magoffin household the headquarters of the United States Boundary Commission.[45] A few years later W. H. H. Davis described Magof-

44. See Miss Drumm's sketch in *Down the Santa Fe Trail* (1926), pp. xx–xxi; Shirley Seifert to H. R. Lamar, Kirkwood, Missouri, December 3, 1961. See also obituary of Samuel Magoffin's daughter, Mrs. Jane M. Taylor, in the St. Louis *Globe-Democrat*, June 1, 1934.

45. John Russell Bartlett, *Personal Narrative of Explorations and Incidents in Texas, New Mexico, California, Sonora, and Chihuahua, Connected with the United States Boundary Commission during the Years 1850–53* (2 vols. New York, 1854), *1*,

fin as "living quite nabob in style in a large Spanish-
built house that reminded me somewhat of an old
mansion of the feudal ages." [46] During the 1850s the
first Fort Bliss was built on Magoffin's property,
which was in turn to become the nucleus of the future
American city of El Paso. Naturally the shrewd merchant was the chief supplier of goods and forage for
the Fort, while engaging in a dozen other mercantile
adventures on both sides of the border.[47] Judge J. F.
Crosby, Simeon Hart, and James were soon noted to
be "three of the wealthiest men in the Southwest." [48]
Financial success seemed to run in the family, for
James' brother Beriah, who was to become governor
of Kentucky in 1859, had such a successful law practice and made such wise investments in Chicago real
estate that he was reputed to be a millionaire.[49]

James' own fortunes were partially eclipsed when
he declared for the Confederacy upon the outbreak
of the Civil War. After General H. H. Sibley's troops
—who had been largely equipped by Magoffin—failed
to take New Mexico during the first two years of the
war, Union forces confiscated Magoffin's properties.
Even so, he survived the war and was well on his way
to economic recovery when he died in San Antonio

143, 193. See also Paul Horgan, *Great River* (New York, 1954),
2, 802–04, 811.

46. William Watts H. Davis, *El Gringo, or New Mexico and
Her People* (New York, 1857), p. 383.

47. *DAB, 12*, 200–01. El Paso *Herald-Post*, November 4,
1948.

48. Keleher, *Turmoil in New Mexico*, p. 147.

49. *DAB, 12*, 199–200. Lewis Collins, *History of Kentucky*
(Covington, Ky. 1878), *2*, 356.

in 1868. His son Joseph carried on the family name in the Southwest by becoming the first mayor of El Paso, where Magoffin descendants live today.

Since *Down the Santa Fe Trail* was first published, a number of recent books have filled in gaps in Mrs. Magoffin's narrative. By and large, however, they all attest to the accuracy and validity of her account. For the reader's reference nearly all these subsequent volumes have been cited in the footnotes to this foreword. In searching out new information which may have come to light about Susan and the Magoffins since her diary was published, I have become indebted to a number of persons and institutions. Among them one happily mentions Archibald Hanna of the Yale University Western Americana Collection, William H. Goetzmann, and Robin W. Winks of Yale, and Miss Shirley Seifert, author of *The Turquoise Trail*, a historical novel about Susan Magoffin published in 1950. The Jackson County Historical Society, the State Historical Society of Missouri, the Missouri Historical Society, the Danville and Boyle County Historical Society, the Kentucky Historical Society, and the Filson Club have kindly offered both suggestions and materials. Above all one is grateful to the late Stella M. Drumm, who first brought to light the Magoffin dairy. In preparing the manuscript for publication Miss Drumm used her own great knowledge of Southwestern history to edit and amply footnote the journal—an excellent piece of research which remains so useful and valid after thirty-five years that her annotation stands unchanged in this new edition.

New Haven, Connecticut
January 1962

INDEPENDENCE, MISSOURI. COURTHOUSE SQUARE

Courtesy Missouri Historical Society.

TRAVELS IN MEXICO

COMMENCING JUNE, 1846.

EL DIARIO DE DONA SUSANITA MAGOFFIN.

MY journal tells a story tonight different from what it has ever done before.

The curtain raises now with a new scene. This book of travels is *Act 2nd,* litterally and truly. From the city of New York to the Plains of Mexico, is a stride that I myself can scarcely realize. But now for a bit of my wonderful travels so far.

This is the third day since we left Brother James's [James Wiley Magoffin]. Tuesday evening we went into Independence;[1] there we stayed one night only at Mr. Noland's Hotel.[2] On Wednesday morning I did considerable business; some shopping—little articles I had thought of only within a few days. I called to see Mrs. Owens,[3] and on my return from there re-

---

[1] Independence, the seat of Jackson County, Missouri, five miles east of Kansas City, was laid out in 1827, and by 1831 had become the western rendezvous for both Santa Fé and Oregon traffic. During the season of departure of the trains it was a place of much bustle and activity.

[2] Smallwood Noland, familiarly called "Uncle Wood." His hotel was the largest and most commodious in Missouri, excepting those in St. Louis; it having accommodations for as many as four hundred guests. Mr. Noland was known from the Atlantic to the Pacific, having been a hotel keeper at this place for many years.

[3] Wife of Samuel C. Owens, the trader. She was Fanny Young, a sister of Eliza Ann, wife of Governor Thomas Reynolds of Missouri. After the death of her husband in the battle of Sacra-

1

ceived two or three visits—next I arranged my trunk "plunder-basket" &c. And after dinner between the hours of 3 and 4 we left the little village of I— [Independence] for the residence of Mr. Barns, a gentleman some ten miles this side of that place. Here we procured a night's lodging preparatory to a final departure. They were very kind to us. Mrs. Barns claims a relationship with me through the Harts; be it so or not I can't tell.

On Thursday morning we left Mr. B's at an early hour. They had us up by day-light, gave us breakfast almost as soon, and by 7 o'clock we were on the road.

Thursday 11th. Now the Prairie life begins! We soon left "the settlements" this morning. Our mules travel well and we joged on at a rapid pace till 10 o'clock, when we came up with the waggons. They were encamped just at the edge of the last woods. As we proceeded from this thick wood of oaks and scrubby underbrush, my eyes were unable to satiate their longing for a sight of the wide spreading plains. The hot sun, or rather the wind which blew pretty roughly, compelled me to seek shelter with my friends, the carriage & a thick veil.

All our waggons were here, and those of two or three others of the traders. The animals made an extensive show indeed. Mules and oxen scattered in all directions. The teamsters were just "catching up," and the cracking of whips, lowing of cattle, braying of mules, whooping and hallowing of the men was a novel sight rather. It is disagreeable to hear so much

mento, she went to live in Platte County, Missouri. She did not long survive Colonel Owens, dying May 31, 1848.

2

swearing; the animals are unruly tis true and worries the patience of their drivers, but I scarcely think they need be so profane. And the mules I believe are worse, for they kick and run so much faster. It is a common circumstance for a mule (when first brought into service) while they are hitching him in, to break away with chains and harness all on, and run for half hour or more with two or three horsemen at his heels endeavouring to stop him, or at least to keep him from running among the other stock. I saw a scamper while I sat in the carriage today. One of the mules belonging to Col. Owens scampered off, turning the heads of the whole collection nearly by the rattling of the chains. After a fine race one of his pursuers succeeded in catching the bridle, when the stubborn animal refused to lead and in defiance of all the man could do, he walked backwards all the way to camp leading his capturer instead of being led. Just as we were about leaving one of the Spanish traders came up and claimed a man (a Mexican) who had gone into the service of Don Manuel [Samuel Magoffin]. The man owed him some five dollars and he was determined to take it out of him by work. The poor fellow refused to go, pleading his last engagement, he had been favoured with the advancement of $20.00 of his wages and could not go in consequence. He came to Don Manuel for a settlement; in a few minutes a dozen Mexicans were assembled around him, all jabbering about the matter. I seldom ever heard as much fuss; finally they concluded to bring the matter to Don Gabriel Valdez, his tent was some three miles off, but notwithstanding we must go there. So we left the wag-

gons and rode over, sending an express ahead to tell
the gentleman we would dine with him. At 12 o'clock
we arrived there, and found him in waiting to receive
us. In a little while the matter was fixed.

Mi alma [my soul] treated him, the Mexican, to a
little grog, ordered him a dinner and offered to pay
him the sum he required of the man. After a stay of
some two or three hours here, we again resumed our
march, and soon caught up with the waggons. We
now numbered, of ourselves only, quite a force. Fourteen big waggons with six yoke each, one baggage
waggon with two yoke, one dearborn with two mules,
(this concern carries my maid) our own carriage with
two more mules and two men on mules driving the
loose stock, consisting of nine and a half yoke of oxen,
our riding horses two, and three mules, with Mr.
Hall the superintendent of the waggons, together
with his mule, we number twenty men, three are our
tent servants (Mexicans). Jane, my attendant, two
horses, nine mules, some two hundred oxen, and last
though not least our dog Ring. A gray hound he is
of noble descent; he is white with light brown spots,
a nice watch for our tent door.

All the evening we drove on well. At half an hour
by sun we came up with the waggons of Mr. Mc-
Mannus[4] and a Spaniard Armigo.[5] They were just

[4] Frank McManus was for many years a merchant in the
Mexican trade. He was at Chihuahua with his fellow merchants,
Connelly and Aull, when news came of the approach of the
American troops and merchant trains, including that of McManus.
About ten days before the battle of Sacramento, fought about
fifteen miles north of Chihuahua, Governor Trias made an order

SAMUEL MAGOFFIN, IN 1845

From a medallion painted on ivory.

preparing to camp at *"The Lone Elm,"* 35 miles from I— [Independence]. This is the first camping place from Fitzu's, which is at the border of Mo. and the place at which our wagons stayed the night before.

There is no other tree or bush or shrub save one Elm tree, which stands on a small elevation near the little creek or branch. The travellers allways stop where there is water sufficient for all their animals. The grass is fine every place, it is so tall in some places as to conceal a man's waist.

sending all Americans seventy miles south of the town. About ten of them succeeded in evading this order by keeping themselves pretty much concealed. At the suggestion of the English Consul, Mr. Potts, they took refuge at the Mint while the battle was in progress. They took with them arms and a large quantity of ammunition to the roof of that building for protection in case of attack by the mob, which they felt sure would follow American defeat.

Here the small party waited in terrible suspense, knowing the great disparity in numbers between the American and Mexican forces. At length the news of Mexican defeat was wafted to them. The next day the American flag floated from the flagstaff on the Plaza and Frank McManus and his friend, Doctor Connelly, reopened their respective stores and proceeded to sell their goods.

[5] Besides General Armijo, there were three others of that name in the Santa Fé trade, namely: J. C., Rafael, and A. J. Armijo. They passed through St. Louis on their way to New York in December, 1845, to purchase their winter outfit. They carried with them over fifty thousand dollars in specie. In March, 1846, J. C. and A. Armijo again arrived in St. Louis on their way East to purchase the goods carried on the expedition described by Mrs. Magoffin.

5

We crossed the branch and stretched our tent. It is a grand affair indeed. 'Twas made in Philadelphia by a regular tent-maker of the army, and every thing is complete. It is conical shape, with an iron pole and wooden ball; we have a table in it that is fastened to the pole, and a little stand above it that serves for a dressing bureau—it holds our glass, combs &c. Our bed is as good as many houses have; sheets, blankets, counterpanes, pillows &c. We have a carpet made of sail duck, have portable stools they are called; they are two legs crossed with a pin through the center on which they turn as a pivot; the seat part is made of carpeting. To be brief the whole is a complete affair.

Well after a supper at *my own table* and in *my own house,*—and I can say what few women in civilized life ever could, that the first house of his own to which my husband took me to after our marriage was a *tent;* and the first table of my own at which I ever sat was a cedar one, made with only *one leg* and that was a tent pole. But as I said after the first supper at *my own* table consisting of fried ham and eggs, biscuit and a cup of shrub, for I preferred it to tea or café—I enjoyed a fine night's rest; it was sweet indeed.

Friday 12th. This morning we were up soon of course. It is fine weather, cool and bracing. I have a cold though, and cannot enjoy it as much as I hope to do. I took it in Independence, though I calculate on the Prairies curing me. We had an early breakfast, and an early start—that is by 7 o'clock. Nothing of importance occurred till noon when we stopped for

6

dinner at "Big Bull Creek." The travellers call this "nooning it." Here we had no wood; there are no trees, and we provided none in the morning so we were obliged to take a dinner of crackers with a little ham fried at the small fire of the wagoners. It went quite well though with a tin cup of shrub. At night we struck camp at "Black Jack," fourteen miles from the last, and 49 from Ind [ependence]. The sun was an hour high when we stoped and as the wagons had not come up we could not strike camp. Being tired of the carriage I got out and took a ramble. I picked numberless flowers with which the plains are covered, and as *mi alma* told me before we started, I threw them away to gather more. I wearried myself out at this, and as the tent was now up, I returned *"home."* There before supper I had a little piece of work to attend to, I mean the feeding of my chickens. It is quite a farm house this; poultry, dogs, cattle, mules, horses &c. Altogether my home is one not to be objected to.

The two companies, McMannus and the Mexicans, are on the other side of the creek to us.

Saturday 13th. This morning we have a dense fog. The other companies are up and off before us.

Noon on the wide Prairie. Well we are going to "noon it" now. We are up on the Prairie with not a tree near us; some are in sight, but none near enough for shelter. The sun is very warm; the oxen are unyoked and are straying off to the water and for grass. This is a good time to write, here in the carriage. I have all the materials, and will take advantage of the time.

This A. M. about 10 o'clock we met an Indian trader returning from "Bent's Fort" up the big Arkansas river. He is returning with his cargo of skins; we stoped and had half hour's conversation with him, respecting the road, war news &c. It is all pretty good. Says the Indians are pretty bad about Pawnee Fork, which is 298 miles from Ind [ependence]. His wagons we met about half a mile back; they are loaded with skins. A negro woman, who is coming up from the fort with them, has been up here to see us.

It is now about 6 o'clock P. M. we are still in the same track. The wagons have started on and most of them are out of sight. The hindermost one has stuck in a mud hole and they are doubling and tripling teams to pull it out, and I believe have finally succeeded and now we will proceed.

Camp No. 3. We have made but a poor travel to day; not more than eight miles. We were late starting in the morning, and stoped at noon quite a long while.

Got off from camp this P. M. by 4 o'clock, but the mud hole detained us two full hours; so to make up in some measure we did not stop till after 8 o'clock tonight. We had to turn out the cattle, stake tent, and make a fire before we could do anything towards supper. It was after 10 o'clock some time before we got it; it made us enjoy it more though.

Camp No. 4. We are out on the Prairie now, with a plenty of water. The oxen were half gone this morning when we got up. The men found most of them

8

though some distance from camp; for the missing ones four yoke we sent two Mexicans. Those wagoners to whom they belonged had to yoke up new ones, which detained us till 9 o'clock. We went on till 1 o'clock when we stoped to noon it, but without water. We left again at four, and continued till precisely sundown this P. M.

This is my first sabbath on the plains!

A very quiet one it has been too, something I had not looked for. But all the men seem to recollect it and hitch in their teams with half the trouble, and I have scarcely heard an oath the whole day. Every thing has been perfectly still and quiet, scarcely a breath of air, or the fliting of a feathered warbler has appeared to disturb the solemn stillness. Ever and anon the sharp whistle of a partridge, the chirp of a lark, or the croaking of a raven in the distant woods, were heard. Save these and the unusually gentle noise made by the waggoners, no other sound conspired to mar the solemn stillness of a sabbath on the Prairies.

The men who went after the cattle have returned with them; found at our last night's camping ground on their way back.

Monday 15th. Noon out on the wide Prairie. The Sun it seems is exerting himself; not a breath of air is stirring, and everything is scorching with heat. We have no water and the animals are panting with thirst; their drivers are seeking shelter under the wagons; while *mi alma* is under the carriage.

We left camp this morning at 6¼ o'clock; have

traveled finely all the morning till 11½ o'clock, when we stoped.

While at dinner the mules and horses all but two got loose and wandered off a short distance, which did not alarm the men any; soon however they were entirely out of sight, and it was only by hard riding they were taken; they were in a fine trot for Ind [ependence].

Last night the oxen made another start for home. Just as we were fixing for a fine night's sleep, they came breaking by our tent from the water, where perhaps they had been frightened by a wolf, with as much noise as 20 empty wagons. The men stood on guard all night after this little fright.

Camp No. 5. At the 110 mile creek, 95 miles from Independence. Tonight is my fifth *en el campo* [in camp]. Oh, this is a life I would not exchange for a good deal! There is such independence, so much free uncontaminated air, which impregnates the mind, the feelings, nay every thought, with purity. I breathe free without that oppression and uneasiness felt in the gossiping circles of a settled home.

We left the noon creek this P. M. at 5 o'clock. While there a company of U. S. Dragoons, who have been ordered out for the protection of the traders to Santa Fé came up.[6] They are some 70 in number, passed on before us and camped about half mile ahead.

---

[6] Captain Benjamin Moore's company of United States Dragoons, which was sent to overtake Albert Speyers' caravan, carrying arms and ammunition to the Mexicans.

The drive today has been pretty well.

The camping place tonight is near a creek, which at present is quite small. A thick woods is just before us which we must pass in the morning; some repairs must be done on it (the road) first, or we should have gone over tonight. Took a little walk this evening while they were fixing the tent, and picked some little pebbles which I shall take home as a specimen of my Prairie curiosities. None of the flowers, of which there are innumerable quantities and varieties, have gone to seed as yet, so I must press them in a book to take home. I fixed some this evening in my journal.

We find some beautiful roses—quantities of wild pinks. One flower to which, for want of a better one, I have given the name of the "hour glass" from its peculiar shape. It is brown and yellow, with a fuzzy pale green leaf. The little flowers, the leaves of which turn in both ways, up and down—the middle is quite small and the whole is quite like an hour-glass, at least my fancy has made it so—but as I was going to say the flowers are very small and hang in a thick cluster only at the top of the stem. I have found wild onions, and a kind of wild bean. The former is very *strong,* rather gluey and grows pretty deep in the ground. The flower and seed resemble the *cultivated* root.

Of Roses there are any quantity. Now at my tent door there are two bushes, one on either side, and inside nearly all the way from the head of my bed to the door are bushes with full blown roses, bursting and closed buds. It is the life of a wandering princess, mine. When I do not wish to get out myself to pick flowers the Mexican servants riding on mules busy themselves picking them for me.

Tuesday 16th. Bridge Cr. 103 ms. from I [ndependence], and 8 from Camp No. 5. Noon. Left camp at 6¼ o'clock—passed through a thick woods at *110.* The soldiers who had encamped on the other side of it, left a considerable time before us. One came over to our camp though "to inquire the way." I think to a bottle of grog, though he said to the next camping place. After his departure we came on ahead of the wagons, to this place. It is a small creek with steep bank, and these covered thickly with trees and smaller undergrowth, for nearly two hours I have been wandering among them picking raspberries and gooseberries, of which there are an abundance. We fixed a line and tried to fish a little but I believe there are none in the stream.

After dinner I layed down with *mi alma* on a buffalo skin with the carriage seats for pillows and took what few ladies have done a siesta in the sun.

Camp No. 6. Rock Creek. Rode on ahead of the wagons, and selected a camping ground. The creek is at present quite low. In high water though it is a bold and deep stream. Its banks are of slate rock mostly. A number of trees are near them, and quantities of small undergrowth. After a ramble of an hour among them, during which time I crossed and recrossed the creek to *mi alma's* astonishment, on the stones lying in it, we fixed a line and hook and made the attempt to fish. Nothing but small minners would bite. So growing weary of catching *nothing,* and being annoyed much by the musquitoes, I left *mi alma* to "fish for himself" and came to my little house, which I found more agreeable to my feelings.

Camp No. 7. Wednesday 17th. Last night I had a wolfish kind of a serenade! May Pan preserve me from the like tonight. Just as I had fixed myself for sleep after faning off to some other quarters the musquitoes, the delightful music began. Bak! ba! gnow, gnow, in such quick succession, it was almost impossible to distinguish one from the other. It was a mixture of cat, dog, sheep, wolf and the dear know what else. It was enough to frighten off sleep and everything else.

Ring, my dear, good dog! was lying under my side of the bed, which was next to wolves, the instant they came up, he had been listening, he flew out with a firce bark, and drove them away. I felt like caressing him for his kindness, but I had another business to attend to just then. Rided of our pest, I was destined to suffer from another. The winged pestilence unsatisfied with having their greedy thirst only half filled, returned with double force and vigor, to the attack. Here went my hands slap, slap, first one side then the other, meeting ever and anon the half closed palm of *mi alma,* who slept between the intervals of the sting. I was but a short time engaged at this when the serenaders began again. Save the mingled and confused noise they made, and the lone screech of an owl no other sound could be heard without. The stock had all ceased their wanderings and the teamsters their watching. The musquitoes, impudent things, had learned

13

more sense than to "buz before the bite." It was solitude indeed. The howling of ravinus beasts, and the screech of not less ravinous birds. I layed perfectly still with *mi alma* breathing a sweet sleep by my side. I could not waken him, just to keep me company, when he was so well engaged. So I remained quiet occasionally knocking off a musquito and listening to the confused sounds without and a wishing that my faithful Ring would not sleep so soundly. Just then, as if he had heard my thoughts and was anxious to prove to me that I was too hasty in my decision as to his vigilence, he gave one spring from his hiding place, and in a twinkling had driven them off entirely. As lonely as I was, I laughed out right. Sleep had entirely deserted me, so I *"kept watch"* till daylight. All the morning I have been noding.

We nooned it at a small creek—the name I do not know—While there we had a visit from an Indian of the *Kaw* tribe. They are a friendly nation. He stayed to dinner, eating I believe at both camps and left the ground when we did. His tribe are wanderers over this part of the Prairie, and often meet and eat with the traders. He was entirely in a state of nudity, except the breach clout which all of them wear. His horse, dog, and rifle were his companions. He smoked his pipe while we were preparing dinner, and watched with a scrutinizing eye. How exceedingly silent he was. I did not hear him speak but two words, and they were telling his name.

Our camp tonight is on a hill, the opposite side of

14

the creek from the wagons; the musquitoes there are too thick to thrive among them.

Bluff Creek Camp No. 8. All day we have been traveling in the rain, not even stoping for our dinner. The oxen travel better in such weather, and Mr. Hall, the superintendent of affairs, wished to push on. As we were quietly joging along in front of the wagons a beautiful little animal of some kind attracted our attentions. I supposed it a dog, or a wolf at first, my dearest after many suppositions settled on its being nothing more than a stone. To settle all doubts we drew the spy-glass—and what was it? Nothing more or less than a timid though curious antelope. It did not run, but all curious as we were about it at first, to know what great objects we were coming toward it, it slowly advanced to meet us, but it advanced to its own destruction, poor creature!

Mi alma had his rifle, loaded only with pigeon shot; as we came within sixty yards of it, he fired with one barrel, and missed, the little thing jumped to the side of the road, and instead of scampering off over the adjacent hill as I should have done had I been in his place, he turned to behold the now still more curious objects. The fire from the other barrel wounded it in the shoulder, and it went limping away. *Mi alma* started back for his bullets, as grape shot were too small, but just then one of the teamsters with his dog came bolting by in pursuit of it. It ran off over the hills, poor creature no doubt to die. Since it was left with life and pain attached to it, I am sorry it was shot at.

15

We stoped about 6 o'clock for each one was anxious to gratify his growling stomach. *Mi alma* and I went as usual to fishing in the little stream, but found nothing. The oxen make a perfect stamper row among the finied tribe, so we were obliged to retreat.

Council Grove, 145 miles from I [ndependence]. Friday 19th. Camp No. 9. We are now at the great rendezvous of all the traders. Council Grove may be considered the dividing ridge between the civilized and barbarous, for now we may look out for hostile Indians. Council Grove is so called from the circumstance of the U. S. agents* who were sent out in the year 1825, to measure a road from Missouri to Santa Fé, from their having met here and held a consultation with some Indian tribes,† who promised in a treaty not only to let go unmolested the traders, but also to lend their aid in defending them against their more ruthless neighbors of the mountainous regions further west.

It is a thick cluster of trees some miles in length, through which runs a small creek called Council Grove Creek. There is a quantity of fine timber consisting of oaks, hickory, walnut &c. Each company coming out generally stop here a day or so to repair their wagons, rest the stock, get timbers for the remainder of the journey; these are lashed under the wagons. They also mould bullets & prepare their fire arms for now they are coming into the region of game.

* Messrs. [Benjamin] Reeves, [George C.] Sibley and [Thomas] Mathers.

† Osages.

16

Another thing is the washing of cloth[e]s; there is a great borrowing of soap and slopping of water now.

We got here about 1 o'clock, just as some two or three companies were leaving. The creek bank, which is short and steep, made some little detention in the crossing of the wagons, they had to double teams several times. It is amusing here to hear the shouting of the wagoners to their animals, whooping and hallowing; the cracking of whips almost deafening.

We struck our camp on the hill. There is a large mound just by us, from the top of which is a splendid view is to be had. On one side, to the west, is a wide expanse of Prairie; as far as the eye can reach nothing but a waving sea of tall grass is to be seen. Out the other, for miles around are trees and hills. I went up onto it at sunset, and thought I had not seen, ever, a more imposing sight.

In our travels today we stoped two miles the other side of Council Grove, at what is called Big John's Spring.[7] The origin of its name I have not learned, but in place of it I found by experience that it is the

[7] Big John's Spring. This was a remarkably fine spring, discovered on June 13, 1827, by and named for John Walker, a member of the party of the three Commissioners appointed to survey the road to Santa Fé in 1825-1827. He was expert in lettering with his pen-knife and tomahawk. Because of his gigantic size he was called "Big John." On the date mentioned Walker took to Sibley some of the water from the spring and asked him what name it should have. The latter directed him to cut in large letters on a big oak that grew near the spring "Big John's Spring." (Sibley, "Route to Santa Fé" in *Western Journal*, vol. 5, p. 178.)

most delightful water we have had on the road. It is
quite a romantic place; just from the side of the hill
around which the road winds, we ascend a rather steep
bank, at the foot of which is a natural basin of half a
foot or more deep, filled [with] cristal liquid as cold
and pure as ever mortal can need. The scenery around
is very wild and rather awing. While I stood apparently very calm and bold as *mi alma* bent down to fix
a little *toddy* with water from the clear flowing
stream, I could not suppress the fear, or rather the
thought of some wily savage or hungry wolf might be
lurking in the thick grape vines, ready the first advantageous moment to bounce upon my shoulders. I
would not tell *mi alma* these foolish fears, for I knew
he would ridicule them, and this was torture to me,
but Ring, my faithful Ring, came by me just then
and I commenced patting his head which made him
lie at my feet and I felt *safe* with this trusty soldier
near me. We took dinner quite late today and in consequence go without supper, for want of appetite. For
my part I am off to bed as soon as it is dark.

Camp No. 10. Still at Council Grove. At early sun
rise this morning Col. Owens and Armijo's company
arrived. Stayed in camp nearly all day. About sun
down Mr. M. took me to see an adjacent spring. It
bursts from the foot of the mound I spoke of yesterday and in a thick clump of high grass. It is rather a
strange place, one comes upon it without ever thinking that such a thing could be near. It is quite deep,
though not larger than half a bushel. The water is
perfectly cool and clear. Besides this we took a long

walk around and through the hills. The scenery is truly magnificent. At one view we have stretched before us lofty hills entirely destitute of shrubbery; at their base gurgled along in quiet solitude a pearlly stream laving the feet of giant trees that looked down with scorn upon the diminutive creature man. In the green and tender grassed meadow just before us the foreground of the scene, were seen quietly grazing hundreds of cattle and mules, while others fatigued from daily toil were seen resting their weary limbs near the shade trees. To the right of us as we stood facing the N. E., might be seen a small *village* as it were, formed though of wagons only. A "corral" had been formed, or in English the wagons were so arranged as to form a great circle into which the stock are some times driven for a night's protection, and always for a "catch up." Around and inside of this the teamsters were actively employed repairing their wagons, and making further preparations for "the road." This view was all to the North and N. E. as we stood on the high and celebrated mound of Council Grove. To our backs lay other and similar scenes, beautiful alike for the artists pencil. We have one in our Company, Mr. Stanley[8] rather celebrated for his

[8] John Mix Stanley made sketches and paintings of the wild scenes encountered on the expedition into the wilderness of the West during the first half of the last century. His works were among the most interesting of that period. The Smithsonian Institution in December, 1852, issued a catalogue of his pictures describing them as "accurate portraits painted from life of forty-three different tribes of Indians, obtained at the cost, hazard, and inconvenience of ten years' tour through the southwestern prairies,

Indian sketches. His acquaintance I have not yet made, but at any rate a sketch of this would do his hand credit.

Camp No. 11, Sunday 21st. We left our two days' camp this morning by 6½ o'clock. The "Diamond Spring"[9] at which we are now lying being but twelve miles distant we made the whole drive at once. Got into camp by 2 o'clock.

The Company today presents rather a more extensive van. We have a strange compound of Americans, Mexicans and negroes; Horses, mules and oxen. This may litterally be considered our start *No. 2*, after

New Mexico, California and Oregon." This catalogue listed 151 pictures left on exhibition. All but five of them were burnt by fire January 24, 1865. One of these five, showing a buffalo hunt, is reproduced in this volume.

Stanley enlisted in Lieut. Emory's detachment, and accompanied him to California. The illustrations in the Senate edition of Emory's *Notes of a Military Reconnoissance,* are the work of John Stanley. In 1853 Stanley accompanied Isaac I. Stevens on his "Explorations for a route for the Pacific Railroad from St. Paul to Puget Sound." A great many of his sketches have been reproduced in Mr. Stevens' Report. (Bushnell, David I., in *Smithsonian Report,* 1924.)

[9] Diamond Spring was discovered by "Old Ben Jones," a hunter of Sibley's party, on August 11, 1825. "It gushes out from the head of a hollow in the prairie and runs among clean stones to Otter Creek." It furnishes enough good, clear, cold water to supply an army, and is superior to the fountain in the Arabian Desert, known as the "Diamond of the Desert"; the name of the latter suggested a good name for this spring, which might well be called the "Diamond of the Plain." Sibley camped there June 10, 1827, and had Big John carve the name on an Elm. (Sibley, "Route to Santa Fé" in *Western Journal,* vol. 5, p. 180.)

a respite of two days and the augmenting of our fources to forty-five wagons. We compose three or four different camps. It is a village on a hill this, for we are strewn in all directions; where the abodes of men are not seen, the stock are in grazing, appearing as much, to the distant spectator, like little dark huts of some kind, while our tents and largest wagons appear like magnificent domes.

Camp No. 12. Ouch, what a day this is! We started in the rain, came in the rain, and stoped in the rain. Last night was a very cold night, and about day-light it commenced raining. We started at 9 o'clock having had difficulty in yoking the oxen. After travelling only a mile two of the wagons stuck at the crossing of a small creek and we were there detained some time, but finally got off, and arrived here by 4 o'clock. This camping ground is called the "Lost spring" from what cause I do not know. It is 12 miles from "Diamond Spring."

We met Capt. Bent[10] this morning, on his return from his fort up the big Arkansas river. While he was in conversation with Mr. M. [Samuel Magoffin] I closed a letter to Papa. It was a hurried affair, for I had only a few minutes to do it in, and then the wind and rain were blowing in my face, blotting my paper, and shaking me so I scarcely knew what I wrote.

This is certainly one of the "varieties of life" as well as of traveling. To be shut up in a carriage all

[10] Capt. Charles Bent left Fort Bent June 12, 1846, and arrived at Independence June 29 following. Leaving St. Louis on July 24, he arrived at Fort Bent August 17, 1846.

day with a buffalo robe rolled around you, and with the rain pouring down at ten knots an hour. And at the close of this to be quietly without any trouble to one's self, into the middle of a bed in a nice dry tent, with writing materials around you and full privellege to write anything and every thing that may chance to enter one's head whether foolishness, as this is, or wisdom. We have rainy days any place and they are not more disagreeable on the plains than in N. Y. I have books, writing implements, sewing, kniting, somebody to talk with, a house that does not leak and I am satisfied, although this is a juicy day *en el campo!*

Camp No. 13. "Lost spring" June 23rd. If I cannot spin a yarn today it is not because I have no field for action! Here I am in the middle of my bed, with my feet drawn up under me like a tailor. I have taken refuge from the rain, which from the time we went to bed last night till this time 3 o'clock P. M. has continued to fall—not exactly in torrents, but quite fast, and driving against the tent as though it would wash us away every moment. But we continue dry over head and that is *something,* for our neighbours over the way, are washed head and foot. We were late rising this morning for we had nothing to do; when we did get up, we eat our breakfast and *came back to bed again;* that is, we sat in the middle of the bed to keep our feet dry. The water ran through the tent like a little spring, so we just turned the carpet up to the pole, and left that part of the house to see after itself.

Alma mia soon grew tired of sitting with his feet

as high as his head, so he put his head into my lap,—
me at my work in the mean time—and dozed a little
and talked a little. Soon we both lay down for a nap,
but just as we were fixed for this our neighbour Col.
Owens, feeling apprehensive for our welfare and
anxious to let us know his own fate, stepped in. He
has been compelled to take up his alls and find another
resting place, for to use his own words "the floor of
his *house* looked as though a parcel of pigs had turned
a trough of slop over in it and then wallowed till it
was a perfect mire." Rather a sad predicament that;
he found us in rather a more *thriving* condition.

As bad as it all is, I enjoy it still. I look upon it as
one of the "varieties of life," and as that is always
"spice" of course it must be enjoyed.

If I live through all this—and I think from all appearances now I shall come off the winner—I shall
be fit for one of the *Oregon pioneers*. We are here
without a stick of wood to get anything to eat, all that
was provided at the last camp having been used last
night & this morning—some of the men though have
gone off, perhaps several miles to find some. I believe
there is not a tree in sight of camp. And this should
no longer be called the lost spring for it is "runing
high" now, and taking all before it.

*Thursday 25th. Camp 15. Cotton wood creek 12
miles.* We are here and as much as a bargain! I have
been trying all day to recollect the scenes of yesterday, for I did not write them then.

I believe I have at length found them at least in
part. We left the Lost Spring about 7 o'clock yester-

day morning with the intention if possible to reach
Cottonwood before night, and without stoping for
dinner. But the previous rains foiled our attempts at
this. The roads were very heavy and often the mud
entirely blocked a wagon wheel. Our speed averaged
not more than one mile per hour. At 3 o'clock P. M.
after a travel of 6 or 7 ms. we stoped to noon it on the
open prairie without wood, save a little that was
saved of our scant supply at the "Lost Spring."

Col. Owens and his partner Mr. Awld[11] were more

[11] James Aull, born in Wilmington, Delaware, in 1804, was
the son of John and Margaret (Elliot) Aull. He removed from
Newcastle, Delaware, in 1836 to Lexington, Missouri, following
his eldest brother, John Aull, who had been engaged successfully
in merchandising in western Missouri since 1819. Later, another
brother, Robert, joined them, and the three, known as Aull
Brothers, conducted stores at Lexington, Liberty, Richmond, and
Independence, Missouri. The brothers were well known throughout the western country, and accumulated great fortunes; John
and Robert being known as the capitalists of western Missouri.
They were energetic, active, and liberal men in the period between 1820 and 1860, and contributed largely to educational and
civic enterprises. James Aull joined Colonel Samuel C. Owens
in the Santa Fé trade, and strangely both of them met violent
deaths on their expedition of 1846. Aull was brutally assassi-
nated by Mexicans in his store at Chihuahua on June 23, 1847.
Being alone in his store one evening, four Mexicans came in
ostensibly to trade, but when he turned his back they stabbed
him to death, carrying away most of his goods and money. A
fine repeating gold watch was overlooked, and this, together
with Mr. Aull's Bible, was faithfully preserved and brought back
to Missouri by his negro servant, Andrew. Mr. Aull was buried
in the Catholic Cemetery at Chihuahua. Unsuccessful efforts
were made by his brothers to locate the remains and bring them

pushing in their attempts. Their ox teams (they have five) passed us and came on I believe safe to this place. But his mule teams (some eighteen or twenty) were from the time we stoped till 6 o'clock passing the little wet weather creek near which we camped. At 6 o'clock we left and about a mile distant found the Col. in a sad predicament indeed. He had one wagon fast in a mud-hole with the tongue twisted off, and two others so much disabled he could not move them; his teams had given out and there he was for the night.

Seeing all this made our wagoners ambitious to get on, so they set to work in right good earnest, and after the usual quantity of swearing, whooping, and cracking of whips, they succeeded in passing their wagons. It was now nearly dark, and they had to drive to the top of a long hill before any kind of a camping place could be found.

When they got there they had neither wood nor water, so the night was spent in fasting and wet cloths.

We drove all of our concern, that is, the little Rockaway carriage we are travelling in, Jane's dearborn

back to Missouri. It was their desire to have them reinterred in the Cemetery Square at Lexington, originally donated by James Aull to that city in 1836.

No man in western Missouri commanded a greater degree of respect and affection in those days, when Independence and Lexington were the starting points for Santa Fé and Oregon trails, than James Aull. He was an elder in the Lexington Presbyterian Church, which was built on the lot adjoining his residence. An unassuming gentleman, of energy and judgment. He never married.

and the baggage wagon, on about half a mile further
to where Col. Owens had one or two more wagons
stuck fast near a small wet weather branch or small
creek. It was now after 9 o'clock and quite damp. So
just as soon as our tent could be stretched and the
bed made, which took us till after 10—I slipped off
to *roost*.

I was so tired I could not sleep; it commenced raining too and beat so near my head, I thought every
minute I must surely get a ducking, but I kept dry
though, and a little before daylight got a short nap.

Soon the wagoners were stirring, anxious to cross
the creek before it should rain any more. The principal pass way was blocked by Col. Owens' wagons,
so they doubled teams and cut around to make one of
their own. Then tent was soon knocked up and off we
came to "Cotton Wood" to get our breakfast, for we
had not a stick of wood to cook with there, and hungry
necessity compelled us to come, we had had nothing
to eat since dinner yesterday. We crossed the creek
without difficulty, the banks are long but not very
steep; the rain has made them quite slippy, but our
little light carriages passed them easy. We got our
dinner, or rather breakfast about 1 o'clock. Seven of
the wagons with doubled teams came over this morning, the others are coming in now, late P. M.

While Jane and I were on a little stroll after
dinner, I carelessly walking along steped almost onto
a large snake; it moved and frightened me very much.
Of course I screamed and ran off, and like a ninny
came back when the snake had been frightened by me

as much as it had me, and had gone I can't tell where.
I came back to look for it.

The last wagon did not get over till 9 o'clock. It
stuck in the mud and when two drivers with eleven
yoke of oxen failed to move it some more hands went
down from camp and they "whiped out" a teamster's
term meaning they fell to work with their whip
handles and beat the poor oxen, whooping and yelling
all the time, till one is almost induced to believe their
throats will split. They continue this till fear of their
oppressors will compel the brutes to pull till they
move it, and as a reward for their preseverance they
come off with bloody necks from the yoke's rubbing,
and their heads and backs well whip-lashed. It is a
hard life both for driver and animals, and this day
has been so especially, the drive was not long but
difficult.

Camp No. 16. I have not yet described "The Cotton
Wood." I went down this P. M., after the little
shower we had, to see it. And such a ramble it was.

The camp ground is on a slight rise, and some three
or four hundred yards down is a steep bank covered
with cotton wood trees, (which give it the name).
Just below rolls a placid little stream, resembling
some the Council Grove, though not so grand or
lively. Its waters were darkened by the recent rain
and perhaps that makes the difference. Just at the
water's edge are quantities of gooseberry and rasp-
berry bushes. They were nearly rifled of their fruits
by the wagoners, before I went to them. Above these
and on the side rather of the cliff, is a thick plumb

27

grove—these too I missed for they are not yet ripe; however I pulled some of them only to say I had picked three kinds of fruits in one spot on Cottonwood creek.

Jane and I climbed entirely down this bank as steep as it was. Women are venturesome creatures! And we found this still more true when we were ready to return. We had difficulties now that were entirely unseen coming down. We had wandered farther up the stream than the place where we descended and there found our road steeper and more slippy. But we took it all in good part and procured long sticks to assist us in our undertaking. I took the lead stoping at every step to laugh at my own picture (an old woman with her back bent double, her cloths held up to her knees and a long staff) and to place my walking stick in a safe place before venturing to rest my precious self on it. We finally reached the land, for we considered ourselves in the water before as one false step would have landed us in the little stream, and to me quite fearful from its dark looks.

One of the prairie pests to me is a green bug, which I can do more justice to in describing by calling it an *aligator in miniature*. Its legs and body are both very long and remarkably slender, and it goes creeping and feeling about everything before it. I am no friend to bugs, worms, or snakes, and though the good people here assure me there is no harm attached to it, its very looks frighten me. I never walk in the grass without holding my dress up high, from fear that its long arm may chance to grapple me. These things, snakes and musquitoes are the only disagreeable parts of my prairie life.

To have peeped into our tent this afternoon one might have been induced to believe I disliked the rain, but the idea is mistaken! It is truly fun for me. I kick up the carpet, put all things from the floor on to the chairs, pull off my own shoes, and then take my seat in the middle of the bed, which I am induced to introduce as my boat, not from its shape, or appearance in any way, but from its keeping me dry from the pond of water below me. I might spin a long yarn and say it is a perfect river, with fishes and great animals, but not so, it runs in a little stream only frightening off the bugs, and this part I don't object to. I am their sworn enemy and it does me no harm to see them floating down the stream.

Camp No. 17. Out on the Prairie with no wood and little water. I am in as good humour this morning as any one can be when they have been kept awake all night by the outward elements. We got to camp last evening rather late and I put off writing till this morning, but I am afraid the *good humour* I am in will not let me recollect the events of yesterday.

I must first record the *trials* of last night—It had something the appearance of rain at dark & accordingly I prepared for a drenching during the night. But it did not come though. But I am sure I should prefer it if I knew that another such was in store for me. The heat at first was so great, I had to pull all but my chemise [off], and even that would have been sent off without regret, had not modesty forbid me.

29

I had just fussed and turned about till sleep came to my relief, but it brought with it a gust of wind that I thought would blow our house, the bed its *inmates* and all into a mass too much on the chaos order to be separated ever. To add to all the pleasure and beauty of this, it commenced lightening, right in my face. It actually seemed that everything was angry with me from some cause or other & were now taking their "satisfaction." The wind carried with it the heat, but put in its place a chilly damp air. I commenced pulling for couver, but that was out of place and after a search in the dark, I found that Mr. Ringling (the dog) had very gallantly made his bed on it. I hoisted him from this berth though, and with my burthen crawled back to my own, to *"make the best of it."*

But for our yesterday's travel. We left at 7 o'clock in the morning—came some six miles, the road tolerably good, nooned it on the Prairie with little water and no wood but that provided at Cottonwood. After dinner to get rid of the hot sun, we spread out a buffalo robe in the little shade made by the carriage, and took a short siesta of a few minutes. The drive in the evening was not so far though quite as good. The roads are very heavy, wagons are sticking constantly in the marshy ground through which we have principally come today.

Saw an antelope this P. M. It was not quite so venturesome as the one we saw at Council Grove and did not come near. Rather a sensible creature that! He knows something of the cruel and wily man!

Camp No. 18 On the wide Prairie. Sunday June

28th, 1846. This is my third Sabbath on the Plains. And how does conscience tell me it has been spent? Oh, may my heavenly father grant me pardon for my wickedness! Did I not in the very beginning of it forget—yes, and how can I be pardoned for the great sin—that it was the Holy Sabbath, appointed by my heavenly father for a day of rest—and classed it so much with the days of the week, that I regularly took out my week's work, kniting. Oh, how could I ever have been so thoughtless, so unmindful of my duty and my eternal salvation!

Passed the whole day with little wood, and no water for the cattle, but some little about in puddles. Had some difficulty in crossing a swampy place, this evening; the teamsters had to mow grass and put in it, before they could pass their teams.

Noon. No. 20. Little Arkansas River. June 30th, 1846. Come my feeble pen, put on thy specks and assist this full head to unburthen itself! Thou hast a longer story than is usual to tell. How we left *Camp No. 19* yesterday (Monday) morning after a sleepless night, our tent was pitched in the musquito region and when will the God Somnus make his appearance in such quarters? It was slap, slap, all the time, from one party of the combatants, while the others came with a buz and a bite.

We traveled till 11 o'clock with the hope of finding water for the weary cattle. The sun was excessively oppressive. Col. Owens' mule teams left us entirely, but his oxen like ours were unable to stand the heat. They were before us and stoped—we followed their

example, as much from necessity as any thing else.
The oxen, some of them staggered under their yokes,
and when we turned out for want of water—there was
none within five miles of us that we knew of—some of
the most fatigued absolutely crept under the wagons
for shade, and did not move till they were driven up
in the evening. One poor thing fell in the road and we
almost gave him up for lost. His driver though, rather
a tender hearted lad I presume, went with a bucket
to a *mud hole* and brought the *wet mud* which was a
little cool, and *plastered his body over with it.* He
then got all the water from the water kegs after the
men had drank, which was not more than two or three
tin cups full; he took this and opening the ox's mouth
poured it down his throat. He then made a covering
over him with the ox yokes standing up and blankets
spread over. In the course of an hour or two the poor
thing could get up, and walk. But his great thirst for
water led him to searching in the deep grass, and when
the wagons started at 5 o'clock, he could not be found.
Roman, the old Mexican who attended the loose stock,
hunted some time for him, but to no purpose. Other
sick ones needed his attention and it was probable this
one had gone back to the last night's camp ground,
and as it was too far to send on an uncertainty and
pressing times, we gave up the search.

It blew up a little cooler towards sunset and we
travelled pretty well, to make water was our object;
both man and beast were craving it. The former could
occasionally find a little to quench his parched thirst,
by searching ravines that were grown up with tall

weeds, this tho' muddy, and as warm as a scorching
sun beaming into it all day could make it, was a luxuri-
ous draught. Now, about dark, we came into the
musquito regions, and I found to my great *horror* that
I have been complaining all this time for nothing, yes
absolutely for *nothing;* for some two or hundred or
even thousands are nothing compared with what we
now encountered. The carriage mules became so rest-
less that they passed all the wagons and switching
their tails from side to side, as fast as they could, and
slaping their ears, required some strength of our
Mexican driver to hold them in. He would jerk the
reins and exclaim *"hola los animal[es] cómo estande
bravos!"* [Ho, animals! how wild you are!] The moon
was not very bright and we could not see far before
us. Suddenly one of the mules sprang to one side,
reared, and pitched till I really believed we should
turn over. Magoffin discouvered something lying in
the road, and springing from the carriage pulled me
out. It was a dead ox lying immediately in our way,
and it is no wonder the mule was frightened.

In my own hurry to get out I had entirely forgotten
the musquitoes, and on returning to the carriage I
found my feet covered with stings, and my dress full,
where they had gotten on me in the grass. About 10
o'clock we came upon a dark ravine, over which *las
caras* [*los carros*—the wagons] would probably experience some difficulty in passing, so we stoped to
see them over. The mules became perfectly frantic,
and nothing could make them stand. They were
turned out to shift for themselves, and Magoffin

seeing no other alternative than to remain there all night, tied his head and neck up with pocket handkerchiefs and set about having the tent stretched. I drew my feet up under me, wraped my shawl over my head, till I almost smothered with heat, and listened to the din without. And such a noise as it was, I shall pray ever to be preserved. Millions upon millions were swarming around me, and their knocking against the carriage *reminded me of a hard rain.* It was equal to any of the plagues of Egypt. I lay almost in a perfect stupor, the heat and stings made me perfectly sick, till Magoffin came to the carriage and told me *to run if I could,* with my shawl, bonnet and shoes on (and without opening my mouth, Jane said, for they would *choke* me) straight to the bed. When I got there they pushed me straight in under the musquito bar, which had been tied up in some kind of a fashion, and oh, dear, what a relief it was to breathe again. There I sat in my cage, like an imprisoned creature frightened half to death.

Magoffin now rolled himself up some how with all his cloths on, and lay down at my side, he dare not raise the bar to get in. I tried to sleep and towards daylight succeeded. On awaking this morning I found my forehead, arms and feet covered with knots. They were not little red places as musquitos generally make, but they were knots, some of them quite as large as a pea. We knocked up the tent as quick as possible and without thinking of breakfast came off to this place, passing on our way our own wagons and those of Col. Owens encamped at Mud Creek.

On our arrival here the buffalo and pillow were spread out and I layed down to sleep and I can say it took no rocking to accomplish the end. The tent was stretched with the intention of remaining here all night. The crossing is quite difficult, the sun extremely warm and it was supposed the oxen could not go on. About 11 o'clock *mi alma* came and raised me by my hand entirely up onto my feet without waking me. The whole scene had entirely changed. The sky was perfectly dark, wind blowing high, the atmosphere cool and pleasant and *no musquitoes,* with every appearance of a hard storm.

At 12 o'clock breakfast was ready, and after drinking a cup of tea I fell on the bed completely worn out. After two or three hours sound sleep I got up washed, combed my head, put on clean cloths—a luxury on the plains by the way—and sallied forth in the cool air somewhat refreshed. I brought out my writing implements and here I am.

Noon. 21. Little Cow Creek. July 1, 1846. According to the calculation of Mr. Gregg,[12] a gentleman

[12] Dr. Josiah Gregg was quite a mechanical genius, as well as a Santa Fé trader, traveler, explorer, and author. On one of his many trips to Santa Fé he was employed by a priest to build a clock in the tower of his church, the contract price for which was one thousand dollars. Dr. Gregg, however, finished the work in much less time than was anticipated by the priest, and he refused to pay more than seven hundred dollars. When building the clock Dr. Gregg placed in it the image of a little negro, which, when the clock would strike, would come outside and dance. Some months after Dr. Gregg's return to the United States he received a letter from the priest stating that the little negro had ceased to perform his mission, and if he would return

who made several expeditions across the Prairies and who wrote a history of the trade &c, we are 249 miles from Independence.

We camped last night at Arrow Rock creek—most of our travel yesterday was after 5 o'clock P. M. till 10—8 miles. I was quite sick and took medicine which has made me feel like a new being today. I am at least *50 per cent better*.

We had a fine dinner today and I enjoyed it ex-

and repair it he would pay him the remainder of his money, according to the original contract. The following spring Dr. Gregg returned to Santa Fé and repaired the clock. Upon inquiry, he learned that the priest's flock had told him the reason the negro would not come out and dance as before was because he had not paid the full price agreed upon. Dr. Gregg received his three hundred dollars and heard no more of the clock.

Dr. Gregg was born in Overton County, Tennessee, July 19, 1806, the son of Harmon and Susannah (Smelser) Gregg. In 1809 Harmon Gregg moved his family to Illinois, and from there to the territory of Missouri three years later, settling in the Boone's Lick Country. Josiah Gregg was a physician, but probably never practiced his profession, as he began life on the plains at the age of twenty-five. He was a war correspondent for American newspapers during the Mexican War. He wrote *Commerce of the Prairies,* which is generally accepted as a great work. His death occurred while on an expedition into the mountains of California in the winter of 1849. He was captain of a party of forty, organized for the expedition, but only eight of them made the start. The others backed down when the Indian guides refused to go on account of an unusually severe storm. The Indians prophesied that snow in the mountains would present an insurmountable barrier, and their fears were justified by the terrible sufferings and casualties which came upon the explorers. Dr. Gregg died of exhaustion, due principally to lack of food.

ceedingly, for I had eaten nothing but a little tea and half a biscuit since yesterday dinner. It consisted of boiled chicken, soup, rice, and a dessert of *wine and gooseberry tart*. Such a thing on the plains would be looked upon by those at home as an utter impossibility. But nevertheless it is true. Jane and I went off as soon as we got here and found enough to make a fine pie. I wish the plumbs and grapes were ripe; there is any quantity of them along all the little streams we pass.

One of the wagoners chased a wolf today. We see them frequently lurking about, ready to come pick the scraps, if the dogs chance to leave any, where we have camped.

Camped tonight at big Cow Creek, three miles from the other which we left at seven o'clock. The crossing here is very bad and took us till moon down to cross. It is good water and wood, so we struck camp.

Camp No. 22. Bank of the Arkansas River. Prairie scenes are rather changing today. We are coming more into the buffalo regions. The grass is much shorter and finer. The plains are cut up by winding paths and every thing promises a *buffalo dinner* on the *4th*.

We left our last night's camp quite early this morning. About 9 o'clock we came upon "Dog City." This curiosity is well worth seeing. The Prairie dog, not much larger than a well grown rat, burrows in the ground. They generally make a regular town of it, each one making his house by digging a hole, and heaping the dirt around the mouth of this. Two are generally built together in a neighbourly way. They of course visit as regularly as man. When we got into this one, which lays on both sides of the road occupying at least a circle of some hundred yards, the little fellows like people ran to their doors to see the passing crowd. They could be seen all around with their heads poked out, and expressing their opinions I supposed from the loud barking I heard.

We nooned it on the Prairie without water for the cattle, within sight of the river, but some six miles from it. The banks are quite sandy and white, having the appearance, at a distance, of a large city. It is shaded by the trees in some places, having very much the appearance of white and coloured houses.

Came to camp tonight before sunset. Col. Owens' Company, which got before us this morning, were just starting after performing the last office to the dead body of a Mexican. He had consumption. Poor man, 'twas but yesterday that we sent him some soup from our camp, which he took with relish and today he is in his grave!

The manner of interring on the plains is necessarily very simple. The grave is dug very deep, to prevent the body from being found by the wolves. The corpse is rolled in a blanket—lowered and stones put on it. The earth is then thrown in, the sod replaced and it is well beat down. Often the corral is made over it, to make the earth still more firm, by the tromping of the stock. The Mexicans always place a cross at the grave.

Our camp is on the bank of the Arkansas tonight. Its dark waters remind me of the Mississippi.—It makes me sad to look upon it.—I am reminded of home. Though the Mississippi is a vast distance from there—it seems to me a near neighbour, compared with the distance I am from it—now three hundred miles from Independence. The time rolls on so fast I can scarcely realize its three weeks out.

Camp No. 23. This has indeed been a long day's travel. We left the Arkansas river, along which we have been traveling far and near since we first struck it, this morning by a little after 6 o'clock, and by 10 o'clock reached the Walnut Creek, a branch of the Arkansas, and eight miles from it. Crossed it with ease, the water quite deep though—and nooned it 4 miles farther near the Arkansas. Today I have seen the first time wild buffalo. A herd of some ten or 12 were just across the river from our nooning place. The teamsters all afire to have a chase started off half a dozen of them—and much to our surprise, for we expected nothing of the kind, killed one—so after all we are to have a buffalo dinner tomorrow.

Started this P. M. about 4 o'clock traveled well till 6 o'clock, when a very hard thunder storm came up and detained us *in the road* till after eight. A thunder storm at sunset on the Prairie is a sublime and awing scene indeed. The vivid and forked lightning quickly succeeded by the hoarse growling thunder impresses one most deeply of his own weakness and the magnanimity of his God. With nothing before or near us in sight, save the wide expanse of Prairie resembling most fully in the pale light of the moon, as she occasionally appeared from under a murky cloud and between the vivid lightning, the wide sea. There was no object near higher than our own wagons, and how easy would it have been for one of them to be struck and consume the whole crowd, for with it was a high wind, sufficient to counteract the effects of the drenching rain.

We traveled on till 12 o'clock and stoped near the "Pawnee Rock"—a high mound with one side of sand stone. It derives its name from a battle once fought there between some company and a band of the Pawnee Indians. It has rather an awing name, since this tribe are the most treacherous and troublesome to the traders.

July 4th 1846. Pawnee Fork. Saturday. What a disasterous *celebration* I have today. It is certainly the greatest miracle that I have my head on my shoulders. I think I can never forget it if I live to be as old as my grandmother.

The wagons left Pawnee Rock some time before us.—For I was anxious to see this wonderful curiosity. We went up and while *mi alma* with his gun and pistols kept watch, for the wily Indian may always be apprehended here, it is a good lurking place and they are ever ready to fall upon any unfortunate trader behind his company—and it is necessary to be careful, so while *mi alma* watched on the rock above and Jane stood by to watch if any should come up on the front side of me, I cut my name, among the many hundreds inscribed on the rock and many of whom I knew. It was not done well, for fear of Indians made me tremble all over and I hurried it over in any way. This

40

I remarked would be quite an adventure to celebrate the 4th! but woe betide I have yet another to relate.

The wagons being some distance ahead we rode on quite briskly to overtake them. In an hour's time we had driven some six miles, and at *Ash creek* we came up with them. No water in the creek and the crossing pretty good only a tolerably steep bank on the first side of it, all but two had passed over, and as these were not up we drove on ahead of them to cross first. The bank though a little steep was smooth and there could be no difficulty in riding down it.—However, we had made up our minds always to walk down such places in case of accident, and before we got to it *mi alma* hallowed "woe" as he always does when he wishes to stop, but as there was no motion made by the driver to that effect, he repeated it several times and with much vehemence. We had now reached the very verge of the cliff and seeing it a good way and apparently less dangerous than jumping out as we were, he said "go on." The word was scarcely from his lips, ere we were whirled completely over with a perfect crash. One to see the wreck of that carriage now with the top and sides entirely broken to pieces, could never believe that people had come out of it alive. But strange, wonderful to say, we are almost entirely unhurt! I was considerably stunned at first and could not stand on my feet. *Mi alma* forgetting himself and entirely enlisted for my safety carried me in his arms to a shade tree, almost entirely without my knowledge, and rubing my face and hands with whiskey soon brought me entire to myself.—My

41

back and side are a little hurt, but is very small compared with what it might have been. *Mi alma* has his left hip and arm on which he fell both bruised and strained, but not seriously. Dear creature 'twas for me he received this, for had he not caught me in his arms as we fell he could have saved himself entirely. And then I should perhaps have been killed or much crushed for the top fell over me, and it was only his hands that kept it off of me. It is better as it is, for we can sympathise more fully with each other.

It was a perfect mess that; of people, books, bottles —one of which broke, and on my head too I believe,— guns, pistols, baskets, bags, boxes and the dear knows what else. I was insensible to it all except when something gave me a hard knock and brought me to myself. We now sought refuge in Jane's carriage for our own could only acknowledge its incapability.

By 12 o'clock we reached this place six miles, when we found all the companies which have come on before us, having been stoped by an order of Government.

Sunday 5th. I am rather better of my bruises today. It is only for a little while though, I fear; such knocks seldom hurt so much for a day or two. I am yet to suffer for it.

We are still at "The Pawnee Fork." The traders are all stoped here by an order of Government, to wait the arrival of more troops than those already ahead of us, for our protection to Santa Fé.

We are quite a respectable crowd now with some seventy-five or eighty wagons of merchandise, beside

those of the soldiers. When all that are behind us
come up we shall number some hundred and fifty.

And it is quite probable we shall be detained here
ten days or a week at the least. I shall go regularly to
housekeeping. It is quite a nice place this, notwithstanding the number of wagons and cattle we have
for our near neighbours. With the great Arkansas on
the South of us, the Pawnee creek to the S. W. and
extensive woods in the same direction. From the west
the buffalo are constantly coming in, in bands of from
three or four to more than fifty.

The sight of so many military coats is quite sufficient to frighten all the Indians entirely out of the
country. So we have nothing to fear either on account
of starvation, thirst or sudden murder.

Monday 6th. Camp No. 26. Ours is quite the picture of a hunter's home today.

The men, most of them, have been out since sun
rise, and constantly mules loaded with the spoils of
their several victories, are constantly returning to
camp. It is a rich sight indeed to look at the fine fat
meat stretched out on ropes to dry for our sustinence
when we are no longer in the regions of the living
animal. Such soup as we have made of the hump ribs,
one of the most choice parts of the buffalo. I never
eat its equal in the best hotels of N. Y. and Philad[a].
And the sweetest butter and most delicate oil I ever
tasted tis not surpassed by the marrow taken from the
thigh bones.

If one cannot live and grow fat here, he must be a
strange creature. Oh, how much Papa would enjoy

it! He would at once acknowledge that his venison camp never equaled it.

Mi alma was out this morning on a hunt, but I sincerely hope he will never go again. I am so uneasy from the time he starts till he returns. There is danger attached to it that the excited hunter seldom thinks of till it over take him. His horse may fall and kill him; the buffalo is apt too, to whirl suddenly on his persuer, and often serious if not fatal accidents occur. It is a painful situation to be placed in, to know that the being dearest to you on earth is in momentary danger of loosing his life, or receiving for the remainder of his days, whether long or short, a tormenting wound.

The servant who was with him today, was thrown from his horse by the latter stumbling in a hole, with which the Prairies are couvered, and had his head somewhat injured. And *mi alma's* horse was quite unruly.

Wednesday 8th. Camp No. 28. This is our fourth day here. It is quite a pleasant and homelike place this. They are busy in the kitchen (two wagons drawn near up and a hole dug in the ground for a fire place), preparations are making for a long jaunt on the Plains—for it seems they intend keeping us out of Santa Fé almost entirely.

The soldiers are coming in, and if we have to travel behind them, it will be poor living both for man and beast. We have all to be allowanced in our provisions from this out, or we shall have none at all.

A band of more than an hundred buffalo came al-

A BUFFALO HUNT ON THE SOUTHWESTERN PRAIRIES

From a painting by John M. Stanley.
Courtesy United States National Museum.

most within gun shot of the camp this morning, and for the first time I had a good opportunity of seeing the little calves. I sat down immediately and wrote to *Papa*.

Camp No. 29. Thursday 9th. We have permission today to go on as far as the ford of the Arkansas, or to Bent's Fort, as we like, and there to await the arrival of Col. Carney[13] the commanding officer. We shall prepare to leave here tomorrow or next day.

The Fort is 180 miles, and the Ford some seventy

[13] Stephen Watts Kearny was born in Newark, New Jersey, in the year 1794. His parents were Philip and Lady Barney Dexter (Ravaud) Kearny. While a student at King's College (now Columbia University) he volunteered for the War of 1812. He was given a commission as first lieutenant of infantry and served under Captain (later General) Wool. Captured by the British at the desperate battle of Queenstown Heights, and later exchanged, he was promoted to a captaincy, and remained in the service after the war. The remainder of his career was in the West and Southwest. In 1825 he went with General Atkinson to the head waters of the Missouri in the "Yellowstone Expedition."

In 1834 he organized the First Dragoons, a new branch of service, and as lieutenant colonel thereof accompanied Colonel Dodge in campaign against the Comanche Indians of the Red River country. The high discipline of this regiment became conspicuous, and General Gaines said: "The First Dragoons are the best troops I ever saw." While in command of the Third Military Department, headquarters at St. Louis, 1842-1846, Colonel Kearny made one of the most extraordinary marches on record. It extended as far as the South Pass of the Rocky Mountains, returning by way of Bent's Fort to Fort Leavenworth. He held successful counsel with many Indian tribes, resulting in protection to persons engaged in the Santa Fé trade. As a consequence of these experiences and achievements, he was put in charge of

or eighty. How long we are to be kept there, it is impossible to tell, perhaps it will be for two or three or even *six* months. Almost the length of time my *grandmother* spent in such a *palace!*

Today for the first time I have had a ride on horseback. It is a treat notwithstanding the jolting horse I was on. I am very much disappointed in my fine,

the "Army of the West" in 1846, during the war with Mexico, with rank of brigadier-general, and ordered to take military possession of New Mexico and California.

The selection of General Kearny for this post sent a thrill of joy and security through every man who expected to engage in that expedition, and volunteers rushed forward to enroll under his standard. This military campaign, including his remarkable march to California, resulted in the conquest of that territory. At the battle of San Pasqual, California, December 6, 1846, he was twice wounded. For gallantry and meritorious conduct he was brevetted major-general.

After his return to Washington in the winter of 1847, General Kearny was sent to Mexico. At Vera Cruz he contracted yellow fever, which undermined his health, and he died soon after the war at St. Louis, on October 31, 1848, in the home of Major Meriwether Lewis Clark.

General Kearny, though not a product of West Point, was a fine disciplinarian, a brave soldier and military genius. He was influential among the Indians and maintained a degree of good fellowship and esprit de corps among his officers and men, which was seldom equalled at any artillery post. He was at all times courteous, bland, approachable, and just; yet stern, fixed, and unwavering when his decisions were once formed. He inspired respect and confidence alike in officers and men in the ranks.

General Kearny married at St. Louis, September 5, 1830, at the residence of General William Clark, Miss Mary Radford, step-daughter of General Clark. She and several children survived him. (*St. Louis Republican,* November 3, 1848.)

noble bay. He walks and paces hard, but I must attribute it to his being spoiled in the buffalo chase. He is constantly on the lookout and requires all my strength nearly to hold him in. And I have grown to be quite an indifferent horsewoman to what I was in *my younger days!*

Friday. Camp 30th. The same routine of meat drying &c. Still lying by at Pawnee Creek—making some preparations though, to leave tomorrow. I have been sick nearly ever since I came here the consequences of my rare celebration of the 4th I suppose.

Saturday 11th. Camp 31st. Oh how gloomy the Plains have been to me today! I am sick, rather sad feelings and everything around corresponds with them.

We have never had such a perfectly dead level before us as now. The little hillocks which formerly broke the perfectly even view have entirely disappeared. The grass is perfectly short, a real buffalo and Prairie dog and rattle snake region.

We left our camp at Pawnee Fork this morning at 9 o'clock. It is 11 o'clock and one of the warmest and most disagreeable days the Prairie ever gave birth to. We stoped as there was plenty water and the oxen tired pulling over those great steep banks. We are nooning it here.

Some twenty of the Government wagons came up. We started again at 3 o'clock and traveled on till 9½ o'clock. Stoped on the prairie with a little water though enough for the cattle, twelve miles from Pawnee creek.

All the companies are before us, or rather they have taken a new road along the River. We are to go along by ourselves across the Prairie with little wood and perhaps no water, as is most generally the case at this point of the road near the Coon Creeks and heart of the buffalo range.

Coon cr. No. 1—5 ms, from Coon Cr. No. 2. Sunday 12th. Camp 32. About 30 miles from Pawnee Fork.

The Sabbath on the Plains is not altogether without reverence. Every thing is perfectly calm. The blustering, swearing teamsters remembering the duty they owe to their Maker, have thrown aside their abusive language, and are singing the hymns perhaps that were taught by a good pious Mother. The little birds are all quiet and reverential in their songs. And nothing seems disposed to mar that calm, serene silence prevailing over the land. We have not the ringing of church bells, or the privilege of attending public worship, it is true, but we have ample time, sufficient reason &c for thinking on the great wisdom of our Creator, for praising him within ourselves for his excellent greatness in placing before us and entirely at our command so many blessings; in giving us health, minds free from care, the means of knowing and learning his wise designs. &c.

We left our camp early this morning and nooned it out on the Prairie with out more shelter from the scorching sun than that afforded by the carriage. I took so much the advantage of this as to take a quiet evening siesta of half hour. A buffalo robe spread out on the ground under the *catrin* [carriage] with the cushions for my pillow, was my whole bed, and quite an acceptable one too.

We drove on till about 12 o'clock, for the morning's drive was not a very good one, and the moon shone so bright that *mi alma* wished to drive *all* night even, and gain as much as possible, but some of the men became refractory and stubborn and stoped in the road, refusing to drive any further because it was night, notwithstanding they had driven (on account of the heat) but a short distance during the drive. So there was nothing to be done but form a corral and spend the night here. *The place is called by Mr. Gregg, Coon Creek.*

Monday 13th Noon. Big Coon Creek, No. 3. Left our last night's camp at Little Coon cr. this morning quite late, after 8 o'clock, traveled steadily on till 12 making about eight or nine miles. The day has been rather cloudy and favourable for the oxen.

Passed a great many buffalo, (some thousands) they crossed our road frequently within two or three hundred yards. They are very ugly, ill-shapen things with their long shaggy hair over their heads, and the great hump on their backs, and they look so droll running. Ring had his own fun chasing them. They draw themselves into a perfect knot switching their tails about, and throwing all feet up at once. When the dog got near to any one of them he would whirl around and commence pawing the earth with not a very friendly feeling for his delicately formed persuer, I imagine.

We have seen several antelope too this morning. It is a noble animal indeed; and there is certainly nothing that moves with more majestic pride, or with more apparent disdain to inferior animals than he does. With his proud head raised aloft, nostrels expanded wide, he moves with all the lightness, ease and grace imaginable.

And we also had a rattle-snake fracas. There were not *hundreds* killed tho', as Mr. Gregg had to do to keep his animals from suffering, but some *two* or *three* were killed in the road by our carriage driver, and these were quite enough to make me sick.

Road to Bent's Fort. Saturday 18th. Camp 38, Bank of the Arkansas. I have written nothing in my journal since Monday, and what a considerable change there has been in affairs.

Tuesday I was taken sick—and recollect that we reached the River at noon that day. Went on about six miles in the evening, struck it again about Sun down, and camped for the night. We now had in company Messrs. Harmoney,[14] Davie,[15] Glasgow,[16] and

[14] Manuel X. Harmony, a native of Spain, but a naturalized citizen of the United States, living and doing business in New York. His firm's name was P. Harmony, Nephews & Co. This firm was engaged in trade with northern Mexico, and in the spring of 1846 sent out its regular caravan, in charge of Manuel X. Harmony. With this train of twelve wagons and teams, laden with merchandise, mostly from foreign countries, he left Independence May 27, 1846. Under the orders of General Kearny he was forced to remain with the other traders at Pawnee Fork, and then to travel in the rear of the army to Santa Fé.

Harmony aided Doniphan in two substantial ways; by communicating information relative to movements and designs of the

two companies of soldiers' wagons. Both Wednesday and Thursday we made pretty much the same travel, reached the crossing Thursday, when we nooned it.

enemy; by giving all his means and credit to supply provisions for the quartermaster and commissary department. Doniphan confiscated his wagons and impressed his men into service. M. B. Edwards, in his unpublished diary, has the following entry about him: "Harmony, a trader, formerly from old Spain, had his mules hid under pretense that the Apaches had stolen them, he wanted to remain behind until our battle at Chihuahua, and then come in as a great friend of the victor." Arriving at Chihuahua, Harmony decided that it was unsafe to remain there after the army should depart, so went with the Americans to join General Taylor. Harmony was given an escort of twenty-five American troops and permitted to travel as he wished, but under orders to keep in communication with the army. To avoid the heat he traveled mostly at night and camped during the day. During the fight of Captain Reid with the Indians at El Pozo, Harmony and his escort came up and entered into the fight. Returning to the United States in the fall of 1847, he filed a claim against the government for $82,956.89, besides a claim of $20,000 for damages for loss of time, use of his money, expenses, etc., because of his detention by the army and for impressment of his teamsters into the service. A committee of Congress reported a bill for his relief.

[15] Cornelius Davy was a prominent citizen and merchant of Independence in the early days. He returned to Independence from the expedition, here described, on July 13, 1847.

[16] Edward J. Glasgow, son of William and Sarah (Mitchell) Glasgow, was born in Belleville, Illinois, June 7, 1820. In 1827 his father moved his family to St. Louis. Edward Glasgow was educated at the St. Louis University and St. Charles (Missouri) College. Before attaining his majority he was appointed United States Consul at Guaymas by President Van Buren. Later, deciding not to remain at that seaport, he resigned. Glasgow went to Mexico in 1840 to take charge of a business in which he

Here we found it rather better to go on to the Fort especially as some two or three companies had gone before us and the Dctr. with them. Made a tolerable drive that evening, and camped on the River again. I was quite sick now took medicine.

Friday morning I was no better, and *mi alma* sent a man ahead to stop the Dr. He returned in the course of four or five hours, having left the Dr. in waiting some twelve miles ahead of us.

We left camp about 2 o'clock P. M. and leaving the wagons to follow on at leisure, hurried on to this place by sun set, (all the companies save Owens and our own wagons are here).

was interested jointly with James Harrison, and his uncle, James Glasgow. He located at Mazatlan and continued in trade there until 1843. In that year he left Mazatlan, sailing around Cape Horn to New York. He then embarked in the overland trade between Missouri and Chihuahua, forming a partnership with Dr. Henry Connelly, and continued in that business for five years.

When Colonel Doniphan organized a battalion of two companies of traders and their employes, Mr. Glasgow was elected captain of one of the companies. He took part in the battle of Sacramento, and entered Chihuahua with the army. Here he remained until the coming of General Price and his troops. During the latter part of 1847 and a part of 1848, Mr. Glasgow served as United States Commercial Agent at Chihuahua. At the close of the war he returned to St. Louis, where he engaged in the mercantile and banking business.

Mr. Glasgow married Harriet Kennerly, October 27, 1856, and of this union two sons were born, Julian Kennerly Glasgow and William Jefferson Glasgow. Two of Mr. Glasgow's sisters married brothers of General William Clark, of Lewis and Clark fame. Mr. Glasgow died in St. Louis, December 7, 1908.

Now that I am with the Doctor I am satisfied. He is a polite delicate Frenchman (Dr. Masure)[17] from St. Louis. He has sandy hair and whiskers, a lively address and conversation—is called an excellent physician *"especially in female cases,"* and in brevity I have great confidence in his knowledge and capacity of relieving me, though not all at once, for mine is a case to be treated gently, and slowly, a complication of diseases.

The idea of being sick on the Plains is not at all pleasant to me; it is rather terrifying than otherwise, although I have a good nurse in my servant woman Jane, and one of the kindest husbands in the world, all gentleness and affection, and would at any time suffer in my stead.

Notwithstanding the hurry in our passing them, and my sickness, I must say something of *"the Caches,"* rather a celebrated place that! They are situated about 20 miles the other side of the crossing, and

[17] Dr. Philippe Auguste Masure was a native of Belgium, and emigrated to St. Louis in 1827. Here by an advertisement in a local newspaper, he "offered his professional services in different branches of physic, surgery and midwifery." He was the son of Victor and Marie Josephe (Parmentier) Masure. Dr. Masure was married in St. Louis to Marie Magdeleine Chenie, daughter of Antoine and Marie Therese (Papin) Chenie, February 18, 1830. Their children were Athalie Masure, who married William Daggett; Therese Masure, who married Constantine Schneer, and Auguste Masure. Dr. Masure was the brother of Dr. Henry Masure, who preceded him to Mexico, dying at Santa Ana in March, 1846. Dr. Philippe Masure seems to have spent the remainder of his life in Mexico, as there is no record of his returning to St. Louis.

are large holes dug in the ground somewhat the shape of a jug. They were made there in the winter of 1812[18] by a party of traders (Beard and others) who were overtaken by a severe winter, their animals died, and these pits called "Caches," a word of French origin, were made, the insides lined with moss and whatever else of the kind they could obtain, and their goods concealed in them till the following spring, when after procuring more assistance, they removed them. They are situated about a quarter of a mile from the River, on rather an elevated piece of ground, and within a hundred yards of the road, which runs at present between them and the river. They are quite as noted as any point on the road and few travellers pass without visiting them. I was rather too much of an invalid, though, to go nearer than the road.

Tuesday (Noon) 21st. A ship-wreck on land, is the theme of my story today.

To begin when I last left off, (on Saturday) is unimportant, since but little has occurred of interest till last night.

We left our camp at 4 o'clock P. M. with a storm blowing over head; we stoped for the night, quite in good time, set up the *house,* which from necessity had but a *"sand foundation,"* and eat supper, and went to bed by a little past 8 o'clock. But this was destined to be of very short duration. In a moment the elements

[18] Mrs. Magoffin is mistaken in this date. It was in the spring of 1823 that James Baird and his party made the *caches.* After his release from Chihuahua prison he returned to the States in 1822, and in the fall of that year he and his friend, Samuel Chambers, started on their second expedition to Santa Fé.

seemed in deadliest warfare. The lightning flashed its awful tongue in all directions, till the whole heavens seemed in one light blaze. The angry thunder raised its coarse notes, peal after peal. And the dark clouds, jealous lest they should be overcome by their two combatants, poured down the rain, till it was quite impossible to hear a word spoken within or without. The tent shook violently and we could almost feel the sand loosening from the pegs. *Mi alma* sprang up, and dressed himself, (I following his example) and "yelled loud and long" till he succeeded in calling to his assistance, for he saw that the whole fabric must soon sink beneath the tempest, our three Mexican servants Jose, Sendavel and Tabino. His object was to have me carried to the carriage before the fall; but it was impossible. Our gallant vessel unable longer to bear the storm gave way in her might, and without a *groan* sunk to the flooded Earth! I was extricated I scarcely know how from the ropes &c., the pole fell on me—and by some means or other found my way to the carriage, though not without a good soaking. I was wet through and through. *Mi alma* rolled me in blankets. There I remained till after midnight, when the storm had entirely abated, and I crept off to Jane's carriage (in which she sleeps) and begged quarters, for our little concern was too small and full of water to think of sitting in it longer. This was cheerfully granted me and I stretched myself out on her bed, not with an eye to sleep, but with a longing heart for *daylight.*

I cannot end "The Ship-wreck on land" though

without eulogizing our Mexican servants for their faithful exertions to shield us from any exposure. They got us in the carriage and pulled it to the baggage wagon and tied their wheels to prevent a turn over, and then gave us their *blankets,* even depriving themselves in a measure, with the hope of keeping us dry. They are truly faithful, and are worthy our sincere thanks.

This morning has been quite eventful too.

A narrow but deep creek detained the whole company for more than two hours. Our wagons were the first to pass, which they did with safety, save the breaking a bow or two on one of them, by running it against a tree limb overhanging the bank. It took a great deal of whooping and cracking of whips to make the oxen pass over without stoping to quench their parched thirst in the cool stream they were wading through up to their very throats.

It is rather a new and novel sight to see *mi alma,* which he did today, mount a bare-back horse without a bridle, with only a halter, and ride through this deep water, with his feet drawn almost up to the horse's back after the manner of mill boys.

We nooned it on this side of the little stream.

A most delightful dinner we had, of *dos patos asado y frijoles cocido* [two roasted ducks and baked beans]. It was a splendid dinner that, and many people in "the States" have set down to worse.—

A thunder storm this evening has made us stop very early. I hope we'll not have another *wreck,* bah!

Bent's Fort, July 27, 1846. Monday noon. I have

been rather negligent in my writing lately. The last I wrote was on Tuesday 21st, after our little ship-wreck. After this was over I supposed an Indian fracas would be our next adventure, for the day following we passed their sign, such as old *mockasins,* and a post set in the ground, with a fork at the other end, in which were a sword and bundle of fagots, *many in number,* representing, as I was told a sign to some other of their tribe passing after them, the army of the whites they were numerous: The sword was painted red, for the use they made with it, and it also had several notches cut in it to represent the number of days since they passed.

We met with no very strange adventure. I was careful enough at every little hill to get out and walk, for the last narrow escape we had is not out of my mind yet.

One evening we had an abundance of musquitoes and another slight thunder storm. It was not so fearful tho' as the other in more than one respect. We had the tent secured by ropes fastened to the top of the pole and to the carriage and *la cara* [*carro*—wagon] wheels.

The road has been very sandy and almost on the river bank, which are poorly timbered till some 120 miles from the crossing it is rather thicker for ten or 12 miles, and taller the trees, with more the appearance of the Mississippi banks. In some places the country is hilly and covered with large stones, but generally speaking it is perfectly level plain, destitute of every thing, even grass, the great reliever of the eye, and making it painful to the sight.

Saturday morning we saw in front of us and many miles distant, perhaps eighty, a mountain called I think James Peak.[19]

In the evening we came on some five miles ahead of the wagons, to where Messrs Davie, Harmony and Hickman[20] were encamped till we have permission

[19] Dr. Edwin James of Long's Expedition to the Rocky Mountains, was the first American to make the ascent of Pike's Peak. This he did on July 13-14, 1820, and in honor of this achievement Major Long thought proper to call the peak by his name. While "James' Peak" appears on the early maps, the name was not acceptable to the mountain men, traders, and trappers, who traversed that country. They called it "Pike's Peak" after General Z. M. Pike, who visited it in November, 1806. On the map in Gregg's *Commerce of the Prairie,* the name is given as "Pike's Peak or James."

[20] James Prewitt Hickman was born in 1814 in Bourbon County, Kentucky, son of Thomas and Sarah (Prewitt) Hickman. At an early age his parents moved to Cooper County, Missouri. Upon reaching his maturity James P. Hickman located in Boonville, and subsequently became one of the leading merchants of central Missouri. His brick buildings were just above the landing of the river on Main street. Later he moved from Boonville to Independence, where he did an extensive business. During this time, as a member of the firm of Allen and Hickman, he also had stores in Fayette and Boonville. In the late forties he took a large stock of goods from Independence to old Franklin, which is now a part of El Paso, Texas. There he established a large store, but later sold all his goods to Santa Fé traders and merchants of Chihuahua. He made many other trips from Independence to Mexico. In time Mr. Hickman moved from Franklin to Chihuahua, Mexico, where he became the leading merchant and banker of that city. After living in Chihuahua for

BENT'S FORT

From Abert's "Journal from Bent's Fort to St. Louis in 1845."

to take a final start. Here we pitched our tent for the night and I believe for the forty-fifth time.

Sunday morning after getting the wagons up there and encamped, some fifteen miles from the fort, we came on ourselves.

Some four miles below the Fort we passed the soldiers encampment, another novel sight to me, perhaps there were fifty or more little tents stretched around in a ring with here and there a wagon, and a little shade made of tree limbs. The idle soldiers were stretched under these, others were out watering horses staked about the camp, some were drying clothes in the sun &c. &c.

At the outer edge of the encampment stood a sentinel, who with all the dignity and pomp, though by no means a Sampson in statue, of his office shouldered his musket marched up, and stoped us with the words "where go you"? We gave him our directions, he reported us to the sergeant at arms, and without farther ceremony we were permitted to pass on. In a little time we were in sight of the Fort[21] and soon after, were in it.

nearly a score of years he retired to San Antonio, Texas, where he reared his family and died in 1893. He was a very genial man, popular in society and quite a beau in his time. His son, James Prewitt Hickman, is still a resident of San Antonio.

[21] Bent's Fort, sometimes called "Fort William" in honor of William Bent, was an important fur-trading post in Colorado, and a base of supplies for the mountain trail to Santa Fé. It was begun in 1828, but was not completed until 1832. The fort was erected by the Bent brothers, William and Charles, and Ceran St. Vrain, a partnership being known as Bent and St.

And now for something of a description. Well the outside exactly fills my idea of an ancient castle. It is built of adobes, unburnt brick, and Mexican style so far. The walls are very high and very thick with rounding corners. There is but one entrance, this is to the East rather.

Inside is a large space some ninety or an hundred feet *square,* all around this and next the wall are rooms, some twenty-five in number. They have dirt floors—which are sprinkled with water several times during the day to prevent dust. Standing in the center of some of them is a large wooden post as a firmer prop to the ceiling which is made of logs. Some of these rooms are occupied by boarders as bed chambers. One is a dining-room—another a kitchen—a little store, a blacksmith's shop, a barber's do an ice house, which receives perhaps more customers than any other.

On the South side is an inclosure for stock in dangerous times and often at night. On one side of the

Vrain. Built in the form of a rectangle about 100 by 150 feet, open in the center, of adobe construction, with walls six feet thick, it was absolutely proof against fire from the exterior. Quoting from Grinnell ("Bent's Old Fort and its builders"): "Over the main gate of the fort was a square watchtower, surmounted by a belfry. The watchtower contained a single room, furnished with a chair and a bed, and with windows on all sides. Here mounted on a pivot was an old-fashioned long telescope or spyglass; here certain members of the garrison relieving each other at stated intervals, were constantly on the lookout." In 1852 the Government attempted to purchase the fort, but William Bent, being dissatisfied with the terms offered, burnt the combustible portions and blew up the walls with gunpowder.

top wall are rooms built in the same manner as below. We are occupying one of these, but of that anon.

They have a well inside, and fine water it is—especially with ice. At present they have quite a number of boarders. The traders and soldiers chiefly, with a few *lofers* from the States, come out because they can't live at home.

There is no place on Earth I believe where man lives and gambling in some form or other is not carried on. Here in the Fort, and who could have supposed such a thing, they have a *regularly established billiard room!* They have a regular race track. And I hear the cackling of chickens at such a rate some times I shall not be surprised to hear of a cock-pit.

Now for our room; it is quite roomy. Like the others it has a dirt floor, which I keep sprinkling constantly during the day; we have two windows one looking out on the plain, the other is on the *patio* or yard. We have our own furniture, such as bed, chairs, wash basin, table furniture, and we eat in our own room. It is keeping house regularly, but I beg leave not to be allowed *that* privilege much longer.

They have one large room as a parlor; there are no chairs but a cushion next the wall on two sides, so the company set all round in a circle. There is no other furniture than a table on which stands a bucket of water, free to all. Any water that may be left in the cup after drinking is unceremoniously tossed onto the floor.

When we came last evening, while they were fixing our room, I sat in the parlour with *las senoritas* [the ladies], the wife of Mr. George Bent[22] and some others. One of them sat and combed her hair all the while notwithstanding the presence of Mr. Lightendoffer,[23] whose lady (a Mexican) was present. After the combing she paid her devoirs to a crock of oil or greese of some kind, and it is not exaggeration to say it almost *driped* from her hair to the floor. If I had

[22] George Bent was the son of Silas Bent and Martha (Kerr) Bent, and brother of the famous Bent brothers, Charles, William, and Robert, of Bent's Fort. He was born in St. Louis April 15, 1814. In 1841 he married a Mexican lady; two children were born of this marriage, a son, Robert, and a daughter. George Bent was greatly esteemed, and possessed unbounded influence with the various Indian tribes with which he traded for many years. He died at Bent's Fort on the Arkansas, October 23, 1847.

[23] Dr. Eugene Leitensdorfer, his brother, Thomas Leitensdorfer, and his brother-in-law, Norris Colburn, were engaged in the Santa Fé trade for a great many years. The style of the firm was E. Leitensdorfer and Company, under which name they conducted a store at Santa Fé. Dr. Leitensdorfer married in Santa Fé, December, 1845, Doña Solidad Abreu, daughter of Santiago Abreu, one of the governors of New Mexico. Dr. Leitensdorfer traveled to Missouri for supplies in the spring of 1846, returning in June of the same year. He was appointed Auditor of Public Accounts for the territory of New Mexico by General Kearny in September, 1846.

Thomas Leitensdorfer married, in Carondelet, Missouri, May 14, 1845, Eliza Michaud. The Leitensdorfer brothers were sons of Gerrasio Probasco Santuario, an Italian soldier of fortune, who fought in many wars; while a prisoner at Milan he escaped to Switzerland, where to avoid detection he changed his name to John Eugene Leitensdorfer. He went to Carondelet, Missouri, in 1811, where in 1812 he married Euphrosine Gamache, who was the mother of Eugene and Thomas.

not seen her at it, I never would have believed it greese, but that she had been washing her head.

We had Cpt. Moore,[24] of the U. S. dragoons, to call this P. M.; he promises me double protection, as an American citizen, and as a Kentuckian; he is from that noble state himself, and even claims a kinship! Both yesterday and this evening we have taken a walk up the River, such as we used to take last winter in N. Y. from Spring to Wall Street.

Tuesday 28th. The Dctr. has just left and I shall endeavour to write a little before dinner. I've been busy all the morning. Wrote a long letter to Mama, which Cpt. Moore says I can send by the Government express. The army affords me one convenience in this. Though I cannot hear from home, it is a gratification to know that I can send letters to those who will take pleasure in reading them.

Dctr. Mesure brought me more medicine, and advises *mi alma* to travel me through Europ. The advice is rather better to take than the medicine, anything

[24] Captain Benjamin Davis Moore, born at Paris, Bourbon County, Kentucky, September 10, 1810; married Martha M. Hughes, daughter of Judge M. M. Hughes, of Platte County, Missouri. He was appointed from Illinois, February 2, 1829, a midshipman in the United States Naval Academy, and resigned January 2, 1832. Entered the army as first lieutenant of Mounted Rangers, November 6, 1832; transferred to First Dragoons September 19, 1833, and promoted to the rank of captain June 15, 1837. Captain Moore was killed in the battle of San Pasqual, California. In the cemetery at Platte City, Missouri, stands a monument erected to his memory and that of his brother-in-law, Thomas Clark Hammond, who also fell in the battle of San Pasqual.

though to restore my health. I never should have consented to take the trip on the plains had it not been with that view and a hope that it would prove beneficial; but so far my hopes have been blasted, for I am rather going down hill than up, and it is so bad to be sick and under a physician all the time. But cease my rebellious heart! How prone human nature is to grumble and to think his lot harder than any one of his fellow creatures, many of whom are an hundred times more diseased and poor in earthly assistance and still they endure all, and would endure more.

Had Capt. Waldo,[25] of the Mo. Volunteers to call

[25] David Waldo, son of Jedediah and Polly (Porter) Waldo, was born April 30, 1802, at Clarksburg, Harrison County, Virginia. Emigrating to Missouri in 1820 he settled in Gasconade County. A few years later he went into the pineries on the Gasconade River and engaged in cutting and hauling pine logs with his own hands. He had the same sawed into lumber, and when he had accumulated enough to form a raft of considerable size, floated it down the Gasconade and into the Missouri to St. Louis, where he sold his logs for $500. With this capital he went to Lexington, Kentucky, and attended the Medical Department of Transylvania University.

In 1821 he served as sheriff of Gasconade County, Missouri, and thereafter filled the offices of clerk of the County Court, justice of the peace, acting coroner and county treasurer, respectively. He also acted as postmaster; held a commission as major of militia, and from 1827 was a practicing physician. The duties of all these offices he attended to personally and discharged with ability. The county of Gasconade comprised at that time a large territory. On that account it was called by many of the inhabitants "State of Gasconade, David Waldo, Governor." Everyone saluted him as Dave.

Removing to western Missouri in 1831, he formed a partner-

this P. M. *Mi alma* is paving his way to "protection" and polite treatment from all the chief men &c.

Wednesday 29th. The same routine today as yesterday, several gentlemen, among the traders and officers called and paid their respects to the "Madam." My health, though not good, is drank by them all, and some times a complimentary toast is ingeniously slipped in. The Fort is not such a bad place after all. There are some good people in and about it as well as in other places. I am not very much displeased with Col. Kearny for sending us here, but he has arrived himself this P. M. and gives the command to leave in three days. The idea of getting onto those rough, jolting roads, and they say this is rather worse, if anything, than the one we have passed, is truly sickening.

I have concluded that the Plains are not very bene-

ship with David Jackson and embarked in the Santa Fé trade. His connection with this trade as merchant, freighter, and mail contractor, extended over a period of thirty years. In this business he amassed a fortune and was estimated to be one of the wealthy men of western Missouri.

During the Mexican War he was captain of a company from Jackson County, Missouri, attached to Doniphan's command. Being a fine Spanish scholar he translated the laws of the United States into Spanish, and what was called the "Kearny Code." He also rendered valuable service in the translation of documents captured from the Mexicans by the Americans. Upon his return to Independence, he married Miss Eliza Jane, daughter of Edward and Margaret (Glasgow) Norris; the wedding taking place March 27, 1849. He died in May, 1878, at Independence, where he had lived nearly fifty years. "His fine qualities, his keen wit in social life in the days before his powers were broken by ill health will be remembered by his friends like the sunlight, but cannot be easily described." (Waldo manuscripts.)

ficial to my health so far; for I am thinner by a good many lbs. than when I came out. The dear knows what is the cause!

Thursday July 30th. Well this is my nineteenth birthday! And what? Why I feel rather strange, not surprised at its coming, nor to think that I am growing rather older, for that is the way of the human family, but this is it, I am sick! strange sensations in my head, my back, and hips. I am obliged to lie down most of the time, and when I get up to hold my hand over my eyes.

There is the greatest possible noise in the *patio* [yard]. The shoeing of horses, neighing, and braying of mules, the crying of children, the scolding and fighting of men, are all enough to turn my head. And to add to the scene, like some of our neighbours we have our own private troubles. The servants are all quarreling and fighting among themselves, running to us to settle their difficulties; they are gambling off their cloths till some of them are next to nudity, and though each of them are in debt to *mi alma* for advancement of their wages, they are coming to him to get them out of their scrapes.

José, our principal Mexican about the camp, and my maid Jane, have had a cat and dog difficulty, he says he can't stand it and she puts on airs, does her business when and how she pleases, leaving a part of it for *me* to do, and here we have it, in addition to all this the Dctr. comes to tell how his men have treated him, therefore we have our own and our neighbours trials to encounter.

The Fort is crowded to overflowing. Col. Kearny has arrived and it seems the world is coming with him. Volunteers are under his command now only as he, on his arrival dispatched them under Capt. Moore ahead, for the purpose of repairing fifteen miles of the road called the Raton, a bed of rocks impassable for wagons, of which there are a goodly No. to pass.

Three Indian warriors came in today; they belong to a large war party of the Arrapaho Indians who are they say some sixty miles off. They are believed by the company to be spies, though they come rather with the appearance of trading.

With the intention of awing them a little Mr. Bent and others are about taking them down to the soldiers' encampment. They hesitate rather saying they have "two hearts on the subject; one of which says go! and the other says don't go"! They are cunning people, and no doubt 'twould be a rich treat to hear, on their returning to their tribe, their graphic account of the American Army "the white faced Warriors."

August. 1846. Thursday 6. The mysteries of a new world have been shown to me since last Thursday! In a few short months I should have been a happy mother and made the heart of a father glad, but the ruling hand of a mighty Providence has interposed and by an abortion deprived us of the hope, the fond hope of mortals! But with the affliction he does not leave us comfortless!

We have permission to "come unto him when our burden is grievous and heavy to be borne; we have permission to pray for more submission and reliance

on his goodness, and in that petition we have an inter-
cessor with the Father, Jesus Christ, who himself
came into the world an infant, after the manner of
man.

Friday morning 31st of July. My pains commenced
and continued till 12 o'c. at night, when after much
agony and severest of pains, which were relieved a
little at times by medicine given by Dctr. Mesure, *all
was over.* I sunk off into a kind of lethargy, in *mi
alma's* arms. Since that time I have been in my bed
till yesterday a little while, and a part of today.

My situation was very different from that of an
Indian woman in the room below me. She gave birth
to a fine healthy baby, about the same time, *and in half
an hour after she went to the River and bathed herself and it,* and this she has continued each day since.
Never could I have believed such a thing, if I had
not been here, and *mi alma's* own eyes had not seen
her coming from the River. And some gentleman here
tells him, he has often seen them immediately after the
birth of a child go to the water and *break the ice* to
bathe themselves!

It is truly astonishing to see what customs will do.
No doubt many ladies in civilized life are ruined by
too careful treatments during child-birth, for this
custom of the hethen is not known to be disadvanta-
geous, but it is a *"hethenish custom."*

In the meantime things have been going on pros-
perously without, so I have been daily informed by
my attendants. The troops *en mass* left about 10 o'c
Sunday morning, and made rather a grand show, at

least *in numbers.* Till their departure the court yard, *el patio,* was thronged. I was not able to look out, but the massive sound that filled my ear the while was quite a sufficient criterion to judge by. Although it was the Sabbath, necessity compelled them to be busily employed. The clang of the blacksmith's hammer was constant. The trumpet sounded oft and loud; swords rattled in their sheaths, while the tinkling spur served as an echo. Ever and anon some military command was heard issuing, and doubtless promptly answered.

Though forbidden to rise from my bed, I was free to meditate, on the follies and wickedness of man! Of a creature formed for nobler and higher purposes, sinking himself to the level of beasts, waging warfare with his fellow man, even as the dumb brute. And by his example teaching nothing good, striving for wealth, honour and fame to the ruining of his soul, and loosing a brighter crown in higher realms. — —

All of the Traders followed on after the troops the next three days.

The Fort is quite desolate. Most who are here now of the soldiers are sick. Two have died, and have been buried in the sand hills, the common fate of man. One must have great faith in their Creator, great reliance on his goodness, not to feel sad and uneasy to see such things passing around them,—their fellow creatures snatched off in a moment without warning almost— and they are themselves lying on a bed of sickness. It requires much prayer for submission, for tranquility, &c.

Thursday.— Another Indian has come in—believed to be a spy, although he tells that he has been lost from his party. He is a warrior well armed with bow and arrows—a quiver full. His dress consists of a striped blanket wrapped around his body, a string of beads, and his long hair tied up with a piece of red cloth. We are quite weak here now, and a large body of these warriors could do us much damage. We only have to be particular in closing the Fort gates, and keeping a watch.

And as we think of starting tomorrow evening we keep the wagons back for safety, instead of sending them on with the troops and other traders, as it is we are quite weak enough, and if they were gone 'twould be bad, depriving us of the service of some seventeen men! In that case, if danger were near, I should be obliged to buckle on my pistols and turn warrior myself, rather a touch above me, at Amazonianism!

The Dctr. thinks I will have to lie down in the carriage, but *lest they should need my services I shall be obliged to decline the treatment.*

There is a little romance attached to my life: taken prisoner, for we were compelled by the soldiers to come here, *confined* in a Fort, and when I left there had to fight my own way through blood thirsty Indians, before reaching a place of any safety.

Friday evening 7th. We are all in a hub-bub—preparing for another move.

My dirt-floored *chamber, dining-room, parlour, reception room* &c. &c. *is* quite dessolate, All things of any size have been moved out to the wagons, and I am now using borrowed propperty.

It is quite strange, and indeed a treat to think of starting. *"The Fort"* is agreeable enough in itself, but with it are connected some rather unpleasant reflections—something rather sad, though I will not murmur at the chasten hand of Providence.

It is just 12 days since we came and eight days since I left my room, within that short space of time many things have occurred, both to myself and others. Many have come and gone; some never to return again to this spot, and others never to return into this world.

What a satisfaction would it be to me now, to know that I shall be as well prepared to leave this mortal, this earthen body as I am to leave this earthen house, and with as much anxiety. That I could know that my daily prayers were not frowned upon by my God, that my Saviour's blood pleads not in vain, and that a seat and white-robe are prepared for me at the foot stool of my Heavenly Father.

If I could feel sure too that my idol is not on earth. That loving my dear husband as I do, I am not excluding an Image more precious to the soul of mortals, than all things earthly. Can I venture to ask myself who has the largest place *here?*

Oh, that there may be no cause for severe judgement against either of us in this thing! but that the deep devotion felt for each other here may be but a small type of that felt for our Redeemer above!

Camp No. 1. Saturday 8th. Second start. **Left** the

71

Fort last evening at 6 o'clock, came six miles up the
River to where we leave it finally. I am now entirely
out of "The States," into a new country. The crossing
of the Arkansas was an event in my life, I have never
met with before; the separating me from my own dear
native land. That which I love and honour as truly as
any whole-souled son or daughter of the fair and
happy America, (for the U. S. are considered to pos-
sess that bright name above) ever did. Perhaps I have
left it for not only the first, but the last time. Maybe
I am never to behold its bright and sunny landscape,
its happy people, my countrymen, again. It is better
always to look on the *bright* side, and it is certainly
wiser to rely more fully on the Wisdom and Goodness
of Providence.

Camp No. 2.—24 ms. from the Fort. Eighteen
miles has been our travel today. Quite long for my
first, and the road is very much changed too; not the
dead plain we had several days the other side of the
Fort, but broken with sand hills. The dust is very
great, and the vegetation so perfectly parched by the
sun that not a blade of *green* grass is to be seen.

A little scrubby bush resembling in some respects
the current bush of the States, is all that seems able
to withstand in any way the scorching heat.

And for the first time I have seen the "Mirages" or
false-ponds. It is so deceiving to the eye, that the
thirsty traveler often breaks from his party with
anxious eyes and heart to gain first the long wished for
luxury, but ere he reaches the brink it vanishes from
his sight. The philosophy of the false-ponds is scarcely

as yet understood. To use the language of my predecessor, Mr. J. Gregg, from whom I have gained my information respecting them, "It has usually been attributed to refraction, by which a portion of the bordering sky would appear below the horizon; but there can be no doubt that they are the effect of refraction upon a gas emenating from the sub-scorched earth and vegetable matter, or it may be that a surcharge of carbonic acid precipitated upon the flats and sinks of the plains, by the action of the sun, produces them."

My life of adventures and sight-seeings is beginning again. Nothing of importance has occurred as yet, save that we were frightened a good deal last night by *el perro* [the dog]. His awful and unearthly yells and howling induced us to believe he was possessed with rabia. *Mi almi* got up for his pistol but finding the percussion caps were in the carriage, he could do nothing but go after them, and now I trembled; for if he should be mad (and he was near the tent door too) he would at once bite any object that approached him. But our fears were soon calmed when he came running into the tent wagging his tail, and seemed perfectly sane. In a little while though he commenced his awful noise again, and to be on the "safe side" we called up José and had him tied.—But then I could not sleep for he continued his yells all night.

Sunday 9th. Camp No. 3. Mountains are coming in sight this morning—we are winding about among large stony hills which finally run into mountains, two of which appear in the distance; the one of these farthest to the north is known to the people adjacent as "Sierral de la madre," the other "Sierra Grande."

They appear disconnected to the eye from the distance at which they are seen, though they are probably united by others too small to be seen from the road, and at the distance of an hundred miles.

They are supposed to belong to the great chain that stretches along the Pacific through North and South America, and known to all geographers as the "Rocky Mountains."

This road is very badly supplied with water. From our last night's camp we came only five or six miles before stoping to noon it, finding water in this place and learning from other traders encamped there that we should find no more for some *twelve* miles at the least, we stoped though it was not ten o'clock. Left at 4 o'ck, in the afternoon and travelled on till 8— (ahead of the wagons) when we stoped at a difficult pass in an *arrodeo* [*arroyo*—dry creek], and waited for the Dctr. and the wagons; the former soon came up, and the moon rising soon after we passed trusting them to their drivers entirely.

At 10 o'ck we came upon some two or three camps, and at a very ugly place in the road: here was water, though no grass, and we stoped for the night.

Camp No. 4. "Hole in the Rock" Rather a place of some celebrity our camp is in tonight.

I have not yet visited the "great well" and therefore cannot describe it according as presented to my own vision, but from what others say it is a large "hole

74

in a rock" filled with clear, cold water, and to which a bottom has never as yet been found. Tomorrow, however, I hope to be able to visit and if I find it different from what I have already said, I will mention it.

We have not traveled since 1 o'k today. As there is no water within fifteen miles it was thought rather wiser to remain here all night where there is an abundance of water and better grass for the stock than they have had for some two or three nights, than to go on perhaps all night before reaching the water and that too without the light of the moon, or stop on the plains without water and in the morning to find half of the oxen missing—Dctr. Mesure this P. M. presented me with two nice hares, quite a treat, although we have a fine antelope, killed by our baggage wagon driver Sendevel, to live on for a day or two yet.

Camp No. 5. The Great Well, alias "Hole in the Rock." We have not moved from our old camping ground today. The cattle during the last night took it into their heads to take "French leave" of us and this morning we are left to pull the wagons ourselves if we *will* start.

Several men after searching all day found 34 of them some fifteen miles from camp, the others were only a short distance off.

So we have lain here in the hot sun with the tent *windows* raised, and eating roast-hare and drinking wine for dinner. In brevity we are quite patient under the circumstances.

Every body is ahead of us and we have the whole

75

road to ourselves; even the polite French dctr. has left us!

Took a walk this P. M. through the pinon woods adjacent &c. This tree which is a specie of pine, has gained celebrity from the little nut it bears. It is about the size of a kidney bean, grows in the *pine trees here,* and has a sweet, rich, oily taste. The Indians, in the Fall of the year, gather large quantities of them, which are quite saleable among their more civilized neighbours.

The tree itself is quite indifferent in appearance, the trunk is scrubby and the leaves short and coarse; this may be attributed though in part to the barren soil and the almost continual drought in this part of the country.

It is quite abundant in turpentine, which is perfectly pure. And I have picked up under the trees balls of rezin the size of a hen's [egg] made by the heat of the sun on the turpentine that drops from the tree.

The Hole in the Rock I found pretty much the same as described: the scenery around it is quite romantic—high rocks covered with cedar trees; shelving and craggy precipices; pearly brooks, and green groves, through which are seen bounding the stately antelope and timid hare; while the ear is greeted by the soft warble of feathered songsters. It is quite the place in which to build a lover's castle and plant his gardens &c.

Thursday 13th. Purgatoire River.[26] *Camp No. 6.*

[26] Rio Purgatoire, "River of the souls in Purgatory," corrupted

We are still lying at the Camp of last night, repairing wagons. Yesterday we made a fine travel some twenty-five miles or more. Left in the morning after 9 o'clock traveled till 4 o'ck. fifteen miles to water. Here we stoped till 6½ o'ck letting the Oxen drink what little water they could find in the little creek, and eat a few blades of grass—we ourselves took dinner.

About Sun set we started again. The night was excessively dark owing to heavy clouds obscuring the Moon. A slight sprinkle of rain, the first we have had for three weeks, refreshed the air very much and laid the dust which had been almost suffocating us during the whole day.

Several times we drove out of the road, being unable to distinguish it in the dark. At the last *mi alma* got out and walked, and I may say almost felt the way. Once we came to a steep little hill and I got out and walked. Often have I done this though, gotten out of the carriage at mid night and walked down such places.

It now grew somewhat lighter and we stoped at this place for the wagons to come up.

The road on to this place is fine, and by 12½ o'k, we reached it. Here we find one or two camps. So al-

by the soldiers into "Picket wire." The Mexicans had two names for the river—Rio Purgatorio and Rio de las Animas. It is a stream of considerable size, heading near the New Mexico state boundary and flowing northeast, across Las Animas and corners of Otero and Bent counties, Colorado. Long states that "we emerged from the gloomy solitude of its valley, with a feeling somewhat akin to that which attends escape from a place of punishment."

though we layed by a whole day our night's travel has made us equal with the others.

Though this stream has rather an awing name it wears a clear smooth face at present. I can't say that it is very appropriate at present, though it may be in stormy weather. Its banks like the Arkansas are covered with cotton-wood and some such undergrowth. Wrote a long letter to Sister Anna.[27]

Thursday Night. Camp No. 7. Left Camp this afternoon early. Came to camp again at Sun Set, and just at the entrance of what is called the "Raton," a difficult pass of fifteen miles through the Mountains.

Our tent is stretched on the top of a high hill, at the foot and on the sides of which I have been rambling accompanied by our faithful Ring, who all the while kept strict watch for *Indians, bear, panther, wolves* &c., and would not even leave my side as if conscious I had no other protector at hand.

Friday 14th. Camp No. 8. It is surrounded by most magnificent scenery. On all sides are stupendous mountains, forming an entire breast-work to our little camp situated in the valley below. To the South is what may be considered "the pinacle" of the Mountains, a great rock towering above every thing around. This, *mi alma,* calls the "wagon mound" from its resemblance to one of the same kind on the old road to Santa Fé and which derives its name from its resemblance to the top of a covered wagon.

[27] Anna N. Shelby, daughter of Isaac Shelby, Jr., born August 5, 1818; married in April, 1840, Beriah Magoffin; died in Lexington, Kentucky, August 7, 1880.

The trees here are assuming a different appearance. Though the pinon is still abundant it is being supplanted by a much taller and more sightly pine. It is very much the shape and appearance of those found in the U. S.

A kind of wild cherry is quite abundant too. It grows on small bushes resembling in the leaf and bark the common domestic cherry tree; the fruit is small, and when ripe is quite black; and though sweet to the taste at first, it is quite as rough as persimons.

We have been rather unfortunate today—a wagon was turned over this morning, and the bed and bows so much broken as to cause a delay of some hours to repair it sufficiently to travel on. "The Raton" is not the best place to keep such articles new; almost every fifty or an hundred yards there are large stones, or steep little hillocks, just the things to bounce a wagon wheels' up, unless there is the most careful driving.

And as for myself, I have been walking till I am covered with dust till instead of being black any longer, I am brown changing back to white again. If exercise will do me any good I must surely be benefited now. Many a one of these long hills do I walk up and down, beside rambling through the bushes, along the banks of the little streams &c. in search of "what I can find." Some times this is a curious little pebble, a shell, a new flower, or the quill of a strange bird.

Saturday 15. Camp No. 9. Still in the Raton, traveling on at the rate of half mile an hour, with the road growing worse and worse. I have scarcely ventured in the carriage this morning; but have "climed the hills" not on my own feet as I did yesterday, but on the back of *my caballo* [my horse]. Horse back exercise is my delight, and of the riding today I shall not complain, though the sun was very warm.

We have an abundance of game, fine turkies, one of which we had roasted for dinner today, prairie chickens, hares, and they say we are to have bear meat soon. Three were seen this morning by the teamsters, and we passed in *el camino* [the road] the carcass of one seeming to have been killed yesterday. I must look sharp when I ramble about through these woods, or I will get myself into a nice hugging scrape with Mr. Bruen. I came very near seeing one this P. M. any how, and set the Mexican boys about the carriage to look out; it changed itself into an ox.

Worse and worse the road! They are even taking the mules from the carriages this P. M. and a half dozen men by bodily exertions are pulling them down the hills. And it takes a dozen men to steady a wagon with all its wheels locked—and for one who is some distance off to hear the crash it makes over the stones, is truly alarming. Till I rode ahead and understood the business, I supposed that every wagon had fallen over a precipice. We came to camp about half an hour after dusk, having accomplished the great travel of *six or eight hundred yards during the day.*

Sunday 16th In our great travel of yesterday, more than one wagon became lame beside the breaking of the *catrin* [*carreton*—little carriage] tongue—this morning we must lay by to repair those evils.

Such a ramble I have had this morning! Up to the

very top of a high hill, the sides of which are not the smoothest I ever climbed. *Mi alma* went off to take his pleasure in some way, and left me alone. So accompanied by Jane who rather doubted my ability to ascend at first, and Ring who appeared surprised, it was poco poco, and when I had gotten to a great rock, which from the ground below I had considered as the ending of my Herculean labour, I found I must ascend at least half as far again before reaching the top.—Not daunted, though the disappointment of not being able to stand on the top of this hugh stone, was some thing we passed on without hesitation to the very top of the Mountain and once there, what a magnificent view I had! Behold to my right as I stood facing the South—that beautiful canon winding (through) between mountains so high, that it was quite impossible though near to them, to distinguish one single tree on the top of it.—In that wild glen is he, who of all else on earth is most dear to me, winding his way through trees and small undergrowth, leaping ever and anon, over the little *arolla* [*arroyo*—dry creek] that winds through it in search of game for our fare.

To my left are high mountains, thickly covered with great white rocks the foundations of the lofty pine that majestically waves its hundred arms above them. In the valley beneath me is situated the little "village of *M*" [Mora]—a thriving, with its nice little cottages and court house in the center. Contentment, ease and peace are apparently inmates of this spot. Off in that mountain meadow is an extensive herd of cattle grazing at their leisure, and anon cooling themselves at the little stream near them. Would I exchange this home for any I ever saw? There are dear friends behind me, and those too, who, if mortals are capable of making by their presence and goodness, a spot on earth happy, any place would be so with them, but there are ties here as strong, a link that binds me to this spot till it is removed may I never leave it.

Left camp at 1 o'k after pulling up and down more than one steep hill, at some of which the carriages were pulled down by the men. We came to camp again at Sun set.

Monday 17th. Camp No. 11. A most beautiful morning this has been—fine for the animals, cool and pleasant and we have traveled well considering it is in "The Raton."

Before we left camp some two hours, one of the traders Mr. Howk[28] of Boonvill[e], Mo. came up with his wagons and passed us, leaving us knocking

[28] Solomon Houck was a resident of Boonville, Missouri, for many years. He was an old Santa Fé trader. In the spring of 1846 he made the trip from Santa Fé to Independence, Missouri, in the remarkable time of twenty days, arriving at Independence in the month of June. There he remained just long enough to purchase supplies for another expedition, retracing his trail in less than a month.

While encamped with Doniphan's command on the Rio Grande, at the entrance to the first Jornada below El Paso, nearly all of his cattle were driven off by the Apache, almost in sight of the Army. He and his men pursued the Indians and succeeded in recapturing most of the animals. Houck killed an Indian and brought back his scalp on a lance.

Mr. Houck owned a large tract of land in Boonville, known as

at wagons and making as much fuss as if it had been a regular ship-yard. We were of course pitied on account of our misfortune, but we were destined not to be alone in it long, for on starting not more than two miles from our camp, we found him at the foot of a little hill with a corral formed, his oxen turned out, a wagon upset and all the bales on the ground. We could only follow his example of the morning, *pitty him and pass on.*

We have had some magnificent scenes before us this P. M. From the greatest hight to which I have yet ascended on horse-back, mountains far more lofty than any I've seen, deep vallies below that looked blue so great was the distance to them; the clouds seemed resting on the mountains around us. Oh, for the genius of an artist that I might pencil such scenes otherwise than in my memory, or the fancy of a Willis[29] that I might trace with this pen a more lively and correct sketch of some of nature's grandest and most striking works.

Tuesday 18th. We are detained in camp this morn-

"Houck's Addition," which extended over a number of city blocks. Some of the main buildings of Kemper Military School now occupy this site. His home was the finest in the town. He was a very tall man, reserved in manner, and indifferent to social life. When thoroughly aroused he was a rough antagonist.

[29] Nathaniel Parker Willis was a popular writer of the day, of whose work Thackeray said: "The prose and poetry of Mr. Willis are alike distinguished for exquisite finish and melody. . . . Many of his descriptions of natural scenery are written pictures, and no other American author has represented with equal vivacity and truth the manners of the age." (Appleton's *Cyclopedia of American Biography,* vol. 6, p. 14.)

ing by a gentle rain which commenced last evening. The road immediately before us is worse than any we have as yet passed, and it is folly to attempt the crossing of these steep hills when they are made slippy by a whole night's rain.

An other company of soldiers has come up today and an express too from Gen. Kearny now about entering Santa Fé. The news he brings is not less favourable than we have formerly received.

A negotiation is being carried on between the two Generals through brother James, who has the confidence of the Mexican Gen. so completely, we may look for pleasant results, and if any thing should go wrong we will be rather the first to receive a warning if it is necessary to remain from Santa Fé, and though we are behind now, if it is necessary to return to the U. S., we will be first.

P. M. Here we are still, they have concluded to have some repairs done to the road before proceeding, as it is almost impassable, so we will not leave till morning. And I have been up on to *the top of an other high mountain.* I shall be quite an experienced climber when we leave the Raton it has been my daily exercise since we entered the mountains and I shall miss it when we reach the plains again.

Wednesday 18th. Camp 13. Rio Colorado. Out of the Raton at last, can it be possible! We have been in it five days, and it seemed that we were never to leave it. This morning the pulling has been worse than ever; some very steep, long, rocky hills, but we passed them without an accident save the breaking of some two or three wagon bows—this cannot be considered an accident though—they caught in the trees that reached their giant arms across the road seemingly with that intention.

We leave behind us Mr. Howk, and the government wagons. I only wish them our good fortune.

And we may now bid good bye to any game; that is one redeeming quality of the Raton—the furnishing us with wild meat. I left it tho' without seeing *un oso* [a bear], (one horse) though they were several times reported by the wagoners as frequenting the little cañons near us.—We have had fine clear, cool water too, and slightly impregnated with sulphur, not a very disagreeable quality to me.

And I must also dispense with my horseback exercise in some measure. Though it is fine in the mountains, I cannot say the same on the scorching plains. I am quite sorry for it too, I enjoy it so much.

Quite cool today for August, more the appearance of October.

Thursday 20th. Noon. Out on the open Prairie again, but with rather more variety than before. We are surrounded, in the distance, by picturesque mountains, a relief to the eye when one is accustomed to behold nothing save the wide plain stretched far on all sides meeting the edges of the bright blue sky and appearing more like water than land.

We left camp this morning at 7 o'clock crossed "Red River," a picturesque little stream winding its way from the mountains, to the great Arkansas, of which it is generally termed the "Canadian Fork."

The water is fine, clear and cool, as mountain streams always are. The banks have some thing of an *"Ash creek"* appearance, a good place to upset a carriage, and as this did not correspond with my feeling, I left the little *catrin,* which I have this morning taken instead of *mi caballo,* and mounting the stump of a tree called *mi alma* to my assistance; he most kindly came and took me up on his horse behind him and with little difficulty I was landed on this side of *Rio Colorado.*

Camp P. M. Oh, the everlasting tongue of that boy Comapu! He is eternally singing, even when he is driving *la carratela* [carriage] over the worst kind of stony, hilly, and muddy roads. But it shows a happy disposition, such as every one has not, and therefore I shall not complain of him, tho' it annoys me much.

Had something of a fright this evening, from the tongue of the carriage, while descending a hill, coming out and letting the vehicle fall so much on the mules as to start them prancing and capering till our lives were really in jeopardy.

Friday 21st. A very cool morning—and last night was so cold we found two pair of blankets and a thick coverlid quite acceptable. There has surely been a hail storm some place, my thick shawl is scarcely as warm as I would like it.

Camp No. 15. Poni creek. Here I am both Madam & Mr. of the whole concern. The recent rains have made the banks of the creek, which are naturally steep, quite slippy, and renders it quite necessary that much care be taken or a wagon may be turned over, (the teams are doubled) therefore *mi alma* after seeing half of them over, placed me on my horse, mounted his own without saddle or bridle only a halter on his neck, and in this manner we crossed what may be termed the second crossing (the first I passed on foot with stepping stones—for the creek is crossed twice in preferance to one place worse than these two together perhaps. On this side we were on landing met by Lieutenant Warner[30] of the U. S. Malitia, who greeted us with a kind smile notwithstanding he has been well drenched in the cold drizzling rain of this P. M. Don Manuel [Samuel Magoffin] now left me to attend to affairs and returned to see the other wagons over crossing No. 1.—So now I had nothing to do but act out the part alloted to me, and after exchanging a few words with Lieu. W. I rode on and with as much dignity as I am capable of commanding, which upon a pinch is not a little in my own opinion, selected a camping ground, and ordered the Mexican servants about in broken Spanish. Now that they are all at work I seize a few minutes to write a letter.

It is quite winterish this evening, with a little ugly rain falling to make it still more gloomy.

In the distance we see a tall mountain whose high

[30] William Horace Warner, born in New York in 1812, and appointed from that state to the United States Military Academy, July 1, 1831. Commissioned second lieutenant of First Artillery July 1, 1836, and later assigned to Topographical Engineers. Brevetted captain December 6, 1846, for gallant and meritorious conduct in California. Captain Warner was killed, September 26, 1849, by hostile Indians in the Sierra Nevada, nine arrows having pierced his body.

crown is white apparently with snow, both to the naked eye and with the glass; this supposition has been confirmed by one of the Mexicans, who appears to know all about it. If 'tis true I have seen snow in August. One of the warmest and most oppressive months of the year, in the States; and the idea of snow there now is absurd in the extreme; and I am sure to tell it there, when they are all suffocating they think with sultry heat, would make the good folks rather doubtful of the person's veracity next time.

Saturday 22nd. Noon at the Rayada Creek. This little creek is a river today; the rain has been quite heavy here, if we may take this as our guide. It is very much warmer too today, and like the rattle snakes after a thunder-storm, we are creeping out in the sun, which to speak the truth is not a bad plan. I don't know that I should have left it so soon either for the carriage, had not the wind driven me. Wrote a long letter to Sister Litty[31] this evening.

Sunday 23rd. Ocate Creek. Camp No. 17. We are getting in among the hills, pigmy Mountains, again. Our camp last night was at the foot of one, which I ascended. At the top I found a thicket of pine trees, and fearing lest a hungry bruen might be lurking in them, or a *tiger cat*—rather the worst of the two when one comes to fighting with them, for while Mr. Bruen will squeeze you gently till all breath has left you, the other will scratch and bite and tear with his long

[31] Maria Laetitia Shelby, fourth daughter of Isaac Shelby, Jr., born September 9, 1829; married James Lawrence Dallam, November 20, 1856.

talons till death comes to relieve the sufferer. I did not dare venture farther, but returned to camp.

This morning I have rode some on horse back—the road has been rough and I found it rather more agreeable than the carriage. *Mi alma* drives today, getting into the settlements has inspired one of our drivers—Sandevel—with new love for his *padre, madre y mujer* [father, mother, and wife]; so last night he petitioned to go ahead to see them, and will meet us at the road, the junta [junction], a place where this and the Cimerrone road joins and the waters of some two or three *arollas* [*arroyos*—streams].

Monday 24th. Camp No. 18. Olla [Ojo] de Gallinas Travelled late tonight and it has been so dark too, it was almost necessary to feel our way—with *mi alma's* careful driving though, I felt little fear.

How cheering it is to one when groping their way in the dark, over roads and through countries he knew nothing about, all bewildered, and not knowing whether he is about pitching over a precipice, or driving into some deep ravine, hole &c., to have the light of the camp fires of those ahead of them, to break suddenly before the eye. It is like drink to a thirsty traveller, or a straw to a drowning man. It gives him new courage; suddenly his path way is opened to his understanding (not exactly the eye) and he pursues his way with a light heart, and rejoicing.

We are surely getting close to the settlements, as an evidence of this we were met this evening by three rancheros, with their *aguardiente*,[32] *quesos, y pan*

[32] Aguardiente—a brandy of very great strength, obtained from the bulb or root of the maguay or *agave Mexicana*. This was

[whiskey, cheese, and bread], to sell: They are like the huxter-women after a steamboat.

Though we had no wood to cook with, and must necessarily go without food till some time tomorrow, it was rather preferable to their *pan,* which they sell. It is made of wheat, and very hard, consequently calculated to keep well. Their cheese is clabber and made on the same principal as the Dutch smerecase, though very tough, mean looking, and to me unpalitable.

Tuesday 25th. Noon. "Mora creek and settlement." And such settlements they are—Here is a little hovel, a fit match for some of the genteel pig stys in the States—it is made of mud, and surrounded by a kind of fence made of sticks; this is the *casa grande* [big house]. Its neighbours are smaller, far more inferior, and to them I have no comparison. They are inhabited by rancheros as they are called, who attend

the common drink throughout that country. The process of manufacture is unique, and is, therefore, given as follows: "A hole is first dug some ten or twelve feet in diameter, and about three feet deep, and lined with stones. Upon this a fire is built and kept up until the stones are thoroughly heated. A layer of moist grass is then thrown upon the stones, and on this are piled the bulbs of the maguay, which vary in size from one's hand to a half a bushel measure, resembling huge onions. These are again covered with a thicker layer of grass; and the whole is allowed to remain until they are thoroughly baked. They are then removed to large leathern bags, and water is poured on them to produce fermentation. At the end of a week the bags are emptied of the maguay and its liquor, which, after undergoing the process of distillation, is ready for use." (Bartlett, *Personal narrative of explorations and incidents in Texas, New Mexico, California, Sonora and Chihuahua,* vol. I, p. 290.)

solely to raising of *vacas* [cattle]. Their food consists
of a little cheese made of thin milk, a little *pan de mais*
[corn bread]—and such little fruits & nuts as they
can collect in the mountains.

We have sent to all of these ranchos, if possible we
may be so fortunate as find *dos or tres huevas o un
pollo, pero no nade* [two or three eggs or a chicken,
but nothing else]. Such things are seldom seen or
heard of here nor any thing else I suspect palitable.
But they say my opinion is formed too hastily, for
within these places of apparent misery there dwells
that "peace of mind" and contentment which princes
and kings have oft desired but never found!

Camp. We only crossed the creek this evening—
the crossing is exceedingly difficult, we had the hounds
of a wagon broken, which must be mended, and therefore necessity compelled us to remain here.

I rode over on horse back while *mi alma* had the
mules taken from the carriage and had it brought
down the almost perpendicular bank, by the man.

*Wednesday 26th. A day of wonders not seen by
every one.* Well, what wonders I have to write tonight! my brain is so full I don't know where to find a
commencement, and if I do begin, how shall I be able
to end? We have passed "the Vegas" and encamped
on this side some three or four miles, with Mr. Houk
and the soldiers, our own wagons being some distance
behind. We left them this morning to come on by
themselves, as we are "going in" sooner than they.

Well now for my Vegas story—We got in there
about 2 o'k. P. M., and dinner was called for, and

while they were preparing it let me take a look around at the premises. We drove down a long hill at the foot of which runs a beautiful clear stream, tempting one whether thirsty, or not to moisten his lips with its cool waters. This circles almost entirely the village of Vegas; crossing it we came immediately in contact with the dwelling houses, pig sties, corn cribs &c.

Here the carriage stoped, and while José, our driver, went in to procure us some little delicacy to eat, I am sure *mi alma* could have made money enough to buy out the whole village, not that his absence was very long, but from the excitement to see his wife a *"monkey show"* in the States never did a better business than he could have done, if he had set me up at even *dos or tres reals* [two or three reals; i.e., 10 or 15 cents] on sight. My veil was ingenuously drawn down, not only for the better protection of my face from the wind and constant stare of *"the natives,"* but also afforded me a screen from whence to beholding my schrutinizing spectators, and while I carried on a conversation with Mr. Houk on the outside respecting them. There were some two or three dozen of children (both sexes) from the infant in the arm up standing around, so thick 'twas hard for any one to pass; none were wholly clad, and some of the little ones in a perfect state of nudity; eyes were opened to their fullest extent, mouths gaped, tongues clattered, and I could only bite my lips and almost swallow my tongue to restrain my laughter.

Mr. H. and *mi alma* were unable to do this, for the idea of my being such an object of curiosity was inducement enough, without seeing the condition of those around them, to provoke the laughter of the most sober heads. When we got out of tʰⁱs place and into "the room" which was pretty much like the "big room" at the Fort, not only the children, but *mujeres* [women] and *hombres* [men] swarmed around me like bees. The women were clad in *camisas* [chemises] and petticoats only; oh, yes, and their far famed *"rabosas."*[33] The latter made of some Mexican woven cotton, mostly blue, the two former of cotton, & red flannel. All *took a look,* and a seat, half of them on the floor, some I talked with as far as my Spanish knowledge extended; some of them had their babies under their rabosas. I shant say at what business. I may venture this much though that the little things were taking care of No. 1. When all that were in were seated, out came the little cigarritas,[34] and the general smoking commenced.

After this some signs of our dinner made its appearance. The old man came in with a blanket which he spread on a little table placed before me, on this

[33] The *rebozo* was worn by all classes at all times. It was a long scarf, about half a yard wide and three or four yards long, fringed at the ends. It was usually thrown over the shoulders and the ends dangled below the waist. It served the purpose of bonnet, shawl, apron, veil, and bodice. Under no circumstances was it laid aside while the owner was awake, being used dexterously even while working or cooking. It never got in the way of any occupation.

[34] Every Mexican, male and female, carried at the girdle a pouch containing a bundle of *hojas* (covering of the ear of Indian corn, cut into oblong pieces about three inches in length and one inch in width), and a small bottle of powdered tobacco.

he spread a clean white cloth, and I thought I was about to have a fine dinner, but woe to me then, for on the top of this he put on an other cloth so black with dirt and greese that it resembled more the common brown, than white sheeting, of which it was really made.

And then the dinner half a dozen *tortillas* [pancakes] made of *blue corn,* and not a plate, but rapped in a napkin twin brother to the *last* table cloth. Oh, how my heart sickened, to say nothing of my stomach, a cheese and, the kind we saw yesterday from the Mora, entirely speckled over, and two earthen *jollas* [*ollas*—jugs] of a mixture of meat, *chilly verde* [green pepper] & onions boiled together completed course No. 1. We had neither knives, forks or spoons, but made as good substitutes as we could by doubling a piece of *tortilla,* at every mouthful—but by the by there were few mouthfuls taken, for I could not eat a dish so strong, and unaccustomed to my palate. *Mi alma* now called for something else, and they brought us some roasted corn rolled in a napkin rather cleaner than the first & I relished it a little more than the *sopa* [soup]; this and a fried egg completed my meal.

As soon after as possible we made our way to the carriage, followed by the whole crowd of men, women, children and dogs. In a little time we were clearly hid from their view by the surrounding mountains, through which our road wound, and joy beat in my heart, to think that once more I was at liberty to breath the pure air of the prairie, and to sit alone in my little tent, unmolested by the constant stare of these wild looking strangers!

Thursday 27. Near San Miguel. We have passed through some two or three little settlements today similar to the Vegas, and I am glad to think that much is accomplished of my task. It is truly shocking to my modesty to pass such places with gentlemen.

The women slap about with their arms and necks bare, perhaps their bosoms exposed (and they are none of the prettiest or whitest) if they are about to cross the little creek that is near all the villages, regardless of those about them, they pull their dresses, which in the first place but little more than cover their calves—up above their knees and paddle through the water like ducks, sloshing and spattering every thing about them. Some of them wear leather shoes, from the States, but most have buckskin mockersins, Indian style.

And it is repulsive to see the children running about perfectly naked, or if they have on a chimese it is in such ribbands it had better be off at once. I am constrained to keep my veil drawn closely over my face all the time to protect my blushes.

We nooned it today at the ojo de Bunal [Bernal]. Had fine fried chicken, corn and bean soup for dinner, not a disagreeable dinner that, and especially when compared with the one of yesterday.

Tonight our camp is among the pine trees at the foot of a mountain, with no other camp near us.

Sent today by the first express that has returned, letters to Sisters Anna and Lettitia.

The news from Santa Fé is that A[r]mijo[35] has fled, and Gen. Kearny, who is in possession of his house, is fortifying the city—so we may just fix ourselves there for the winter.

Friday 28th. This has been rather a more agreeable day than yesterday, though we met with a little acci-

[35] In spite of his various ranks of dignity, both as soldier and statesman, Manuel Armijo was by habit and training essentially a merchant and trader. His peculiar cunning in this field of action gave him the position and power to gain ascendancy in politics and in the ranks of the Mexican Army. From all accounts of him, the methods he adopted in business were decidedly dishonest. His career began with petty larcenies, and while still a youth his business of stealing sheep grew into large proportions. He was born and raised at or near Albuquerque, his parents being persons of bad repute. A large plantation owner in that neighborhood, by the name of Chavez, conducted a business of purchasing sheep from his poor neighbors at very reduced prices, and he collected so many herds that he could not get time to mark them. He had no means of recognizing his own sheep, simply kept them in the charge of shepherds, who were supposed to watch the sheep and prevent their being lost, by straying, or theft. Armijo adopted the method of stealing these sheep while the shepherds were asleep, and of bribing the wakeful ones, so that he accumulated considerable property. In due time he would sell the stolen property back to Chavez, who thus paid for his own property over and over again. With these ill-gotten gains and considerable luck in gambling, he managed to build up quite a fortune. Later he launched into the trade along the Santa Fé trail, purchasing his goods in the East, or in St. Louis, and starting, as the others did, from Independence.

It appears that while Governor of New Mexico, and while the Mexican War was in progress, Armijo had a train of goods, consisting mostly of ammunition, in command of Speyers, which arrived at Santa Fé June 24, 1846. Speyers brought the informa-

dent this morning. At the little creek the other side of San Miguel the carriage tongue broke entirely out, and we were in rather a critical situation as to travelling, till Lieu. Warner came up with his wagons, and we got two carpenters he had with him to make a new tongue. This required some two hours' time, and

tion that American troops were approaching and Armijo sold his interest to Speyers. Captain Waldo had reported to General Kearny that "Governor Armijo has about $70,000 worth of goods near the head of the Cimarron that left Independence about a fortnight since."

Armijo's first accomplishment in politics was his appointment as collector of customs at Santa Fé. He later became lieutenant-governor, and then, following the assassination of Governor Perez, was made governor, which office he retained, excepting a short interval, until the American invasion. In these official capacities he became commander of the troops. He ruled as a despot, and was a man of cruel nature and oppressive both to foreigners and to his own people.

While Governor Armijo left the way open for Kearny to enter Santa Fé, he had previously filled the minds of his people with hatred and dread of the Americans; telling them that the United States intended to rob their churches, desecrate their altars, and visit every kind of oppression upon them. Colonel James Magoffin seems to have been able to dispel this falsehood and reconcile the people to a change in government.

After the war, General Armijo was tried at the city of Mexico for cowardice and desertion in the face of the enemy. Witnesses were brought from New Mexico, but the trial resulted in his acquittal. An English traveler named Ruxton, in his book, *Adventures in Mexico*, p. 118, speaks of meeting Armijo on his way north from the city of Mexico, the year following Armijo's flight from Santa Fé, as follows: "I stopped and had a long chat with Armijo, who, a mountain of fat, rolled out of his American 'dearborn' and inquired the price of cotton goods in Durango, he

97

as usual the villagers collected to see the curiosity, and I did think the Mexicans were as void of refinement, judgement &c. as the dumb animals till I heard one of them say *"bonita muchachita"* [pretty little girl]! And now I have reason and certainly a good one for changing my opinion; they are certainly a very *quick and intelligent people.* Many of the *mujeres* came to the carriage shook hands and talked with me. One of them brought some tortillas, new goat's milk and stewed kid's meat with onions, and I found it much more palitable than "the dinner at the Vegas." They are decidedly polite, easy in their manners, perfectly free &c.

The village of San Miguel is both larger and cleaner than any we have passed; it has a church, and public square, neither of which are in the others.

Nooned it on this side some three or four miles.

The road this P. M. has obliged me to ride on horseback again, and I find it quite as agreeable as when in the Raton. The pure air of the Santa Fé mountains is doing me great good. I love dearly to spend half an hour or an hour in rambling over and among them in the evening when we stop, and before starting. Nature

having some seven wagon-loads with him, and also what they said of his doings in Santa Fé, alluding to its capture by the Americans without resistance. I told him there was but one opinion respecting it expressed all over the country—that Gen. Armijo and the New Mexicans were a pack of arrant cowards; to which he answered: 'Adios! they don't know I had but 75 men to fight 3,000. What could I do?' " General Armijo died at Limitar, New Mexico, December 9, 1853.

RUINS OF THE DESERTED VILLAGE OF PÉCOS

From Abert's "Report of his Examination of New Mexico, 1846-1847."

furnishes beautiful reflections for the mind as well as pictures for the eye, in the grand scenes before me.

Saturday 29th. I have visited this morning the ruins of an ancient pueblo,[36] or village, now desolate and a home for the wild beast and bird of the forest.

It created sad thoughts when I found myself riding almost heedlessly over the work of these once mighty people. There perhaps was pride, power and wealth, carried to its utter most limit, for here tis said the

[36] This was the ancient town of Pecos, the largest and most populous of the pueblos of New Mexico. It was situated on an upper branch of the Pecos River, about thirty miles southeast of Santa Fé. At the time of Coronado's visit, in 1540, Pecos contained about 2,500 inhabitants. It consisted of two pueblos, or communal dwellings, each four stories high, one containing five hundred and seventeen and the other five hundred and eighty-five rooms on their respective ground floors. The buildings were erected on a terrace arrangement and must have contained a tremendous number of rooms, so as to make the modern apartment house pale into insignificance. The population in this place dwindled down until 1790, when there were only one hundred and fifty-two souls. It is supposed that most of them were killed in a raid by the Comanche Indians, and that epidemics contributed largely to the depopulation of the place. In 1838 there were only seventeen survivors, who went over the mountains and joined a tribe at Jemez. It is said that they carried with them some of the sacred fire, and in the days of this journal were still maintaining it.

Pecos was once a fortified town, built upon a rock somewhat in the shape of a foot. At one end of the rock, or promontory, were the remains of the Aztec temple, which contained the sacred fire, and at the other end were the remains of the Catholic church, so close that the incense from the Aztec fire was sent through the altars of this Christian church. The place where this sacred fire was kept, known as the *estuffa*, was forty feet in

great Montezuma once lived, though tis probably a false tradition, as the most learned and ancient American historians report that great monarch to have resided much farther south than any portion of New Mexico.

At any rate these pueblos believed in and long-looked for the coming of their king to redeem them from the *Spanish yoke*. And I am told by persons who saw it, that tis only within some two or three years since it was inhabited by one family only, the last of a once numerous population. These continued to keep alive "Montazuma's fire," till it was accidently extinguished, and they abandoned the place, believing that *Fate* had turned her hand against them. This fire, which was kept in vaults under ground, now almost entirely filled in by the falling ruins, was believed to have been kindled by the king himself, and their ancestors were told to keep it burning till he returned, which he certainly would, to redeem them, and it has been continued down to this time, or within a few years.

But now something of what my own eyes witnessed. —The only part standing is the church. We got off our horses at the door and went in, and I was truly

diameter and must have required an enormous amount of labor to keep replenished.

The bones which have been dug from the floor of the Aztec temple, in modern times, were of gigantic size. There is a tradition that this temple—which is supposed to have been in existence over five hundred years before the time mentioned by the diarist—was built by a race of giants, fifteen feet in height, which preceded the Aztecs.

awed. I should think it was sixty feet by thirty. As is the custom among the present inhabitants of Mexico, this pueblo is built of unburnt bricks and stones. The ceiling is very high and doleful in appearance; the sleepers are carved in hiroglyphical figures, as is also the great door, altar and indeed all the little woodwork about it, showing that if they were uncivilized or half-civilized as we generally believe them, they had at least an idea of grandure. Some parts of it, too, have the appearance of turned work, though it is difficult to decide, it is so much battered to pieces. From the church leads several doors, into private apartments of the priests, confession-room, penance chambers &c.

One of them only has a fire place in it, and this is exceedingly small. All around the church at different distantes are ruins; the side of one house remains perfect still, and 'tis plain to see a three storied building once was there. The upper rooms were entered by ladder from the outside—and in case of an enemy's coming these ladders were drawn up, and no communication being afforded below they were perfectly secure to cast stones or any other missil at their not so well protected enemy.

Mi alma pointed out to me the door of a room in which he had once slept all night in some of his trips across the plains, and while some of the inhabitants still remained. It was in the second story of a house, which is now entirely fallen in, and the doors so entirely closed by the rubbish (except this room) that it had nothing of the appearance of having been a house.

101

The place too has the appearance of having been once fortified, from the number of great stones lying all around it, and which they must have used in this way as they are too large for the building of houses.

They say this is our last evening out, that tomorrow we will see Santa Fé. And to this I shall not object, if we are to stay there a whole winter, or even till winter, I must be in and preparing my house.

I do think I have walked three or four miles today; before noon I rode on horseback over all the bad places in the road, but this P. M. I have walked. It will not hurt me though, and especially as much as jolting in the carriage over the hills and rough road we have passed, and being frightened half to death all the while.

An other Spanish beauty, I saw this evening, with her face painted, a custom they have, among them when they wish to look *fair and beautiful* at a "Fandango," of covering their faces with paint or flourpaste and letting it remain till it in a measure bleaches them. These I saw one of them had paste—and with it more the appearance of one from the tombs than otherwise. Another had hers fixed off with red paint which I at first thought was blood.

Santa Fé. August 31st 1846. It is really hard to realize it, that I am here in my own house, in a place too where I once would have thought it folly to think of visiting. I have entered the city in a year that will always be remembered by my countrymen; and under the "Star-spangled banner" too, the first American lady, who has come under such auspices, and some of

ARRIVAL OF THE CARAVAN AT SANTA FÉ

From Gregg's "Commerce of the Prairies."

our company seem disposed to make me the first under any circumstances that ever crossed the Plains.

We arrived last night, and at such a late hour it was rather difficult for me to form any idea of the city. I know it is situated in a valley; and is to be seen from the top of a long hill, down which I walked; this leads into "the street," which as in any other city has squares; but I must say they are singuarly occupied. On one square may be a dwelling-house, a church or something of the kind, and immediately opposite to it occupying the whole square is a cornfield, fine ornament to a *city,* that. A river runs through the place, affording me a fair opportunity to enjoy that luxury to the fullest extent. The church is situated at the Western end, and though I cannot answer for the grandure of the inner side—to say nothing of the "outer walls"—I can vouch for its being well supplied with bells, which are chiming, it seems to me, "all the time" both night and day. Though Gen. Kearny has come in and taken entire possession, seated himself in the former Governor's chair, raised the American flag and holds Santa Fé as a part of the United States, still he has not molested the habits, religion &c. of the people, who so far are well pleased with their truly republican governor.

Nuestra casa [our house] is situated under the shadow of *"la inglesia"* [the church], and quite a nice little place it is. We have four rooms including *la cochina* [the kitchen], our own chamber, storage room, and the reception room, parlour, dining-room, and in short room of all work. This is a long room with dirt floor (as they all have) plank ceiling, and nicely white-washed sides.

Around one half to the height of six feet is tacked what may be called a schreen for it protects ones back from the white wash, if he should chance to lean against it; it is made of calico, bound at each edge, and looks quite fixy; the seats which are mostly cushioned benches, are placed against it—the floor too at the same end of the room is covered with a kind of Mexican carpeting; made of wool & coloured black and white only. In short we may consider this great hall as two rooms, for one half of it is carpeted and furnished for the parlour, while the other half has a naked floor, the dining table and all things attached to that establishment to occupy it. Our chamber, at one end of the "big room," is a nice cool little room, with two windows, which we can darken, or make light at pleasure, and I must say it is truly pleasant to follow after the Mexican style, which is after dinner to close the shutters and take a short siesta; it both refreshens the mind and body, one is then prepared, without fatigue, of the morning's labours, to go about the duties of the evening.

After our arrival last evening Dctr. Conley,[37] a trader, and formerly of Ky. and Col. Owens called.

[37] Dr. Henry Connelly was a native of Nelson (now Spencer) County, Kentucky, where he was born in the year 1800. He was graduated as a doctor of medicine from Transylvania University in 1828, and soon afterwards opened an office in Liberty, Missouri. However, the lure of the trail, coupled with the family tendency toward trading and mercantile pursuits, was too strong for him, and before a year passed he had abandoned his office and joined

Brother James [Magoffin], received us at our door, and supped with us on *oysters* and *Champaign,* for 'twas too late to prepare a warm supper, and this by the bye was not a very bad one, though cold. And he dined with us today too. As he is the fore-runner of Gen. Kearny, he is to start for Chihuahua tomorrow, a day before the Gen. – – – "Speak of something & his imps will appear," is what I have heard in my life, and it has been the case this P. M., for just as I fin-

a party bound for Chihuahua. These men endured great hardships, but finally reached their destination. Dr. Connelly became clerk in a store and afterwards bought out his proprietor. In this business he had occasion for many years to travel back and forth to the Missouri River; first with pack mules, and later with his own wagon train.

In 1843 Dr. Connelly formed a partnership with Edward J. Glasgow of St. Louis for the overland trade between Chihuahua, Mexico, and Independence, Missouri. Dr. Connelly acted as an emissary of Armijo in communications with General Kearny, before the latter had advanced to Santa Fé. He was later arrested at El Paso and taken to Chihuahua, but there released without trial. He was probably a naturalized Mexican citizen, as he made an effort to become such in 1832. However, after the war with the United States, he moved to New Mexico, where he passed the remainder of his life, dying of accidental poisoning in July, 1866. He established the largest mercantile business in New Mexico, having houses at Peralta, Albuquerque, Santa Fé, and Las Vegas. In 1861 he was appointed Governor of New Mexico by President Lincoln and reappointed in 1864. His influence is said to have kept New Mexico out of the Southern Confederacy.

Dr. Connelly's family were Irish, but came to America in colonial days, settling at Albemarle Point, South Carolina. He was the son of John Donaldson and Frances (Brent) Connelly. Dr. Connelly was twice married, both times in Mexico and to Mexican women.

ished writing *General,* an hour ago, he came walking in, accompanied by Mr. Thruston[38] of Ky. formerly.

I had made up my mind that the Gen. was quite a different man in every respect; he is small of statue, very agreeable in conversation and manners, conducts himself with ease, can receive and return compliments, a few of which I gave him; as I hope, & *mi alma* thinks, they were of the right kind, and in their time and place, so I am satisfied. He says as he is the Gov. now I must come under his government, and at the same time he places himself at my command, to serve me when I wish will be his pleasure &c. This I am sure is quite flattering, *United States General No. 1* en-

[38] Lucius Falkland Thruston. A contemporary said of him: "He stood six feet, six inches in his moccasins." He was born in Louisville, Kentucky, July 18, 1799, son of John Thruston and Elizabeth Thruston Whiting; his father and mother being cousins. His father (son of Reverend and Colonel Charles Mynn Thruston of Gloucester and Mary Buckner) served as a cornet in George Rogers Clark's campaign in the Illinois country during the Revolutionary War. Lucius Falkland Thruston went to New Mexico about 1827 and spent the remainder of his life in the Mexican country. He was arrested and confined in jail at Chihuahua by reason of a letter of introduction, directed to him, having been found among the papers of a member of the ill-fated Texas-Santa Fé Expedition of 1841. After the American occupation of Santa Fé, General Kearny appointed him a Prefect, because of his knowledge of the Spanish language and his acquaintance with the Mexicans. Mr. Thruston had some years previous become a citizen of Mexico. He belonged to the prominent Thruston family of Kentucky, of which a well-known member is Hon. R. C. Ballard Thruston of Louisville. The name is often confused with that of Thurston.

tirely at my disposal, ready and will feel himself flattered to be my servant.

Mr. T. [Thruston] is a friend of Gen. Kearny's and I believe about to receive an office from him, he is a gentleman I should judge who had seen a good deal of the world; is easy and familiar in his manners. As he leaves with the Gen. day after tomorrow, he will be happy to call on me on his return two weeks hence, and learn something of his old friends in Ky., a number of whom I am acquainted with. . . . This has been my evening's. business to receive these gentlemen, write of it, and to receive a visit from an American lady formerly a resident of *"Illinois"* I may speak of her anon.

This morning a Mexican lady, Dona Juliana, called to see me. She is a woman poor in the goods of this world, a great friend to the Americans and especially to the Magoffins whom she calls a *mui bien famile* [*muy buena familia*—very good family]. Though my knowledge of Spanish is quite limited we carried on conversation for half an hour alone, and whether correct or not she insists that I am a good scholar.

Tuesday September 1st. Today has been passed pretty much as yesterday, in receiving the visits of my countrymen. Dr. Mesure called early, before I had pulled off my wrapper, to congratulate me on my good fortune in getting through the Raton without a fractured limb.

Mr. Houck called too. Brother James dined with us, and also supped on oyster-soup and champain. Like the rest of his brothers he is quite lively, and this

evening he appeared unusually so, cracked jokes and
spun yarns, laughed, drank &c. He thinks because I
take the slow way of travelling and frequent deten-
tions so coolly, that I am quite a phylosophic old
woman, and will do to travel any place. He leaves
tonight for the *Rio Bajo* settlements[39] to prepare for
Gen. Kearny's arrival; and from thence he goes to
Chihuahua to prepare for us, at least he is to get a
house & necessary articles for house-keeping as he did
here.

Dona Juliana called again this P. M. to see *mi alma*
who was out yesterday. I rather retired from the conversation, save a little which *mi alma* interpreted to
her. She is a great rogue to win the respects, good
wishes, and esteem of *la nina* [little child], as she
flatteringly spoke of me to my good husband, who by
the way took it all well. *"A que Don Manuel, la
Senora es muy linda, muchachita, la nina! Y que es
major, ella es muy afabla, muy placentera, muy
buena."* [Ah! Don Manuel, the lady is very pretty,
only a little girl, a child: And what is more, she is very
affable, very pleasing, very good.] Of course I heard
none of this.

*Wednesday 2nd Don Manuel esta muy malo todo
el dio, y yo esta mui triste.* [Samuel has been very sick
all day, and I am very sad.] Brother James has gone
and no one has been here today, save Mr. Robert

[39] All settlements below Santa Fé were collectively known as
Rio Abajo. They comprised over a third of the population and
the principal wealth of New Mexico. The settlements up the
river were known as *Rio Arriba.*

Spears[40] of Missouri, who called this morning before breakfast.

Here I have sat all day brooding over and exerting all my energies to relieve by bathing and other outward applications, the severe pains in *mi alma's* head; but the relief is only momentary, and oh, how it hurts me to see him lying in such pain and my poor hands are so entirely worthless.

Mi alma is rather better tonight. Lieu. Warner called as we sat down to tea and took it with us.

Thursday 3rd. Una Senora [a lady] called to see me today, *mi alma* was in and interpreted for me, so my tongue was *vale nada* [no account]. Her name I do not know as yet, but her *lengua* [tongue] I do, for she kept in constant motion all the time of her visit, which lasted an hour and a half, very fashionable! She is a good old lady I dare say; speaks in favour of the foreigners, and without hesitation says Gen A[r]mijo is a *ladrón* [thief] and coward.

She has great confidence in her own knowledge of *the men,* as she speaks of those staple objects of Creation, and says she wishes we could understand each

[40] Probably the same Robert Spears, of Doniphan's command, who was killed by Navaho Indians near Fray Cristobal, November 26, 1846. The army had a large flock of sheep, which was driven off by the Mexicans or Navaho. Spears and James Stewart followed the trail of the sheep and overtook them, but being without arms the Indians fell upon and killed them. One was pierced with thirteen arrows and the other with six or seven —the arrows were broken off and the barbed heads left in the wounds. Their heads were mashed with rocks and their bodies treated in a shocking manner.

other sufficiently well that she might give me some advice respecting their snares! She could lesson me to the fullest limit, I'd venture to say.

We are having fine protection near us in case of danger; the soldiers have made an encampment on the common just opposite our house, and though we are situated rather "out of town," we have as much noise about us as those who reside in the center of the city.—We have constant rhumours that Gen. A[r]mijo has raised a large fource of some five or six thousand men, in the South, and is on his march to retake possession of his kingdom. The news has spread a panic among many of his former followers, and whole families are fleeing, lest on his return they should be considered as traitors and treated accordingly.

In other families there is mourning and lamentations, for friends they may never again see on earth. A day or two before Gen. Kearny arrived, A[r]mijo collected a fource of some three thousand men to go out and meet him, and even assembled them ready for a battle in the canon some twelve miles from town, but suddenly a trembling for his own personal safety seized his mind, and he dispersed his army, which if he had managed it properly could have entirely disabled the Gen's troops by blockading the road &c. and *fled himself!* While all these men, the citizens of Santa Fé and the adjacent villages, were assembled in the canon, and their families at home left entirely destitute of protection, the Nevijo [Navaho] Indians came upon them and carried off some twenty families. Since Gen. K.— arrived and has been so successful,

110

they have petitioned him to make a treaty with them, which he will not consent to till they return their prisoners, which 'tis probable they will do thro' fear, as they deem the Gen. something almost superhuman since he has walked in so quietly and taken possession of the pallace of the great A[r]mijo, their former fear.

Friday 4th. Mi alma has been away all day, and though entirely alone, I cannot say I have grown lonesome, for both my mind and body have been actively engaged.

I have my *housekeeping* to attend to now; and the opportunity for growing lonesome or sad in any way is rather poor. I've been teaching one of the Mexican servants his business how he is to do it &c., and though we have considered him one of the *numbskulls,* I have found him both willing and apt in learning. The great virtue of these servants is their ever pleasant faces; they never begin their work sullenly, and you may change it as often as you please or make them do it over, and over, and they continue in the same good humour, never mouthing and grumbling because they have too much to do, but remain perfectly submissive, and indeed it is a pleasure, when an underling is so faithful, to do them any little favour. Mine is a quiet little household, the servants are all doing their duty, the great bugbear to most house-keepers; and if I can do my duty so well as to gain *one* bright smile and sweet kiss, from my good, kind husband, on his return my joy will be complete for I trust my spiritual business has not been neglected.

Wrote a long letter to Mama, (to be sent to-morrow) telling her of my sickness at Bent's Fort.

Saturday 5th. Let me see what has transpired today within the little circle of my vision. After an early breakfast *mi alma* went out on business (not afraid to trust all things to his own *"little one"*) and as usual I commenced my daily task—the superintending of the general business of house-keepers, such as sweeping, dusting, arranging and re-arranging of furniture, making of beds, ordering dinner, &c. &c. &c. This part being completed, I took up my sewing.

In a little while though I was called up to buy some vegetables from a little *muchacha* [girl], and a cunning piece she was too, knows well how to make her *granos* [small weights], *cuartillos* [close figuring], &c. the idea of her offering me four squashs for one real, and half a dozen ears of *mais verde* [green corn] for *un real y media* [a real and a half—7½ cents]. One must look out for themselves, I find if they do not wish to be cheated though only of a few cents, and called *tonta* [stupid], into the bargain. I shall know the next time better how to deal with them. – – – And I had a visit from an Indian chief too, but what is his name? Well at any rate his tribe is known as the Comanche. He speaks quite good English and some Spanish, and our conversation was carried on in both languages! he was well dressed in new boots, pants, hat, and white blanket-coat. He told me he was a friend to Don Manuel, had come to see me, asked if I was "good" *meaning well,* and among other questions—said he was bearing a letter to Gen. Kearny

112

(and showed it to me) from some of the officers here. I suppose it is something of a treaty.

Sunday 6th. I hope the first sabbath in the city of Santa Fé has been passed, so far as opportunities would admit, in a way deserving it. The morning was spent in reading the Bible and other pious books, and in serious reflections.

Though the sabbath, two gentlemen, Lieu. Warner & the aid de camp of our Gen. [called]; with the latter I had some conversation in regard to the neglect of this day by people generally, the traders and soldiers, especially, on the Plains; the advantage of a pious leader to the latter, and this called forth the information of the strict piety of Gen. Kearny an Episcopalian. This is truly fortunate, and increases doubly the already high esteem I have for that General.

Monday 7th. Received early this morning four mammoth bunches of purple grapes with the regards of Lieuts. Warner and Hammond,[41] the latter aid to

[41] Thomas Clark Hammond was born at Fort McHenry, Maryland, August 19, 1819. Entered the United States Military Academy July 1, 1837, and graduating therefrom served as second lieutenant in the Dragoons. Lieutenant Hammond married, January 28, 1845, Miss Mary A. Hughes, daughter of Judge M. M. Hughes, of Platte County, Missouri. The marriage was clandestine and took place on Pilot Knob, near Fort Leavenworth, Kansas; the ceremony being performed on horseback. The "angel baby" referred to (p. 146) was Thomas C. Hammond, Jr., born at Bee Creek Mills, May 22, 1846, and later a prominent physician of Platte County. Lieutenant Hammond was killed, December 6, 1846, in the battle of San Pasqual, California. A monument has been erected to his memory at Platte City, Missouri. (*History of Clay and Platte Counties, Missouri*, p. 945.)

113

Gen. K.— They are very sweet though smaller than the common grape of the States.

And today I've been constantly engaged, with my needle, market people, of whom I have gained some little information as to the names of different vegetables, prices &c.

What an everlasting noise these soldiers keep up— from early dawn till late at night they are blowing their trumpets, whooping like Indians, or making some unheard of sounds, *quite shocking to my delicate nerves.*

Tuesday 8th. No one has called today! surely we are not to be deserted thus! I've sat alone a good part of the day, thinking of those at home; how I should like to step in unawares upon them, and give what I know would be an "agreeable surprise," and how I would like for *some* of them to see me now how very happy and contented I am, how I am delighted with this new country, its people, my new house, or rather my *first* house, *which 'twas supposed* I should not be capable of managing, and last of all what a good, attentive, and affectionate husband I was fortunate enough to choose, though "young and wholly inexperienced."

Tonight we took a walk to the *plazo* [*plaza*—public square], the first time I've been there; my opportunity for seeing was not very good, for the night was dark, and they have no public lights. The plazo or square is very large—on one side is the government house with a wide portal in front, opposite is a large church commenced by the predecessor of Gov.

Armijo, 'tis not finished—and dwelling houses—the two remaining sides are fronted by stores and dwellings, all with portals, a shed the width of our pavements; it makes a fine walk—and in rainy weather there is no use for an umbrella.

They have a circle of trees around the square, leaving a wide street between them and the portal.— Within a few days past the American soldiers have erected a very tall pole in the center of the square; the flag is run up occasionally.

Wednesday 9th. Una Senora called this morning, and as usual when *mi alma is out.* I talked a good deal, she thinks I both speak and understand *bastante* [sufficiently] What an inquisitive, quick people they are! Every one must know if I have *una madre un padre, hermanos e hermanas* [a mother, father, brothers, and sisters], their names &c. They examine my work if I am engaged at any when they are in, and in an instant can tell me how it is done, though perhaps 'tis the first of the kind they have ever seen.

The market affords us fine *durasnos* [peaches] and delicious grapes, which though quite small are remarkably sweet and well flavoured; also good melons, the apples though, are inferior.

Thursday 10th. A cool day this, such weather though as we have had for more than a week. The air is fine and healthy; indeed the only redeeming quality of this part of New Mexico is its perfectly pure atmosphere, not the damp unhealthy dews of the States. One can walk through the deep grass here, and his shoes will never show at any time, either late in the evening or at early dawn, the slightest moisture. We have occasionally a little thunder and slight sprinkle of rain, enough to settle the dust.

News is received that Gen. Kearny will be here by the 12th and that Col. Price,[42] who has command of an other detachment of Malitia from the States, will

[42] Sterling Price was a member of Congress from Missouri when the war with Mexico became imminent, and resigning therefrom he returned home for the purpose of raising troops. President Polk gave him a commission as colonel, and the troops raised by him were afterwards organized into the Second Missouri Regiment of Mounted Infantry. This regiment was permitted to elect its own officers, and much to the gratification of Price the men elected him to the chief command. This regiment followed Kearny, and with its train of baggage and provision wagons started to move in August, 1846, and after fifty-three days on the march, reached Santa Fé. Colonel Price and his staff preceded the main body, reaching Santa Fé September 28, 1846. For his gallantry and meritorious service in this war, Price was promoted to the rank of brigadier-general on July 20, 1847.

Price was a Virginian, born in Prince Edward County, September 11, 1809, and received his education at Hampden-Sydney College. In 1831 he traveled with his father's family to Fayette, Howard County, Missouri, and there entered the tobacco commission business. On May 14, 1833, he was married to Miss Martha Head. Later he conducted business in the town of Keytesville, Chariton County, and finally settled on a farm near the town, which was always thereafter his home.

Sterling Price was a member of the Missouri Legislature in 1836, 1840, and 1842, and on the last two occasions was chosen Speaker. He was a Democrat, and as such was elected to Congress in 1844. The popularity of General Price increased rapidly after his return from the Mexican War, and in 1852 he was elected governor of Missouri, being the anti-Benton candidate. The salary of governor was then two thousand dollars per annum,

be in soon, he is now within a few miles of the city. Lieut. Warner has waited on me this A. M. with an invitation to attend a Spanish ball given by the officers to the traders. As the only *traderess*, it would be

and at his suggestion was raised to twenty-five hundred dollars, but he refused to accept the increase for himself.

In 1861 events in the life of General Price ran a rapid and devious course. He was elected to the convention held in Missouri to decide the question of secession, and was chosen president of that convention. He opposed secession in and out of the convention, strongly advocating neutrality. On May 10, following, the state troops, in annual encampment at St. Louis, were made prisoners by Captain Lyon of the United States Army. On May 18 Governor Claiborne Jackson appointed Sterling Price major-general in command of the Missouri State Guard. The course of events brought General Price to decide upon joining the Confederate Army. He was made major-general by the Confederate Government, and led his troops with great skill and success in the battles of Wilson's Creek, Missouri; Pea Ridge, Arkansas; and Lexington, Missouri. In the latter engagement he had his men fight behind bales of hemp, moving them toward the enemy as they advanced. This movable fortification proved a great institution, and was unique in the annals of warfare.

General Price and his command were distinguished at Iuka and Corinth, but most of their operations were west of the Mississippi. The duties of the Trans-Mississippi Department consisted in keeping the Federal troops away from Texas, the great source of Confederate supplies, and in getting these transported across the Mississippi. In this the service of Price's army was of great value, and eminently successful, even after the opening up of that river by the Federals.

General Price was a soldier in every sense of the word, a strict disciplinarian and a great general. He was a handsome man of very large physique and very kindly nature. His troops spoke of him affectionately as "Old Pap Price" and idolized him.

offending in me after so polite a request, not to exhibit myself at the *managerie,* along with other bipeds of curiosity.

Friday 11th. What did I write of last yesterday? The managerie, well, now for a little critical view of it. I went in of course somewhat prepared to see; as I have often heard of such a show, I knew in a measure what to look for. First the ballroom, the walls of which were hung and fancifully decorated with the "stripes and stars," was opened to my view—there were before me numerous objects of the biped species, dressed in the seven rain-bow colours variously contrasted, and in fashions adapted to the reign of King Henry VIII, or of the great queen Elizabeth, *my memory* cannot exactly tell me which, they were entirely enveloped, on the first view in a cloud of smoke, and while some were circling in a mazy dance others were seated around the room next the wall enjoying the scene before them, and quietly puffing, both males and females their little cigarritas a delicate cigar made with a very little tobacco rolled in a corn shuck or bit of paper. I had not been seated more than fifteen

If any one asked what the men were cheering about, the answer would be: "It is either a rabbit, or General Price moving along the line."

After the war General Price went to Cordova, Mexico, where he received a grant of land from the Emperor Maximilian. He was joined there by many Confederates, but upon the fall of Maximilian they returned to the United States. General Price died in St. Louis of cholera, September 29, 1867. In 1911 the state of Missouri erected a bronze statue to his memory at Keytesville, Missouri.

minutes before Maj. Soards[43] an officer, a man of quick perception, irony, sarcasm, and wit, came up to me in true Mexican style, and with a polite, "Madam will you have a cigarita," drew from one pocket a *handfull of shucks and from an other a large horn of tobacco,* at once turning the whole thing to a burlesque.

Among the officers of the army I found some very agreeable, and all were very attentive to me. Liuts. Warner & Hammund, the principal managers of affairs did themselves credit in their interested and active movements to make the time pass agreeably to their visitors.

El Senor Vicario [the priest] was there to grace the gay halls with his priestly robes—he is a man rather short of statue, but that is made up in width, which not a little care for the stomach lends an assisting hand in completing the man. There was "Dona Tula"[44] the

[43] Major Thomas Swords, born in New York City, November 1, 1806, and graduated from the United States Military Academy in 1829. After serving in various parts of the Southern States, on March 3, 1839, he was promoted to the rank of captain and served on the frontier with General Henry Leavenworth against the Indians in the Southwest. On April 21, 1846, as major quartermaster, he was assigned to Kearny's command. When General Kearny's forces reached San Diego in January, 1847, Major Swords went to the Sandwich Islands to obtain clothing and supplies for the soldiers. He rose to the rank of colonel, and on March 13, 1865, was brevetted brigadier-general for faithful and efficient service in Quartermaster Department during the Civil War. General Swords retired February 22, 1869, and died in New York City, March 20, 1886.

[44] Gertrudes Barcelo, familiarly known as "La Tules." She was

principal *monte-bank keeper* in Sant Fé, a stately
dame of a certain age, the possessor of a portion of
that shrewd sense and fascinating manner necessary
to allure the wayward, inexperienced youth to the hall

a native of Taos and went to Santa Fé in search of "fame and
fortune," where she found both. She was considered the most
expert monte dealer of her time. Of fascinating manners and distinctly Spanish type of beauty, she became a great favorite in
official circles. In her long sala balls were given, where the
officers attached to the Mexican garrison disported themselves as
inclination demanded; these entertainments, however, being by
invitation only. The card rooms were patronized by the *élite,* and
hundreds of thousands of dollars were won and lost in this
"sporting emporium," where this goddess of chance ruled supreme.
During the American occupation she was a great favorite among
the American officers, and having received information as to the
conspiracy of December, 1846, through a mulatto servant, she
gave warning to the military authorities. (Twitchell, *Old Santa
Fe,* 338.)

It is said that this woman made a loan to the United States
Government, through Colonel David D. Mitchell, who had been
ordered to open communications between General Wool, supposed to be at Chihuahua, and the Army of the North. The
Government not having, at Santa Fé, the thousand dollars necessary to purchase supplies for his men, Colonel Mitchell was at a
loss how to raise the money. He finally thought of Senora Tules,
but she proved obdurate. He got into her good graces, however,
by escorting her to a ball, walking into the room with this
notorious woman on his arm, which so flattered her that she consented to make the loan.

Monte was played with cards, suits being clubs, swords, suns,
and cups, all delineated in their own proper colors and figures.
Each suit numbered ten cards (like American) from ace to seven,
and then knave, horse standing in the place of queen, and king.
The mysteries of the game could be learned only by losing at it.

of final ruin. There was Col. Donathan,[45] a native of
Ky. "as you will see by my *statue* Madam," leaving
unknowing listeners to believe that state the mother
of a giant tribe. There, too, circling giddily through

[45] Alexander William Doniphan was a lawyer by profession,
who gained great distinction as a military officer, although he had
no military education and no knowledge of military tactics. He
assisted Governor Edwards of Missouri in recruiting troops to
fill the quota of that state for the Mexican War. Doniphan himself
enlisted as a private in a company from Clay County, which was
one of the eight companies united to form the famous First Regiment of Missouri Mounted Volunteers. This regiment numbered
one thousand men from the best families in the state, and contained the best raw material imaginable for military service in
time of war. It became part of the force commanded by General
Kearny.

After a few weeks of drill this regiment started on the march,
June 26, 1846. They entered Santa Fé, marched from there into
the country of the Navaho Indians, whom Doniphan treated with,
and then through deep snows to the eastern slopes of the Rocky
Mountains. After accomplishing the objects of the expedition,
fighting in the meantime the battles of Brazito and Sacramento,
they marched to Chihuahua, Mexico, to form a junction with
General Wool. Not finding General Wool, Doniphan reported to
General Taylor, and later embarked with his troops for New
Orleans. Some of his men wanted to remain in Chihuahua until
the arrival of General Wool; others suggested a retrograde march
to Santa Fé; most of them, however, were in favor of pressing
homeward by way of Monterey, but Doniphan impatiently said,
"I am for going home to Sarah and the children." This expression
took hold and became a popular one in the army.

In twelve months Doniphan's command marched about four
thousand miles, performing a military feat said to be without
parallel. Fighting and marching with continued success, his men
were without uniforms, tents, or military discipline. His officers
and men, with sunburnt faces and grizzled beards, had a strange

121

the dance, Cpt. M[oore] of [First] Dragoons; if necessary we can be sure of at least one person to testify to the "virtues or vices" of what has been graphically called "the ingredient." There in that

uncouth appearance when they returned home. Their ill-made clothing, having fallen from them piecemeal, had been substituted from time to time with whatever the wild beasts and chance threw in their way.

Colonel Doniphan, the youngest of ten children, was born in Mason County, Kentucky, July 9, 1808, and died at Richmond, Missouri, August 8, 1887. His father, Joseph Doniphan, was a native of King George County, Virginia, and his mother, Anne Smith, of Fauquier County, Virginia. Alexander was educated at Augusta College, Kentucky, graduating with high honors at eighteen. He studied law in the office of Martin Marshall, of Augusta, Kentucky, and moved to Missouri in 1829. He entered the practice of law at Lexington, and four years later went to Liberty. He was in the legislature as a Whig in 1836, 1840, and 1854. In January, 1861, he was appointed by the Missouri Legislature one of five delegates to the Peace Conference at Washington, and during his absence was elected to the convention held in 1861, to decide upon the question of Missouri's seceding. He joined the convention at St. Louis, and from the outset was a Union man, although an outspoken champion of State's Rights, as indicated in his unpublished autobiography.

Doniphan acquired fame as a criminal lawyer and was employed in every case of importance in northwest Missouri during his career. He was a man of surpassing eloquence, and it has been said that he was well-nigh invincible before a jury.

One of Colonel Doniphan's legal efforts was in behalf of the Mormon, Orrin P. Rockwell, who was charged with conspiring with Prophet Joseph Smith to assassinate Lilburn W. Boggs, former governor of Missouri. Seventeen shots had been fired at Governor Boggs, while he was sitting in his home in Independence, Missouri; he was severely wounded, but later recovered.

corner sits a dark-eyed Senora with a human foot-stool; in other words with her servant under her feet—a custom I am told, when they attend a place of the kind to take a servant along and while sitting to use them as an article of furniture.

The music consisted of a gingling guitar, and violin

The jury found Rockwell guilty, but he was sentenced to only five minutes in jail.

Doniphan had previously taken part in the war between the state of Missouri and the Mormons, serving as commander of the First Brigade under General Samuel D. Lucas. When the army neared the town of Far West, the Mormons saw that defeat was imminent and asked for a compromise. General Lucas told their commander that his instructions from Governor Boggs made it necessary for them to surrender up Prophet Joseph Smith and certain other leaders of their church, to be tried and punished. Their commander, Colonel George M. Hinkle, agreed to this, but neglected to confide in his brethren. Instead he told Smith and the four others designated that General Lucas wanted to confer with them. He accompanied them to General Lucas, who immediately made them prisoners. A short time afterwards they were court-martialed and General Lucas ordered Doniphan to take them into the public square of the town and shoot them at nine o'clock the following morning. Colonel Doniphan, in a high state of indignation, replied to his superior as follows: "It is cold-blooded murder. I will not obey your order. My brigade shall march for Liberty [Missouri] tomorrow morning at eight o'clock, and if you execute these men I will hold you responsible before an earthly tribunal, so help me God!" General Lucas rescinded the order. These, and other Mormon prisoners, were kept by the militia for some time, and then turned over to the civil courts. After being further imprisoned for several months, the Mormon leaders were permitted to escape.

In his autobiography Colonel Doniphan did not mention his connection with the Mormon war.

with the occasional effort to chime in an almost unearthly voice. *Las Senoras y Senoritas* [the ladies
and girls—young ladies] were dressed in silks, satins,
ginghams & lawns, embroidered crape shawls, fine
rabozos—and decked with various showy ornaments,
such as hugh necklaces, countless rings, combs, bows
of ribbands, red and other coloured handkerchiefs, and
other fine *fancy* articles. This is a short sketch of a
Mexican ball. Liuts Warner & Hammond called this
evening to see how I *enjoyed* the dance (not that I
joined [in] it myself).

Saturday 12th. William[46] arrived this morning, and
oh, how provoked I am with him; he had letters for me
and instead of bringing them left them in his trunk
at the wagons. I may almost expect some by the express by the time they get here, the wagons have that
ugly Raton to pass through, and to be broken all to
pieces, and mended before they get here. Men are such
provoking animals when they take it into their heads.
I must be more expert in my Spanish, that I may
receive the advice that la Senora [the lady—Mrs.]
Ortis wishes to give me respecting them; how I shall
punish them for their misconduct, spoil them for their
good deeds, & other little fixings—

[46] William Magoffin, youngest son of Beriah Magoffin. After
returning from this expedition he took up the study of medicine.
He served in the Confederate Army during the war between the
states; married, in Savannah, Georgia, Miss Anne Patterson.
Practiced his profession for a while in Georgia, then removed to
Minnesota, where he lived for many years. William Magoffin died
at the home of his brother, Governor Beriah Magoffin, in
Harrodsburg, Kentucky.

Two of the officers called tonight to while away a few hours in social chat. Capt. Turner[47] is a gentleman of extensive information; exceedingly polite, endeavours to make himself agreeable and to interest the company with his interesting narations; he spent a year in France, and has traveled in Prusia—his con-

[47] Henry Smith Turner was born in King George County, Virginia, April 1, 1811. In 1830 he was admitted as a cadet at West Point, and graduated in June, 1834, receiving the brevet of second lieutenant in the First Dragoons. On March 3, 1837, he was appointed aide-de-camp to General Atkinson, serving in that capacity until July, 1839. Then he was sent by the War Department, with two colleagues, to the cavalry school at Saumur, France, to study cavalry tactics, and prepare a manual of instructions for that arm of the service in the army of the United States. Upon returning to the United States two years later, he married Miss Julia M. Hunt, daughter of Theodore Hunt and Ann Lucas Hunt of St. Louis. He was promoted to the rank of captain of the First Dragoons, April 21, 1846, and served as the acting assistant adjutant of General Kearny's Army of the West. At the battle of San Pasqual, California, on December 6, 1846, Turner was badly wounded, but none of his comrades knew of his injury until after the battle. He was brevetted major for gallant and meritorious conduct in this affair; was in the conflicts at San Gabriel and Plains of Mesa, California. Major Turner was an essential witness in the trial by court-martial of Colonel Fremont, and was detained in attendance on that court at Washington until after the treaty of peace in 1848. In July of that year he resigned his commission and devoted himself thereafter to civil pursuits. In 1852 he embarked in the business of banking, in partnership with Captain (afterwards General) William T. Sherman and James H. Lucas. The firm opened a branch bank in San Francisco, California, of which Major Turner took personal charge and remained there for several years. He died in St. Louis December 16, 1881.

versation is both interesting and improving to his hearers. - - - Mrs. Turner is a niece of one of the Lexingtonians, Mr. John W. Hunt.

The name of the other officer I do not recollect—he is from Baltimore though—and one of the plain independent, blunt spoken men, just exactly the reverse of his companion. If he has not the brilliant mind and great command of language that the other has to interest he at least can amuse with his droll sayings.

The military have been very punctual in calling, some of them nearly every day; our similar situations —the separations from friends and relations—seems to create within us all a kind of sympathetic feeling that makes each other's society agreeable, and quite desirable to be sought after in this foreign land where there are so few of our countrymen, and so few manners and customs similar to ours, or in short anything to correspond with our *national* feelings and *fire*-side friendships.

Mr. Glasgow—a trader—called this morning and soon talked away a half hour; he is quite an agreeable St. Louisan, and interested me with a description of the manner in which *The Gen.* was received in the lower settlements.

Sunday 13th. An other Sabbath in Santa Fé—we have intended the whole week to visit the church today, but the best hour for attending mass (there are two or three) not being known we have declined it till an other day.

Dr. Conley and Mr. Thruston called about 11 o'k. sat with us half an hour. The latter has spent several years in this country in different parts; some times talks of returning to Louisville Ky. his former home, but I suspect he has become so well iniciated in the *manners of living* and *ways* of Mexico, he will not be in much of a hurry to visit his native land. They give us some news just arrived from Chihuahua, viz: That Peredes[48] the new President and General in the field has been taken prisoner by his own troops while on his way from the city of Mexico to give battle to Gen. Taylor at Montere [Monterey], and has been lodged

[48] Mariano Paredes y Arrillage was born in the city of Mexico, January 6, 1797. He entered the Spanish Army as a cadet January 6, 1812, became captain in 1821, at which time he joined Iturbide. In 1831 he was promoted to colonel and the next year brigadier-general. Was elected president of Mexico, January 20, 1846.

Paredes was frail, slight in form and not ungraceful, though maimed by the wounds of many battles. He was known throughout the Republic as "El Manco," or the wounded hand. He was considered the Murat of Mexico, as he knew no fear in his almost mad and reckless daring. He was once banished to the United States as an exile, studied our institutions and worshiped our enterprise. His American feelings were strong. It was his skill, energy, and indomitable courage that made Santa Anna president of the Mexican Republic, and when Santa Anna trifled with the liberties of his beloved country, it was Peredes who hurled the dictator from place and power, and banished him. He was a favorite with the people—a favorite with the army. As commander of the forces and governor of one of the richest departments of the republic, his influence was seen and felt throughout the land. When war with the United States brought about Mexican defeats in the battles of Palo Alto and Resaca de la Palma, a mutiny under General Mariano Salas took place. This resulted in President Paredes being deposed and the restoration of Santa Anna to power.

in prison, and that General Santa Anna,[49] a former President, for some years a traveller in the U. S. and Cuba, has been recalled to take the power of government into his own hands, and as his feelings to our government is rather more lenient and peaceable than

[49] Don Antonio Lopez de Santa Anna was born at Jalapa, in the Department of Vera Cruz, February 21, 1795, of an obscure and indigent family. In early life, with an inadequate education, he joined the army. With a natural suavity of manners, refined by his intercourse with the best society of Vera Cruz, and the discipline of a studious and observing mind, he acquired a facility of address that rendered him at once conspicuous in camp, and secured favorable notice of his superiors, both in the army and the society in which he was admitted. In 1832 he was elected president. On April 6, 1836, he stormed the Alamo fort at San Antonio, killed its defenders, afterwards massacred the garrison at Goliad, and for several weeks was victorious. But on April 21 he was surprised at San Jacinto and totally routed by the Texas army under General Houston. He fled, but was captured three days afterwards. On May 14, he signed a treaty with the provisional president of Texas, recognizing the independence of that state. He was a prisoner for eight months, but was finally sent by General Houston to the United States. Returning to Mexico later, he was coldly received, and retired to his farm.

The French invasion of 1838 once more put the warrior into his saddle, at the head of the Mexican army before Vera Cruz. There, in his charge upon the enemy, he gloriously retrieved his character, but lost his left leg below the knee. The wily general saw an opportunity to climb to the top of the political ladder with his dismembered limb, and accordingly sent his fallen leg to his fellow citizens in the city of Mexico, accompanied by an eloquent letter, full of patriotic sentiments.

From 1839 to 1844 Santa Anna was again in power, in one form or another, either as president or military dictator. In the latter year a mutiny resulted in his flight, capture, release, and

Peredes, he is to petition for quarters. This if true, is as favourable as we could desire, and it is the general opinion that ere this a minister to that effect has been sent to our Government. I trust it may be so indeed.

Wrote a long letter to Sister Anna this A. M. and now if I could only have those she sent me by Wm. what a treat 'twould be.

Monday 14th. Gen. Kearny and Mr. Glasgow called this A. M., found me in the kitchen with my hands in something for dinner. I sent Jane in to seat them, and in a little while went in with my sun-bonnet in my hand and frankly told the gentlemen they had caught me attending to my household duties. The Gen. seemed delighted with my candour, met me half way across the floor with out stretched hand, and when seated gave me a very graphic account of his reception at the lower settle⁸ how he paraded through some little village in the priests procession, carrying

retirement to Havana. After the defeats by the United States troops, when President Paredes was deposed, Santa Anna was recalled to the command of the army, and in December, 1846, again became president. On December 21, 1853, he had himself appointed president for life, with power of nominating his successor. After many revolutions, aroused by his despotic rule, he fled and finally settled on the island of St. Thomas.

He made several efforts to promote revolts and finally died in the city of Mexico, June 20, 1876.

Santa Anna has been described as a hale-looking man with an "Old Bailey" countenance and a well-built wooden leg. His countenance was said faithfully to depict his character in portraying oily duplicity, treachery, avarice, and sensuality. He always paid courtly attention to the fair sex and won great favor with them.

as did all his officers a lighted candle lightening the
train of the Virgin Mary, and to use his own words
"making a fool of himself." He told of his fine feasts,
the balls, Indian sham battles &c.

On leaving asked if I had any commission to the
upper Calafornia he would be at my service, and I requested him to select me a fine situation, which business he promised faithfully to attend to, provided I
would give my word to reside there, or at least to take
possession. He gave me permission to send a letter by
the mail which goes out on Thursday.

Liut. Warner called this evening and sat an hour
with me; he leaves for Touse [Taos] tomorrow, where
he is to take the latitude and longetude of this and
other places. What an odd man he is to talk; giving
such out-of-the-way details of his travels &c.

Tuesday 15th. What a polite people these Mexicans
are, altho' they are looked upon as a half barbarous set
by the generality of people. This morning I have
rather taken a little protege, a little market girl—Sitting at the window and on the look out for vegetables,
this little thing came along with green peas the month
of *Sept.;* she came in and we had a long conversation
on matters and things in general, and I found that not
more than six years old she is quite conversant in all
things. On receiving her pay she bowed most politely,
shook hands with a kind *"adios"* and *"me alegro de
verte bien"* [I am glad to see you in good health], and
also a promise to return tomorrow. Just to see the
true politeness and ease displayed by that child is
truly [amazing], 'twould put many a mother in the

U. S. to the blush. And she is so graceful too, her rabozo was thrown to one side and a nice white napkin of pease set down from off her head with quite as much grace as some ladies display in a minuet. Donna Julienne called this evening; took a great fancy to my cape because it is *high in the neck,* and will return for the pattern; she dislikes, she says, to go into the *plazo* where there are so many *Americanos,* and her neck exposed.

Cpts. Johnson[50] and Waldo called tonight—they belong to the militia, and not to be too severe a critic, I shall only say I think I have had some more talkative, interesting and agreeable visitors.

Thursday 17th. I wrote nothing yesterday and now I do not recollect any of the transactions now, or at least they were of but little importance, no visitors I believe & nothing to do but sit here all day and read &c. &c. &c.

And today I have been engaged with market people in the first place, here is my little protege, with her nice napkin of * *y totos* [*tortas*—little cakes]; how the little thing excites my sympathies and I can almost say affections; she is pretty in her face and in her manners, and though her garments are not the best

[50] Abraham Robinson Johnson, born in Ohio in 1815, and graduated from United States Military Academy. Served on frontier duty as first lieutenant of Dragoons at Fort Leavenworth 1837-1846. In the war with Mexico was aide-de-camp to General Kearny, and on June 30, 1846, was promoted to the rank of captain. Captain Johnson was killed in the combat of San Pasqual, while gallantly leading a charge against the enemy's lancers.

* [Missing in manuscript.]

and in something of a tattered condition, she is the possessor of some extraordinary qualities.

Next is a half grown boy with mellons—here he asks me "dos reals por una" [two reals for one] believing me to be like some of my countrymen entirely young in such matters, but he found me different. I looked at him straight till he fell to *un real media* [a real and a half], when I said *"hombre"* in a long voice, as much as to say "man have you a soul to ask so much!" and without hesitation he *gladly* took *una,* the regular market price, and I dare say he will return another time since he was not able to play the cheat, and I am a pretty prompt customer.

Cpts. Johnson and Turner called tonight and sat with us some half hour or more, in pleasant conversation & the former makes rather a more agreeable impression than in his first call.

Friday 18th. This has been quite a day of little scenes one way & an other; the gentlemen *mi alma* & William have been absent most of the whole day and all the visitors I have received alone. The Gen. & Mr. Thruston called to pay me an especial visit. How candid and plain spoken the general is; he speaks to me more as my father would do than any one else— it is very kind of him too; so much better than stiff formality. I complimented him a little and my own dear *Kentucky,* at the same time by asking him, for my own private information, if he [came] from Ky. as I believed most or all of the great men were from there, or connected with her in some way. In an instant he replied, "Madam though I am not a native Kentuckian, I have visited there, and Mrs. Kearny is from there," at once taking the compliment to himself, but as I meant it so, 'twas all right.

Mrs. Leitendorfer (whom I saw at the Fort) and her sister called to see me. They were both dressed rather in American style; with bonnets, scarfs & parasols and dresses made after the fashions there. We carried on quite a sociable chat, and she thinks since she saw me last that my progress has been exceedingly rapid. We are invited to dine, with the Gen. & principal officers of his staff, at her house tomorrow at two o'k—that is to be the first entire Mexican dinner I take.

While sitting here alone reading this afternoon, some one tapped at the door to which I, on raising my head, responded "good evening" and in walked an American whom I supposed to be a wagoner wanting employment, but soon discovoured my mistake, for instead of asking for Mr. Magoffin as such men always do, he took a seat unasked and said in half English & Spanish "are you Merican." I looked at him straight and briefly replied *"yes"!* He now discouvered his *mistake* that instead of being in the house of a *low* Mexican he was in that of an American gentleman, and stammering out something as to his surprise in seeing an American lady, and if I was "satisfied at living here," with a most uneasy twist in his chair for without paying any attention to his words, demanded "if he had any business with Mr. Magoffin the gentleman of this house," and I may venture to say the poor

fellow's frightened looks showed that he heartily
wished himself in other quarters. It was a perfect reel
from his chair to the door, and all the while stammering, "now Mam—if you will pl—ease excu—se my
int—trusion"—at the door he doffed his beaver and
said, "may I wi—sh you go—od even"; he received
no other answer to all this than a stern look. Once
across the door sill he soon found other quarters.

My little protege too has been here, on leaving she
adopted her native manner of saluting, and put her
arms around my waist for she could reach them no
higher.

Saturday morning. A written invitation to dine
with Mr. & Mrs. Leitensdorfer today has just been
received, and as I am to be somewhat an object of
wonder 'twould be best that I put on my best manners, looks, conversation &c.

Well the dinner is over, and can I give a little sketch
of the proceedings? I shall try.—

We left here at fifteen minutes to 2 o'clock P. M.
passed through the plazo, of course atracting the attention of all idle bystanders—my bonnet being an
equal object of wonder with the *white* woman that
wore it. We arrived at Mr. L's door followed by the
Gen. and his little party of officers, after Mexican
style, I suppose, we were met by *tres Senoras*, Mrs.
L. and two sisters. We entered the dining room where
we found a number of gentlemen seated around on
the cushioned benches, and waiting to partake the
dainty viands now being placed en la mesa [on the

table]. My bonnet and shawl were soon removed and we seated ourselves at table.

One custom I cannot admire among them, 'tis this the ladies are all placed on one side by themselves, while the gentlemen are also alone; 'tis not at all congenial to my sociable feelings, there is much more enjoyment for the company generally, much more taste, and more sociability when all seat themselves promiscuously around.

But now for the dinner; first came *sopa de vermicile* [vermicelli soup], then *sopa de otro* [another kind of soup], this is their custom to bring on something light preparatory to the more weighty dishes. This *sopa* is pretty much a substitute for our fine *soups.* The rice is boiled, dressed with little butter, salt &c. and then covered over with slices of boiled eggs.— Next came the several dishes of *carne de asado, carne de cocida* [roasted meat, boiled meat], and some other *carnes,* all of which they placed in plates before me, and of course I *tasted* them. The champain went round without reserve. The Gen. drank and enjoyed it, he has been under the Dctor for some days past and consequently could now do justice to the dishes before him after his fast. For desert we had a dish made of boiled milk and seasoned with cinnamon and nutmeg, and it was very good, the recipe I should like. An other of cake pudding—both Mexican and new to me, fine cool grapes, to which we all did justice. Our General gave us a toast, with the permission of our host, "The U. S. and Mexico—They are now united, may no one ever think of separating." It was translated into Spanish by Mr. Rubidor,[51] the general's interpreter. 'Twas responded to by Mrs. L's brother, while the Mexican gentlemen around the table cried out *"viva" "viva."* After dinner, which lasted some two hours and a half or three, we, the ladies, passed into an adjoining room, took seats on the low cushions

[51] Antoine Robidou (the name is frequently spelled Robidoux), son of Joseph Robidou and Catherine Rollet dit Laderoute, was born in St. Louis, September 22, 1794. He was a brother of Joseph Robidou, the founder of St. Joseph, Missouri, and of François and Louis Robidou, prominent fur traders of the Northwest and Southwest. In 1828 Antoine Robidou married Carmel Benevides at Santa Fé, who accompanied her husband on many trips from Santa Fé to St. Joseph.

Antoine Robidou joined General Kearny's "Army of the West" in June, 1846, and acted thereafter as interpreter. Accompanying Kearny to California, he participated in the battle of San Pasqual, where he was severely wounded. Lieutenant Emory tells of sleeping next to him after the battle, and of the grave doubts of his recovery. Early the morning after the battle Robidou awakened Emory and asked him if he did not smell coffee, and expressed the belief that a cup of that beverage would save his life. Not knowing that there was any coffee in the camp, the lieutenant supposed a delirious dream had carried him back to the cafés of St. Louis and New Orleans. But much to his surprise, upon investigation, he found his cook heating a cup of coffee over a small fire. Lieutenant Emory continuing says: "One of the most agreeable little offices performed in my life, and I believe in the cook's, to whom the coffee belonged, was to pour this precious draught into the waning body of our friend Robidoux. His warmth returned and with it hopes of life. In gratitude he gave me what was then a great rarity, the half of a cake made of brown flour, almost black with dirt, and which had for greater security been hidden in the clothes of his Mexican servant, a man who scorned ablutions. I ate more than half without inspection,

placed around the wall, immediately *cigarrettos* were brought, this part I declined. After a little more champain the gentleman joined us, and by the time a half hour's chat was over 'twas time to depart, they to their respective occupations, and we to return the call of Don Gespar and Senora Ortis. The latter only was at home; we stayed but a short time, in consequence of a threatening thunderstorm.

Madam Ortis is a very talkative and agreeable lady, her house I suppose is one of the best in the city. The entrance first is into a large court-yard (the fashion of all the houses) with portals all around. The long salon to the front, is the sitting room. This is furnished with cushions, no chairs, two steamboat sofas, tables a bed and other little fixtures.

Sunday 20th. I accompanied the general to church today with the view of seeing the church, but this was not accomplished, for they placed me around in a recess a seat from whence I could see nothing. The women kneeled all over the floor, there being no pews, while the men stood up, occasionally kneeling and

when, on breaking a piece, the bodies of several of the most loathsome insects were exposed. My hunger, however, overcame my fastidiousness, and the *morceau* did not appear particularly disgusting until after our arrival at San Diego, when several hearty meals had taken off the keenness of my appetite, and suffered my taste to be more delicate."

Robidou had a trading post in Taos in the twenties; built a fort in Colorado in the late thirties, and one in Utah some years later, which was in use during the forties. A stream in Colorado, and a pass in the Rocky Mountains are both named for him. He died at St. Joseph, Missouri, August 29, 1860.

crossing themselves. The priest neither preached nor prayed, leaving each one to pray for himself; he repeated some latin neither understood by himself or his hearers. The latter repeated their aves and pater nosters—ever and anon whispering to a next neighbour and giving a sly glance to the American spectators. Their music consisted of a violin, which all the time they continued to tune, and a thumming gingling guitar; the same tunes they had the other night at the fandango, were played. It is a strange mode of worship to a protestant who has been raised to regard the Sabbath with strictest piety, not even to think of a dancing tune on a violin, let the hearing of it alone. There are some defaced pictures hanging about the Altar, the designs of which, for the numberless scratches and fingerprints, I could not unravel. There is also a statue of Christ covered with a net to protect it from injury—near it is a large waxen doll dressed as a priest and is bearing a cross. As soon as the Priest left the altar, after an hour's stay, we took our departure from the Church and thus ended my first lesson in Catholicism!

Monday 21st. Mi alma quite sick in bed all day, and how lonely the day has been, the house is like some vacated castle; no noise is heard save now and then the quick but gentle scamper of a mouse embolden by the silence of the larger inmates, as he steals out from his covert in the earthen floor, to pick a crumb or other morsal around the room. I have read most of the day and watched by the sick bed.

Tuesday 22nd. He is better today and out of his room.

Gen. Kearny with his aid Cpt. Johnson and the adjutant General, Cpt. Turner, called tonight and sat a long time in pleasant chat. The Gen. delights in reminding me of my Calafornia tour, says he will write and give me the required information resting the sight for my house, and I must let him have my word that I will go (there will be a little romance in that—and I think we might on the strength of it bring forth a novel, with Capt. Johnson, who they tell me is a good writer to handle the pen). The Gen. will call tomorrow at 10 o'clock to take me to see Fort Marcey.[52]

While the gentlemen sat here we had a fair opportunity of testing the dry virtues of our Mexican house. A hard thunder storm came up and detained them some half hour or more longer than, I presume, they would otherwise called. We continued in pleasant and

[52] Fort Marcy. This fort was on an elevation commanding the city of Santa Fé, and was located by Captain Emory, designed by Lieutenant Gilmer, of the Topographical Corps, and L. A. Mac-Lean, a volunteer of Reid's Company. It was built by the volunteer troops, a certain number of men being detailed each day for the purpose. The fort was within six hundred yards of the heart of Santa Fé and nearly one hundred feet above that city. It was of such a size as to accommodate a great number of cannon and one thousand soldiers. The walls were built of adobe blocks, two feet long, one foot broad, and six inches thick, and was very strong and massive. It was named for Secretary of War W. L. Marcy. (Hughes, *Doniphan's Expedition*, p. 123.) Efforts are being made by the Historical Society of New Mexico to restore the old fort.

merry chat, when suddenly the rain came pating onto the General, from the ceiling, and of course caused a very unceremonious jump, and an inquiring glance to know the meaning of that. The mystery, new alike to all was soon explained by a bolder stream coming through in an other place. Soon we were leaking all around, the mud roof coming with the water, and had the rain not stoped when it did we might soon have been left without a canopy, save the dark forbidding sky.

Wednesday 23rd. Agreeable and punctual to his promise, the Gen. mounted on a splendid bay charger, reached our door as my faithful time-piece marked the hour of 10. My horse was soon in trim & leaving *mi alma* "Madam" of affairs, we commenced winding our way through the clogged streets of Santa Fé; first we found ourselves inspecting the artillery, arranged in two rows on one side of an outer street—from this we wound our way along by the barracks, formerly for Armijos troops, where a small party of soldiers were engaged, as the Gen. passed they all touched their beavers with profoundest respect, while he kindly returned the salute. We now ascended a long and rather steep hill, on the summit of which stands fort Marcey, sole master of the entire plain below. It is the most perfect view I ever saw. Not only every house in the city can be torn by the artillery to attoms, but the wide plain beyond is exposed to the fullest view—and far beyond this still are the majestic mountains some of which we passed in coming in. The Fort occupies some two acres of ground, has double walls built of adobes, the space between being filled with stones and morter. Dwellings, store houses &c. are to be built within the wall, in the center under ground is the magazine for ammunition. Under the wise superintendence of Lieutenant Gilmer[53] of the U. S. Corps of Engineers, will be, when completed a stronghold as well as a prettily improved spot. – – – On leaving the Fort we rode to the opposite side of the city (*to the West*) to see the Gloriatta, an inclosed public walk.

[53] Jeremy Francis Gilmer, born in Guilford County, North Carolina, February 23, 1818. Graduated at the United States Military Academy in 1839. Receiving the rank of second lieutenant of engineers, he served in the military academy as assistant professor of engineering until June, 1840, and then as assistant engineer in the building of Fort Schuyler, New York harbor, until 1844, following which he was assistant to the chief engineer at Washington, D. C., until 1846. During the Mexican War he was chief engineer of the Army of the West in New Mexico, constructing Fort Marcy at Santa Fé. He was promoted to the rank of captain July 1, 1853. As a member of various commissions of engineers, he was continually engaged in fortification work, and in the improvement of rivers throughout the South until 1858. From that time Captain Gilmer was in charge of the construction of defenses at the entrance of San Francisco Bay until June 29, 1861, when he resigned to join the Confederate Army. He was commissioned lieutenant-colonel, corps of engineers, in September, 1861; was severely wounded in the battle of Shiloh. Subsequently he was promoted to brigadier-general, and on August 4, 1862, was made chief engineer of the department of northern Virginia. A few months later he became chief of the engineer bureau of the Confederate States War Department. In 1863 he was promoted to major-general. After the war he engaged in railroad and other enterprises in Georgia, and from 1867 to 1883 was president and engineer of the Savannah Gaslight Company. He died December 1, 1883, at Savannah, Georgia.

It was commenced by *Gov. Gen. Garcia Conde*,[54] being planted altogether in indifferent looking Cotton-woods it is quite susceptible of improvement—a Yankee's ingenuity and *Kentuckian's* taste is wanting to make it a beautiful place. Leaving this little spot we wound our way home again after a ride of an hour's length. The Gen. came in and sat half hour with us—in the mean time an ambassador from the Comanche Indians called with his staff of treaty, and as this was a business to be transacted at home he left for "The Palace" with his Indians friends. – – –

Lieutenant Warner, who has been in Touse [Taos] on duty (surveying) for a week, called to bid me "good bye" as he leaves in The Calafornia expedition on the 25th. He is a warm-hearted good kind of a man—a true friend I should think from the little I've seen of him—he regrets deeply that we will may be not see each other again, but hopes that in the long run of things, my travelling so much, and his being stationed in all parts of The U. S. chance may bring us together again.

Thursday 24th. This morning's work is to tell of the ball last night, given to the Gen. & his Corps by the

[54] General Pedro García Condé was an accomplished engineer and one of the commanding officers at the battle of Sacramento; planning the whole Mexican defense in this action. He held many important positions under his government, being at various times Secretary of War and Navy, director of the Military College, deputy to the Mexican Congress, and Mexican commissioner in the United States-Mexican Boundary Commission of 1850. While serving in this last mentioned office he died at Arispe, Mexico, on December 19, 1850. He was but forty-seven years old at the time.

newly appointed officials and citizen merchants. It is rather too long to go through the whole, so I'll sketch it slightly. 'Twas given at the Government house, "The Palace,"[55] the first I've ever been in.

On entering the room every one turned to look at me and seemed particularly attracted by a scarlet Canton crape shawl I wore, to be in trim with the "Natives." I was conducted to a seat by Mr. Smith,[56] one of the managers, and soon was surrounded by the Gen. and officers of his staff. Maj. Swords, Capts. Turner, Johnson, Clark,[57] (who I was introduced to

[55] "Palace of the Governors." This old building has seen governors and governments come and go, from 1698 to the present day. Until 1886 it was the home of the governor and seat of government both under Spanish and American rule. Subsequently it became the home of the Historical Society of New Mexico. It is said that Governor Lew Wallace wrote the last chapters of *Ben Hur* in one of the rooms of this building. The building is of adobe construction and extends east and west along the north side of the Plaza, presenting a front of about three hundred feet, with a depth of forty feet. It is one story high, has walls three feet thick, and a portico along the entire front.

[56] William T. Smith. He was a clerk for John Scolly, trader and merchant in Santa Fé.

[57] Meriwether Lewis Clark, son of William Clark, of the Lewis and Clark Expedition, and Julia Hancock, was born in St. Louis, January 10, 1809. He was appointed a cadet in the United States Military Academy July 1, 1825. Served in the Black Hawk War as colonel and assistant adjutant-general of Illinois Volunteers from May 9 to October 11, 1832, and was wounded in action. Colonel Clark resigned his commission May 31, 1833, and entered civil life as a civil engineer. He was a member of the House of Representatives of Missouri from 1836 to 1838; recorder of the city of St. Louis, 1843; and United States surveyor-general for

for the first time, a fine looking gentleman, with au-
burn hair & whiskers; claims kin with me, through his
wife, who was a Miss Churchill of Louisville, Ky.),
Lieutenants Gilmer, Hammond, Warner and Peck,[58]
beside many gentlemen of the city. It kept my tongue
constantly going to keep them entertained, and I
trust my efforts were not ineffectual, as I think there
is nothing more pleasing than to see a lady agreeable
and entertaining in her conversation, and I am sure
as it is *mi alma's* wish that I should excell, it is never

the state of Missouri, 1848 to 1853. At the outbreak of the war
with Mexico he was commissioned major of a Missouri battalion
of artillery. Was in the battle of Sacramento, and during the occupation of Chihuahua he took up his quarters in the Palace Library. While there he found that the books were not properly
classified, so with his penchant for doing things thoroughly he
ordered a detail to do the work properly. He was honorably
mustered out June 24, 1847. Colonel Clark served in the Confederate Army as colonel and aide-de-camp from 1861 to 1865.
He married, first, Abigail Churchill, and second, Julia David-
son. Colonel Clark died at Frankfort, Kentucky, October 28,
1881.

[58] Lieutenant William Guy Peck was born in Litchfield, Connecticut, October 16, 1820. He was graduated at the United
States Military Academy in 1844 at the head of his class, and was
assigned to the topographical engineers; served in the third expedition of John C. Fremont through the Rocky Mountains in
1845. During the war with Mexico he was with the Army of the
West. He was a mathematician of note, and resigned from the
army in 1855 to accept the professorship of physics and civil
engineering in the University of Michigan, remaining there until
1857, when he accepted a position in Columbia University. He
was the author of a number of school and text books on mathe-
matics. He died February 7, 1892.

an exertion but the greatest pleasure to make myself so.

The company of ladies, they say, was not so large or select as on some other occasion owing to the death of an old gentleman, a few days since, the relation of half the city. They were dressed in the Mexican style; large sleeves, short waists, ruffled skirts, and no bustles —which latter looks exceedingly odd in this day of grass skirts and pillows. All danced and smoke cigarrittos, from the old woman with false hair and teeth, (Dona Tula), to the little child. "The Cuna"[59] was danced, and was indeed beautiful; it commences with only two and ends when the floor gets too full for any more to come on—One lady and gentleman danced a figure (the name I now forget, but it resembled the "old Virginia" negro shuffle). We left at 11 o'clock, and soon after our arrival home it commenced raining hard and this morning it is disagreeably cold, snow is to be seen on the adjacent Mountains, and we are in the valley living on fine vegetables, and most delightful peaches, grapes, melons &c.

Lieuts. Warner & Hammond called since tea to bid us good bye, they are of the Calafornia expedition. The latter, (I do not mean to slander him at all) has taken a little more of "the ingredient" than he can well bear. He constantly talked of the American

[59] The Mexicans' favorite dance, and appropriately called *Cuna,* or cradle. It is somewhat similar to the waltz. The couple stand face to face, the gentleman encircling his partner's waist with both arms, the lady's similarly disposed, complete the sides of the cradle, which is not bottomless, for both parties lean well back as they swing around.

women, *their strict virtue, which he said could not be said of the men,* said he had written to his wife all about me, and I am afraid the poor woman, if his account of the letter is true, will, if she ever sees me, be tempted to kill me. Said his was a run away match, and they "were married *on horse back on top of a very high hill."* Talked of his "angel baby," then flew off on to the War, and almost went off into extacies on the subject; he is all eagerness for a fight, and says he has done all things in his power to provoke one. And then he commenced eulogizing every body, flew again to what he had written his wife of me, and ran on at such a rate I absolutely became frightened, and giving *mi alma* the *nod, turned him over* and commenced conversation with Warner. How he happened to be in such a *fix* tonight, is strange, for he is a most perfect gentleman when *sober.*

Friday 25th. The Army is leaving today. Cpts. Johnson, Turner and Clark called to bid me farewell, and to wish me a prosperous and pleasant journey to the South—While "I hoped they might meet with the same good fortune in Calafornia and be safely restored to their happy families." Three more gentlemanly, polite and intelligent men have not entered our house in Santa Fé. The Gen. found so much business to do he was unable to see me, so he sent his adieus, respects &c. by *mi alma.*

Saturday 26th. Gabriel Valdez, brother James' brother-in-law arrived this morning with brothers J's, & W's wagons. He became sick with chills & fever, a sickness in which I truly sympathize with him—ex-

perience the best of teachers, has taught me that the
shaking and quaking of bones is not a very agreeable
sensation. I must therefore turn his nurse and relieve
if possible a brother sufferer.—First here is "Sappington's celebrated fever and ague pills."[60]

Wrote a letter to Sister Mary[61]—first since I left
Independence—rather shameful treatment that I
must allow, and can only excuse myself by fears as to
the result of her peculiar situation, having heard not
one word whether she might be dead or in fine health
&c. I hesitated long as to my course, and wrote at last
after reading a long expected letter from Sister Anna,
in which (dated June 28th) she says "Sister Mary is
still on her feet—not yet in the straw" accordingly my

[60] About 1840 the most popular medicine in Missouri was Sappington's anti-fever pills. Most of the people lived along the
creeks and in the river bottoms, and suffered from malaria. Dr.
John Sappington mixed pills, in the preparation of which quinine
was used. He wrote a book entitled *Theory and Treatment of
Fevers,* which was published at Arrow Rock, Missouri, in 1844.
It was commonly called "Sappington on Fevers." Dr. Sappington
was one of the most remarkable pioneer citizens and physicians
of central Missouri of his day; his practice covering a wide area,
including half a dozen counties in the state and an occasional
visit to Arkansas. His reputation as a physician extended far
beyond Missouri. Three of his daughters became, in succession,
the wives of Claiborne Jackson, governor of Missouri. It is related that on the Governor's asking him for the third daughter,
the doctor replied: "Yes, you can have her on one condition, that
if you lose her, you will not come back for her mother."

[61] Mary Pindell Shelby, daughter of Isaac Shelby, Jr., born
May 2, 1822; married Henry Lloyd Tevis, July 5, 1843; died in
1861.

147

imagination saw her well and a happy & safe termination of the long dreaded hour.

October 1846. Thursday 1st. Oh how dreadfully slow this week goes by, and nothing scarcely occurs worth noticing.

Report today says that Gen. Peredes is again at the head of government and making all possible preparations to prosecute the war with vigor. We may give what credence to this we please.

One would think we made entire associates of drunken soldiers, if they could have chanced to look in here at two particular times only. While sitting here alone this P. M. some one knocked at the door, and thinking it a Mexican I had just seen in *el patio* [the yard], I said *"passa y Senor"* ["come in, Sir"] when in *staggered* a man, I wont say gentleman, with "why you speak Spanish already," and with as much familiarity as though he had been an old acquaintance, and I had never seen him before. Introducing himself as "Lieut. Woster[62] of the Army" and he had intended calling on me some time, staggered to a seat where he sat and ran on with foolishness and impudence to which I paid but little attention, and *mi alma* coming in he took him off my hands. He by and bye took a notion to start and accordingly got up,

[62] Charles F. Wooster was appointed a cadet to the United States Military Academy, from New York, the state of his nativity, July 1, 1833. Served as first and second lieutenant from July 1, 1837, to June 10, 1842. He was brevetted captain February 28, 1847, for gallant and meritorious conduct in the battle of Sacramento; and promoted to captain September 27, 1850. Captain Wooster died February 14, 1856.

staggered about the floor & at length departed. I do think some of my countrymen are disgracing themselves here.

Friday 2nd. News is received today that Peredes is not again in power contradicting the report of yesterday, but that peace has been made. Gen. Taylor recalled from the South, &c. I only hope it may be true, 'tis too soon for us to have received the news from the U. S.

We will start on though in a few days with good faith believing all things for the best. The greatest fears is of Indians, who still continue their mischief, in the Rio Bajo, driving off stock, and killing the inhabitants if they have the opportunity, notwithstanding the troops now among them.

Monday 5th. My back is like a broken stick, I can't do work of any kind but that it cripples me up like a rheumatic—we start tomorrow and as usual, there is much to be done. I've packed and packed, and besides have partly made a dress for the road; this is an other piece of trouble, cutting, fitting &c &c.

I am most tired of Santa Fé & do not regret leaving.

Tuesday 6th. Well we cannot leave today, not exactly ready.

Wednesday 7th. Camp No. 1. El rancho de Delgado. Lo, we are camping again! and after all it is quite as good as staying in Santa Fé. I was impatient to leave. Gabriel [Valdez] and William [Magoffin] are with us now. The wagons are all on ahead, and we'll not reach them yet for some days. Left Santa

Fé about 12 o'k. came on fifteen miles to this place—
a little farm, called a rancho—rather a poor place,
only a little corn, beans, and an abundance of *chile
verde* [green pepper], a few goats, sheep and jacks—
the beast of all work—they pack wood on them, ride
them, take all their little "fixings" to market in
baskets or bags swung on the long-eared animals back
&c &c. We camped pretty near the house and of course
the peepers are not a few.

The women stand around with their faces awfully
painted, some with red which shines like greese, and
others are daubed over with flour-paste. The men
stand off with crossed arms, and all look with as much
wonder as if they were not people themselves.

It is quite cool and our little tent is comfortable
enough—it is a fine thing.

Thursday 8th. As we advance farther South more
civilization on a small scale is to be seen in the dress of
the people, manners, houses &c.

Friday 9th. The boys have been out all day with
their guns trying to shoot grullas (sand hill crains)
which abound here in the river bottom, feeding off
the rancho cornfields—but they returned to be laughed
at only—They shot, each, some eight or ten times only,
and good sights too, but all were fruitless.

The "table-planes of Mexico," of which from my
youngest school-girl days, I have heard so much, are
full in view now—rather different though from what
I had expected to see—instead of the perfect plains
rising like regular steps one above an other—a plain
is only seen in the distance, on arriving at which by
descending into a valley, and then rising to the top of

150

a hill—you find almost a mountain, uneven and rough
travelling—little bushes & cedar trees of small growth
—We have much pulling through sand and we stop
earlier tonight, on the bank of the Rio del Norte—it
resembles the Mississippi much, muddy and dark, the
banks are low, with no trees—we are buying wood
every day—a small arm-full for *un real.*

A parcel of Indians are around the tent peeping in
at me and expressing their opinions. It is a novel sight
for them. These are the Pueblos or descendants of the
original inhabitants—the principal cultivators of the
soil—supplying the Mexican inhabitants with fruits,
vegetables &c.

Saturday 10th. In passing through a little town this
A. M. called Sandia, *my* Indian friend—the one who
called to see me once in Santa Fé—who lives there, the
big man—head chief among the tribe, stoped the carriage and pressed us to get out and go into his house—
he had been expecting and preparing for us. We had
no time for this though—and only accepted some
grapes at the carriage—he with his family, squaw &
children saw us eat them, with pleased faces, and after
a little compensation we left them.

Report comes to us that Brother James has been
robbed of *all* his things, carriage, mules, trunk, clothes
&c &c. by the Apache Indians and escaped with his life
only—how he escaped is a miracle to us. In robbing
they always want the *scalps,* the principal part of the
business.

I hope it is all a falsehood—though every person
we meet confirms it. The last we heard he was in the

little town at the Pass of the Del Norte—without a
hat.

We have fine grulla today—our hunters have better
luck today. They are tender and nice after being boiled
nearly all night—the meat is black as pea fowls.

Sunday 11th. Started out on a little walk this morning, but it was cut short by the little sand burrs sticking to my feet and dress till I was entirely unable to
walk; they are quite as sharp and hurt as much as
briers. I stoped and called for Jane to come to my
assistance—after a long time she succeeded in picking
them out. My fingers are sore now with the little
thorns.

Passing through one of the little towns, Albaquerque we stoped for a few moments at the store of
Don Raphel Armijo, which notwithstanding the Sabbath was opened.

While they were counting some money *mi alma* was
receiving, I steped in to take a look at the premises.
The building is very spacious, with wide portals in
front. Inside is the patio, the store occupying a long
room on the street—and the only one that I was in.
This is filled with all kinds of little fixings, dry goods,
groceries, hard-ware &c.

Over took Brother James's wagons this P. M.

Monday 12th. Stoped to noon it today for the first
time since we started. The pulling has been altogether
through sand & of course the animals are quite fatigued, and after a hard pull of two miles through
entire sand, they fare much better to stop. Our resting
place is on the river bank opposite to an Indian village
on the other side, and the warriors and squaws are

coming over in flocks to see the wonderful objects of curiosity—They bring things to sell—eggs, sandias, tortillas, grapes and the like. They wish to trade for bottles instead of money. They readily give *four bits a piece* for an empty bottle, making a fine proffit for the owners. We can buy in the States the filled bottles for three or four dollars a dozen, drink the liquor, and then sell the empty bottles for six dollars per doz. They peep into the carriage at me, and talk among themselves, and are altogether curious in their inquiries of how some things about the carriage and my clothes are made.

We camp tonight in a large piece of woodland belonging to some of the Chavez's—the ricos of New Mexico. The trees are all cotton-woods, which I suppose from the sterility of the soil, are much stinted and from the manner of their situation they resemble an apple orchard—and especially from a distant sight.

Tuesday 13th. Noon. This morning we called to see the widow of Don Mariano Chaviz,[63] who was one of the chief men in New Mexico till his death, about a year since. His wealth was immense, and his lands (for

[63] Don Mariano Chavez y Castillo was of the most wealthy and influential family in New Mexico. He was a gentleman of rare qualities and a leading citizen. Don Chavez was acting governor of New Mexico in 1835, and was one of five citizens nominated in 1845, from whom it was arranged a central government should select a permanent governor, but he died five weeks after the nomination. It is said that he aided Col. Cooke's division of Texas prisoners, by supplying them with provisions and clothing. His wife also is said to have supplied comforts to the Texans, having crossed the river from the village of Padillas, the place of their residence. (Gregg, *Commerce of the Prairies,* vol. 2, p. 172.)

Mexico) were improved accordingly. The house is very large—the sala measuring some — feet. This is well furnished with handsome Brussles carpet, crimson worsted curtains, with gilded rings and cornice, white marble slab pier tables—hair and crimson worsted chairs, chandelebras. And all the Mexicans have the greatest passion for framed pictures and looking-glasses. In this room of Chavez's house are eight or ten gilt-framed mirrors all around the wall. Around the patio are chambers, store-room, kitchen and others. All is exceedingly neat and clean.

La Senora met us and opened the *great door,* she was very polite, friendly, and invited us to spend sometime with her. All was with true hospitality, and I truly regret we were not able to do so.

We had more squaws to see us this morning—they came trading with *tortillas; cebollas* [onions] watermelons, and *manzanas* [apples]. Bottles are their great passion, and especially thick black ones. One old woman took a fancy to me, and so we got to trading. *Mi alma* told her he did not want her to have it, (in a joke only) but *I* made him give it, it pleased her so much she called me *"comadre"* [godmother] all the time, and on separating we parted almost like old friends. She *presented* me with some *tortillas.* I warrant if I should see her ten years hence she would recollect her *"Comadre"* and the *black bottle.* We hear that Calafornia has been taken by Com. Stockton,[64]

[64] Robert Field Stockton was born in Princeton, New Jersey, August 20, 1795, and died there October 7, 1866. He entered the navy as midshipman September 1, 1811, and served in the War of 1812. December 8, 1838, he was promoted to the rank of

and that Gen. Kearny will send all his men back, save one hundred dragoons as his body-guard principally. A vague rumor also comes that Gen. Wool[65] has taken Chihuahua.

captain, while sailing with Commodore Hull in the Mediterranean Squadron. October, 1845, found him commander-in-chief of the Pacific Squadron, on the eve of the Mexican War. Commodore Stockton assumed command of all the American forces on the coast by proclamation, July 23, 1846. Organizing a civil government in California, he appointed John C. Fremont governor. On January 17, 1847, he started homeward, and on May 28, 1850, resigned from the navy. He was elected to the United States Senate in 1851, served two years, resigned and retired to private life.

Commodore Stockton always took an interest in politics, and also in the turf. He imported from England some of the finest stock of blooded horses.

[65] John Ellis Wool, born in Newburgh, New York, February 20, 1784; died November 10, 1869. Raising a company of volunteers in Troy, he was commissioned captain in the 13th United States Infantry, April 14, 1812. He greatly distinguished himself at Queenstown Heights, October 13, 1812, and on September 11, 1814, he received the brevet of lieutenant-colonel for gallantry. On April 26, 1816, he was made inspector-general of the army with the rank of colonel. Colonel Wool was sent abroad in 1832 to inspect the military establishments of Europe for the benefit of the United States. On June 25, 1841, he was appointed brigadier-general. At the beginning of the Mexican War he was active in preparing volunteer forces for the field. He was General Zachary Taylor's second in command at Buena Vista. For gallant and meritorious conduct in that battle he was brevetted major-general February 23, 1847, and for his services during the war with Mexico Congress awarded him a vote of thanks and a sword of honor. From 1848-1853 he was in command of the eastern division of the army, and from 1854-1857 of the department of the Pacific, putting an end to Indian disturbances in

Wednesday 14th In our travel today we have met many Indians with their backs loaded with *muchas cosas a vender* [many things to sell]. They fill their *serapes*—[Mexican shawls or wraps for men] with whatever it may be, and start off in the trot natural to the Indian, and it is a remarkable thing that nearly every Mexican (of the lower class) and the Indians are either knock-kneed or pigeon-toed. And they have such an odd way, when asked where and how far to such a place, of tooting out their lips in the direction of the place, with a pigish grunt and *cuenta* [answer].

Thursday 15th. Came up with our wagons today at Noon. All is going on smoothly. Nooned it near the River, and as usual had some of the country people to see us. We are kept constantly supplied with eggs and small fruits. The apples all seem to be of one kind, and are not good, having a sickening sweet taste and very tough.

I have opened a regular *mantua* makers [dressmaker's] shop on the Plains. I am sewing on a dress every day at noon and will soon finish it. And I must not wear it out before I get home either—for I wish them to see that I have been doing some thing else

Washington and Oregon territories. General Wool had charge of the Department of the East in 1860, and at the opening of the war between the states saved Fortress Monroe by timely reinforcements, afterwards commanding there at the head of the Department of Virginia. He was promoted major-general in May, 1862, and retired from active service August 1, 1863, being long past the age of retirement. General Wool was a rigid disciplinarian and had no superior in the United States as an organizer of troops.

than roll along idly in the carriage. . . . Came up
with Mr. Harmony's wagons this P. M.

Saturday 17th. Left our last night's camp this
morning, came only about a mile, over an ugly hill and
sandy road—this side found a fine place for the animals and stoped for the whole day, "as we are in no
hurry." There is a little town near to us and we are
living on the fine Mexican *tortillas*—and they are fine
indeed they are.—The process of making them is
worth knowing—the corn is first soaked in ley [lime]
till the husk is off, 'tis then mashed into a paste with a
large flat stone and a small roller made for the purpose; this mixture is passed into the hands of a second
woman (by whom they are always made) from the
hands of the first, and is made into round cakes like
our batter-cakes, and thrown on to a griddle of thin
iron or stone; in a few minutes they are done through
and *the third person,* in a napkin takes them on to the
table, where with a good dish of Frijoles[66] or any thing
of the kind, one does not eat a bad dinner.

Sunday 18th. This day has been passed at the same
camping place of yesterday, resting the animals for a

[66] "Pronounced *freeholeys* by the Mexicans. From the simi-
larity in the pronounciation, the Americans always called them
freeholders. A species of dark beans of large size, stewed or fried
in mutton fat and not too highly seasoned, wind up the substantial part of a dinner, breakfast, or supper, and seldom is
this favorite and national dish omitted. In fact frijoles, especially
to the lower order of Mexicans, are what potatoes are to the Irish
—they can live very well so long as they have them in abundance,
and are lost without them. A failure of the bean crop in Mexico
would be looked upon as a national calamity." (Kendall, *Narrative
of Texan Santa Fé Expedition,* vol. 1, p. 31.)

long pull we are to have in a few days without water—
a hard drive.—Had a visit from some of the elite here,
this morning. They are real old *comadres,* with few
teeth and gray hairs, one of the young ones brought
her baby—they asked if I had one and when I said *no,*
they asked *how long I had been married,* and on my
telling her a year, they opened their eyes with a *"mui
muchachita"* [very young girl]. They are very young
to be asking me such questions.

Though very inquisitive and prying, I can perceive
some thing more of refinement in them than those of
the settlements nearer to Santa Fé. Take them all together they are certainly the most inquiring, prying,
searching people I ever saw.

Tuesday 20th. More of the *natives* to see me this
morning. Three of them came—with a little one of
course—just as I was starting out on a *walk in the
cotton-wood orchard,* and turned me back. They
talked about all things—took hold of, and examined
the dress I am making—thought it some thing entirely
new.

Wednesday 21st. We have come to a new camping
ground six miles farther on. It is near to an other little
town and the people are coming and squatting all
around the tent door to see the little concerns within.
There is one man of middle age, the curiosity of the
crowd; he is waiting to escort the remainder of the
troops coming with Capt. Cook,[67] to Calafornia—He

[67] Philip St. George Cooke was born at Leesburg, Virginia,
June 13, 1809. Graduated from West Point in 1827. His first
active service was in the Black Hawk War, being in the battle of
Bad Axe August 1, 1832. The next year he was commissioned

is a considerable oddity and apparently a great friend
of the Americans—talked much of Gen. Kearny and
some of his officers—*mi querido* [my darling] told
him to get a *superior mule,* and all things attendant,
that Armijo was coming to take possession again, that
he would the first thing call out *los amigos de los
Americanos* [the friends of the Americans]—*his*
name would come in no. one on the paper, and if his
steed was not the quickest, his eyes the sharpest, the
next thing would be *"mata la" fuera con el* [kill him—
away with him]. He winked slightly and cutting up
his mule called out "never mind me"—a grand scamp
—he is prepared with all things and Armijo is a sharp
man ever to catch him.

Thursday 22nd. Mirabile dictu [wonderful to re-
late], how these people annoy me. This whole afternoon I have been sitting here, an object of curiosity

lieutenant of the Dragoons, and saw much service on the plains.
During the Mexican War he was with Kearny in New Mexico
and California; was detailed by Kearny to carry a letter to
Governor Armijo, and to serve as escort for James Magoffin.
Returning from California he entered the city of Mexico, in
1848, with General Scott's army. During the fifties he served on
the Kansas frontier. At the outbreak of the war between the
states he decided for the Union, and commanded the cavalry in
the Peninsula Campaign. At the close of the war he commanded
the departments of the Platte and the Great Lakes. He retired
in 1873, having served continuously for forty-six years. He was
brevetted lieutenant-colonel February 20, 1847, for meritorious
conduct in California; and major-general March 13, 1865, for
gallant and meritorious service during the war between the states.
A daughter of General Cooke became the wife of J. E. B. Stuart,
afterwards famous as a cavalry leader and general in the Confederate Army.

to them—*querida mio* [my darling] was reading to me when they commenced *flocking* about the tent and we thought for him to continue they would soon leave, but it only attracted them more, and in a few minutes they were peeping under the sides of the tent, which had been raised to let in the air—as thick as some flocks of sheep and goats I see here.

They whispered among themselves, picked at my dress—a great curiosity—fingered the bed clothes, the stools, and in short every thing *"en la casa bonita"* [in the pretty house] as they call this. Here they staid and apparently with the intention of remaining till the dark curtain of night should hide me from their view, till *mi alma* got up and ordered the tent to be staked down, and they went off to think and talk for the next *muchos anos* [many years].

Friday 23rd. Moved camp today three miles—the road is entirely of sand and exceedingly hard pulling and as we are in but a very little hurry only, we are moving very slowly. Mr. Harmony has crossed the river with his wagons and we are alone now, at least for a few days at least.

I've made the good graces of another old comadre this morning—an old half Indian, half Mexican—she came in soon after we stretched the tent, and sat a good long half hour or more. We talked of all family concerns from the children down to the dogs. She asked if I had mother, father &c. and said I had run off from them *"just for a husband,"* but I laughed and said *"peres es mejor nos"* [Well, is it not better], and with a hearty laugh she assented both to this and my other little question *"el marido es todo del mundo a los*

mujeres" [the husband is the whole world to women].
She thinks though I am *young,* I am old enough.

An express comes to us this evening from all the
traders camped below us some thirty miles, with intelligence that a large force is coming up from Chihuahua to take us—that they themselves are about
corraling together and sinking their wagon wheels to
the hubs for a breast-work in case of an attack—that
they have taken the men, whom they suspicion as spies,
prisoners—rather a bold step for peaceable traders
to take.

And the Express went on to Santa Fé, with a letter
to Col. Donathan [Doniphan], the officer in command
there, to send down his troops, who are set apart for
Chihuahua to protect them. They say all communication has been stoped at "the pass" by the Mexican
troops there, no one is allowed to go in or to come out,
and the traders on this side are determined to play the
same game, and let no one pass their encampment,
whom they in the least suspicion as carrying intelligence to the Mexican army.

Saturday 24th. I've had a real tramp this morning
through the mud, sliping down the River bank, jumping the *saquia* [*acequia*—ditch or canal], which last,
by the way, is quite a feat—and in fine doing all sorts
of wonders of the kind. It has been my desire through
curiosity only to get onto a sand-bar in the River, so
soon after breakfast, notwithstanding the wet grounds
from last night's heavy rain, I put on my rubbers and
sallied forth. The first adventure was a long slide
down the slippy bank of the saquia—completely
mired. I found some difficulty in again recovering my

balance—this completed however, although tired enough to have come home, I clambered up the opposite bank—steeper than the other but not so slippy, after two or three other ups and downs I found myself standing on a sand-bar and the wide Rio Grande curling its dark waters around me. There is something wildly sublime in the wild deep murmur of a mighty river, as it rolls by us with stately pride, its course pending to the fearful Ocean.

An other Express comes from the camp of Mr. Harmony still behind us, to know what to do; he is frightened at the News of yesterday. We hear he is about to cash his goods and returning to Santa Fé, and we, what shall we do, if the Mexican troops should come upon us, we must make a corral of *our own, sink our wheels &c.*

Sunday 25th. Moved our tent today to an other spot —and are lying by till some news is received to justify our travelling on. The day has been passed in reading my "Bible," "the writings of Josephus," and "Morris's Sermons."[68] The author of the latter work, is a bishop in the Methodist church—a resident of Cincinnati. They are plain of speech, though beautiful— his motives all seem of the purest and most faithful. And if the hearers and readers of these Sermons would but hear and see profitably the good way in which they should walk, pointed out to them by this good man, how many would be the souls saved, and crowns prepared for him in Heaven!

An other old comadre has been to see me this eve-

[68] *Sermons On Various Occasions,* the author being Thomas Asbury Morris, a bishop in the Methodist Episcopal Church.

ning—like the rest of her kind she is curious, and loves to talk—the old lady gave my neck a stinging pinch to see if it was truly as fat as it looks to be, and it surprised her to find it so solid.

Tuesday 27th. How impatiently we are waiting the return of the Express from Santa Fé to see and hear the news.

This has been a dark, gloomy, rainy day—quite enough to give one the hippo, even the sage and philosophical face of *mi alma* is elongated at least an inch—and what must my case be! phaw, what nonsense!

Wednesday 28th. A little Mexican boy of nine or ten years came this morning to *mi alma* to *buy him.* His story though affecting is soon told.—Three years since the Apache Indians beside depredations to other families, murdered his father (his mother was then dead) and carried him off prisoner. After three years of hard servitude among them, the little fellow ran off and found his way to the house of an old Mexican, who resides here on the bank of the River in a lone hut the picture of misery. Here this boy has been for two months under the fostering care of the old *compadre* [godfather], but growing weary of this life, which was not better than that with the Indians, he now wishes to be bought with *the sum of $7.00* which he owes the old man for his protection. Tomorrow the money is to be paid & hence forth Francisco is our servant.

Noviembre, 1846. En San Gabriel.

Tuesday 17th. You have been sadly neglected, my poor journal, this last three weeks. I have been sick with fever and you have layed quietly and patiently on the shelf till now. I was sick in the tent several days taking medicine all the time, and on getting a little better *mi alma* rented a house here in the village and moved me to it. A physician was sent for to the camp of the traders below us, and Dctr. Simpson[69] of the dragoons, came to my relief. He prescribed blue pills, oil and other nauseating doses, and though they relieved me some, the chief cure was "Dctr. Sappington's Pills," which I must ever eulogize as a medicine of fine qualities. One box of them administered by *mi alma* cured me, or at least broke the fever. After great prostration of body I am again creeping about.

In the mean time what has happened at home and abroad. One thing I have had a letter from *home,* yes, all the way from Lex.[ington, Kentucky]! It bears date as late as the 10th of Sept., and brings good news respecting every thing; it almost makes me long to be there, they seem so happy—But I won't be impatient, if we live, the time is coming around for us to be together again.

No news is yet received of Gen. Wool's arrival at Chihuahua, and the traders are likely to be detained here all the winter from all appearances. No express has been sent—no one is allowed to go into the Pass or to come out, and we are in rather a dumb predicament. If we remain here during the winter, I must learn a good many of the New Mexican ways of living, manufacturing *serapes, rabozos,* to make *tortillas,*

[69] Dr. Richard French Simpson, born in Virginia; entered the army from that state as assistant surgeon, August 1, 1840, and was commissioned major surgeon June 23, 1860. Dr. Simpson died July 4, 1861.

chily peppers, and cholote [chocolate], which by the way I do know a little something about—I made myself a passable cup this afternoon.

Wednesday 18th. This is the first day I have dined at table for *two whole weeks.* I found my way out as dinner came in, and sat down to table. Our dinner of chily with *carne de carnero* [mutton], stewed chicken with *cibollas* [cebollas—onions], and a dessert made of bread and grapes, a kind of pudding I suppose, was furnished by our landlord and lady. This is a great feast day with the good people of the village, and they have been preparing their danties for a week. This morning Don José, the owner of our house, came and told us to cook no dinner, and as we obeyed his command, at noon he brought us the repast just named.

Tonight the Priestly portion of the community followed by a crowd, has paraded the patron St. of San Gabriel, with the cross bourn before it, around the plazo, which was illuminated by many small heaps of burning wood and torches bourn by the procession. As I could not go out, I saw from our door the whole proceeding; the music I believe consisted of a kind of *drum,* violins and I suppose the ever constant accompaniament of the triangle, though I could not distinguish it at that distance. The procession is broken up now, and all have gone off to the *bayle* [*baile*—ball], *monte* &c.

It is rather odd to see the women coming from other towns in ox-carts, alias, *Rio Baja* steamboats. The whole family, wife, children, servants, dogs and all get, or rather pile themselves, up in the vehicle of all work and the *dueno de todos* [their lord and master], with his long pole gets his horned animals under way, and off they start squeaking, squealing, barking an other noises accompaning such crowds. Once into town they begin to jump out, or pulled out, turned and tumbled out, and a happier set never got together.

But my new house as yet goes undescribed. Here is the long sala or hall common to all the houses,—it has a nice little fire place in one corner, a door opens, at the same end into a room, which we have not the use of. I dare say though it is nicely whitened and kept in fine order—perhaps 'tis used as a sitting room by the family when they are [all together], now 'tis occupied by the sundries of the house-hold, and kept locked. At the opposite end of the sala are two doors, —one opens into a fine nice little kitchen—this is as white and nice about the walls as any part of the establishment—it has in it what I have seen for the first time in my life, viz. the stones used in grinding corn for tortillas, called *mola* stones. They are wedge-shaped, some eighteen inches in length by six or eight in breadth—the next thing is to see some of the natives at work with them.

The next place is my bed-room—a cozy little place it is, walls covered with pink rosetts, pictures, two or three paintings of Saints, and two waxen figures each about twelve inches in height. One is some saint; the other represents our Savior's mother, with a crown on her head, and standing with her hands raised as if in the act of blessing some poor mortal. There is one window and this is filled in with izing-glass, which I suppose they find out in the hills as we do in the states.

Take the whole together we have quite comfortable winter quarters if we are compelled to remain in New Mexico during the whole winter.

Wednesday 25th. A memorable day this, the anniversary of our wedding—and though perhaps already forgotten by many present at the ceremony that made the "twain one," still 'twill ever be fresh in the minds of those most concerned. Yes, we have been married a whole year today! and what a short one it has been. Mrs. Green would say 'tis the novelities of matrimony that has made it so. Whether that or those of travelling—for we have not been stationary any time since that event—I know not but this I do know that I cannot remember one as short. And it has been a happy one too. I shall be contented if all we pass together are like it. Have written to Aunt Susan today,[70] first time since we left.

Thursday 26th. The wife and daughter of Don José, the owner of this house, came today with their mola stone and corn to show me how to make tortillas. What a deal of trouble it is too. I had not thought half the work. The corn had been previously soaked in lay till the husk was off, and it made some what soft. She placed a handfull or two on the stone, which is some what hollow in the center, about eighteen inches in length, and a foot wide. With an other oblong stone of some eight or ten pounds weight, she continued (on

[70] Susanna Shelby, daughter of Governor Isaac Shelby, born in 1791, died 1868. She married four times: first, James McDowell; second, James Shannon, minister to Mexico and *chargé d'affairs* to Central America; third, Col. John McKinney; and, fourth, Rev. James Fishback.

her knees all the time, a position most fatiguing to the back and indeed the whole frame) to rub the corn up and down on the other till it was ground to a paste. This was slipped off onto a broad, and thin piece of iron lying at the other end of the stone, more corn was put on and ground till the whole stew panful disappeared. The [entire] mass was now put on and ground still finer, being occasionally wetted with a little water. A third time it was put on, and as she ground she divided it into little pieces the size of a biscuit, each of which were taken from the plate, now supplying the place of the sheet of iron, which was now placed over the fire as a griddle, by an other senorita and patted out into the tortillas. She greased the griddle a little, and layed one on it, she turned this over several times while she patted out an other which took the place of the cooked one, now layed on a plate. In this way the whole mass was disposed of. When they were finished the good lady presented me with a plate full of fine tortillas. I have now seen the whole operation from beginning to end. The old lady also brought over her knitting, which like the tortillas is done in a way tedious enough, notwithstanding, for curiosity to those at home, I learned how she did it. On showing her the much easier mode of the U. S. she seemed much surprised and delighted.

Saturday 28th. Mi alma has opened a bale of calicos, and the women of the village like children in a toy shop are nearly run crazy. They are coming in by the dozen for several days, and it seems they cannot see or buy enough. The whole bale of some forty-five pieces, will not last many days longer, I imagine. The flashy

colours take best, and how the husbands are obliged
to bring in their money, bags of corn, flour &c &c.

December, 1846.

Tuesday 1st. News comes in very ugly today. An
Englishman from Chihuahua, direct, says that the
three traders, Dr. Conley, Mr. McMannus and
brother James, who went on ahead to C. have been
taken prisoners, the two former lodged in the calaboza
[calabozo—jail] while Brother James is on a *trial for
his life,* on account of his interview with Armijo at
Santa Fé, which they say was one cause of the latter's
having acted as he did in regard to the American
Army—and also on account of a letter from President
Polk introducing him to Gen. Wool and saying he
had resided in the country some time and might perhaps be of service to him in his operations. This makes
him appear in their eyes something as a spy, though
his intentions were of an entire different nature, and
his motives, his feelings to all parties of the purest
kind. 'Tis a hard case and distressing to us; how, or
when, or where 'twill end is unknown to us. Let us
hope and pray, therefore, that our Almighty Father,
The Just Judge will be with him, and deliver him from
the hands of his enemies.

We also learn that Gen. Taylor has taken Monteray, after a very severe battle, in which he lost one-
sixth of his little army of six thousand men; that there
is now a cessation of arms for eight weeks, which time
has now expired, as it commenced the first of Oct.

Wednesday 2nd. No news today more than a confirmation of that we heard yesterday, we are lying

here in a state of silent anxiety, what a day may bring forth we know not, tomorrow may turn us back to Santa Fé.

Thursday 3rd. A man from the Pass comes with news that a large army is coming from Chihuahua to carry us off prisoners and to *retake* New Mexico—that Gen. Wool has been ordered to join Gen. Taylor, and that on Sabbath last they were to have had a battle with Santa Anna himself, the last one having been fought by Gen. Ampudia[71]—Santa Anna has been long preparing for this, and will doubtless render Gen. Taylor's strongest efforts necessary to save himself from defeat. He also bring news that Gen. Wool has been ordered to join Taylor, and that the Chihuahuans are in consequence coming on to us with a large force.

If this be true, and news should come that Taylor's army had been defeated, we will certainly have to retrace our steps to Santa Fé and enter Fort Marcy for safety, for 'twill inspire this fickle people with such confidence as to his superior and almost immortal skill

[71] General Pedro Ampudia was a Cuban by birth. He joined the Mexican Army in 1842, and served at the head of a regiment during the Texan-Mexico War. He fought several battles against the army of Texas, capturing Generals Fisher, Green, and Murray. During the war with the United States General Ampudia was in command of the army of the north, and capitulated at Monterey to the Americans. Because of this surrender he was court-martialed by Santa Anna, but was acquitted and reinstated as general. He fought against the Americans at Angostura, and against the French Army during the War of Intervention. He died August 7, 1868. (From information supplied by Benjamin M. Read of Santa Fé, New Mexico.)

that en mass they will rise on our heads and murder us without regard. This is rather a dark picture to be painting.

Sunday 6th. An other Sabbath day has been permitted to pass over our heads, and has it departed without doing some good, without making one solemn impression on my mind as to its holiness. Have I "remembered the Sabbath day to keep it holy." I fear justice will raise her hand against me. I have read my Bible 'tis true, (and religious books), but not, I fear, with that fervent longing for and praying for light to see my way clearly, to be guided in the strait and narrow way that leads to life eternal.

I have not clung to it and poured over it with that thirsting desire to believe in and to see the face of the Lamb that sittith in Judgment, that is by him required of one who would see his face. I have not prayed with sufficient fervour to have my weak faith strengthened, my preseverance to find religion increased—to have this "stony heart taken away and to receive a heart of flesh." I have joined in merry and useless conversation. I have spent time foolishly that should have been spent in doing good. I have "left undone those things which I should have done, and have done those things which I ought not to have done." When *conscience* tells me that this is true, a just condemnation, what must be the wrathful sentence of my Judge above? Let me flee and hide myself from the thought and "seek relief in prayer."

Tuesday 8th.

Thursday 11th. We learn today that Col. Dona-

171

phan, the officer left in command by Gen. Kearny, has returned from the Navijoe [Navaho] country,[72] where he has for some time been engaged in making a treaty, and is now preparing to march on to Chihuahua, to meet Gen. Wool, who we learn by an other post from the U. S. is on his march there, instead of being with Gen. Taylor as we heard.

The traders, except ourselves, are on fire for him to start, as they can then follow. *Mi alma,* who perhaps has more knowledge of the people and country than any of them, thinks 'twill be a rash step for him to leave here before he has heard positively by an express from Wool himself, that he is near to Chihuahua. He may be misinformed as this news comes not from Government, and if he should march on and even take the city he cannot hold it with *fifteen hundred men.* Why the whole *State,* which is neither small or thinly populated, would rise against him in a day, and not only his whole force cut off, but the traders along with *him.* Will he walk into the calabozo, rather a different place from the *mint* into which they are going—*"cuindado"* ["caution"], I think should rather be their motto. We

[72] The treaty was signed November 22, 1846. In the negotiations a young chief named Sarcillo Largo represented the Indians, and Doniphan, through an interpreter, the United States. The latter explained to them that by reason of the conquest of New Mexico by the United States, the Indians, as well as other inhabitants, became subjects of that government; that the government would not permit the warfare which was constantly going on to be continued, and unless they would agree upon terms, he was instructed to make war upon them. These Indians observed the treaty for a short while, but, on the whole, it proved of little value.

shall remain here, if he goes alone, and if the thing ends well, then we can follow immediately, if not we are near enough to retreat to *Fort Marcy*.

William is very sick with fever, a dctr. sent for from the soldiers' camp below.

Tuesday 15th. I am merchant today. *Mi alma* has gone over the River to see some of the troops now passing down to join Col. Donaphan, and also to find a physician to see William, who continues, notwithstanding much physicing, very sick. . . . Some women came in to purchase dresses, but we could not agree as to the price. One of them in particular was a hard customer, but I think she found her equal. I did not yield one *pedazo* [bit] in the price, although she insisted that *mi alma* sold for less,—which was a mistake by the way,—and I told her it was wrong *if* he let calico go *for two bits,* when the price was *dos e media* [two and a half], and that because he did it I could not. So she concluded to wait till he comes. It is my simple opinion she will find the same hard case to deal with then; 'twill be as hard to persuade him into her measures as 'twas to *frighten* me.

The home folks would think me a great favorite, if they could see how the good people of the village are sending me tortillas, *casas* [*quesos*—cheeses], *dulces* [sweets], and the like.

I learned last night their mode of giving a sweat. The patient is made to sit with his feet in warm water, in which has been boiled some *wheat-brand,* with blankets thrown over him till a profuse perspiration is produced, assisted by drinking some warm tea or hot lemonade. After persevering in this some fifteen minutes, he is covered up in bed, some *dirt* is now put into a plate, a little fire on this; a few pounded annice seed and black pepers are then thrown onto it, and it is set under the bed cloths till the invalid, bed and all become perfectly *hot* from it. It is both a simple and good method.

P. M. Wrote a long letter to Aunt Susan, to send off tomorrow, the letter of the 26th Nov. was not sent.

Dctr. Hope from Col. Mitchell's[73] company of volunteers has arrived, and finds it necessary to give more medicine to his patient,—to remain with him tonight.

Wednesday 16th. 'Tis a pity we cannot govern our tempers at all times. Nothing hurts me more than to have a cross, ill-tempered servant about me. Jane is in a pet this morning has a little more work to do than usual. William's sickness, the dctr's being here, and one of the soldiers who came as an escort to him, of course makes a little more cooking and brisk movements. On giving some necessary directions about

[73] David Dawson Mitchell was born in Louisa County, Virginia, July 31, 1806. He came to St. Louis when quite a young man and had a long and honorable career in the fur trade, first as a clerk and then as a partner in the upper Missouri outfit of the American Fur Company. He was the builder of Fort McKenzie in 1832. Colonel Mitchell became United States superintendent of Indian affairs, Central Division, with headquarters at St. Louis, September 20, 1841, and held the position at intervals until 1852. He entered the volunteer service during the war with Mexico and was elected lieutenant-colonel of the 2d Missouri Regiment of Volunteers. Colonel Mitchell was conspicuous in the battle of Sacramento. He married Martha Eliza Berry, daughter of Major James Berry of Kentucky, in 1840, and died in St. Louis, May 31, 1861.

breakfast, without real cause or provocation her in-
solent answers which I cannot repeat, arose to such an
extent that for peace sake I was obliged to leave my
work half done and retire from the kitchen. And how
shall I tell *mi alma* of this, if he could have heard it,
he would be very angry I know.—It is a trifling matter, and I shall not trouble him. I can manage my
own domestic concerns without worrying his already
perplexed mind, with my little difficulties. The only
way to treat a turbulent domestic, is to look above
them too much to answer them back, or even to hear
their impudence, till it becomes correctable by the rod.
In this case I generally have to wait till the effects of
an extra dram wears off.

Col. Owens and Mr. Glasgow called this P. M. on
their way from Santa Fé. The[y] are crazy to get on
notwithstanding the danger they may be rushing into.
We learn that Maj. Gilpin[74] with some two or three
hundred volunteers, has gone into the jornada as
scouts, and will perhaps go on to El Passo, what a
blind step, when they may meet a large force!

[74] William Gilpin was born in Delaware County, Pennsylvania,
October 4, 1812. He was educated at the University of Pennsylvania and United States Military Academy. He served in the
Seminole War, but afterwards resigned from the army. He settled
in St. Louis, having charge of the *Missouri Argus,* and espoused
the cause of Thomas H. Benton. A few years later he moved to
Independence, Missouri, and entered the practice of law.

The troops supplied by the state of Missouri for the Mexican
War were received by General Kearny at Fort Leavenworth.
Gilpin wanted to be an officer in that contingent, but was not a
favorite with General Kearny. However, through gaining entrance as a private to one of the companies, he placed himself in

Thursday 17th. William is some what better today, the Dctr. after spending a day and two nights with him, has left, pronouncing him in a fine way to recover.

We send a boy with the Doctor to bring us what news they may have at the lower camp, the movements of the army &c. &c.—I thought *mi alma* should not know of my difficulty in the kitchen yesterday morning, but it would come out. I found her this morning dipping into a keg of brandy siting in my room, and knowing it to be the cause of her insult, I determined to tell him, which determination was backed by the fact that *I had never concealed anything from him,* and how could I keep this back?

Friday 18th. The boy has returned from Col. Mitchell's camp with a letter saying the troops will all leave tomorrow for the pass, and the traders will follow. 'Tis a momentous time for us; we are alone, for they have heedlessly [gone] into the very jaws of the enemy. That jornada—(a travel of two or three days for those heavy wagons without a drop of water) may be called the enemy's breastwork, the traders are going *within* it, to be cut to pieces perhaps and we are

position to be chosen by the Volunteers as one of the officers. In this manner he succeeded in being elected major of the 1st Regiment Missouri Volunteers.

It is said that he was the only man in Jackson County, Missouri, to vote for Abraham Lincoln in 1860. He was appointed by Lincoln governor of Colorado, 1861-1863. On February 12, 1874, he married Julia Dickerson, a widow, and the daughter of Bernard Pratte of St. Louis. Gilpin died in Denver, Colorado, January 19, 1894. (Bancroft, *History of the Life of William Gilpin,* San Francisco, 1889.)

here ready for them, when they have devoured that portion of their prey, to destroy as they please.

I wonder what tomorrow will bring forth? We'll see. *Mi alma* dispatches an other courier tomorrow early to remain with them till something more is to be heard.

It is a strange people this. They are not to be called cowards; take them in a mass they are brave, and if they have the right kind of a leader they will stem any tide. Take them one by one and they will not flinch from danger. This man who goes for *mi alma* tomorrow is a sample. For a very small compensation, (which by the way has no weight with him, as he at first offered himself to go not for money, but with the desire to serve only; the reward I may say is gratis) he will go over a road, (perhaps on foot,) infested with Indians, by whom he is liable to be murdered at any moment,—he will perhaps have no water for some days,—at the pass, if he goes so far, he may be taken by his own countrymen, and if found in the employ of an American he will be shot. I am sure the brand of a coward will never stick to him.

Saturday Morning early 19th. What is the news this morning! A man strait from the Pass—he can be relied on too, as he lives here, is well known as a man of integrity and comes to give the news and to take care of his family in case of an attack—says that there are actually seven hundred regular dragoons now in the Pass, all determined resolute men, and *three thousand* more are leaving Chihuahua to come and take us. There is our little army of only *nine hundred* and perhaps three hundred of these (Maj. Gilpin's command) are already prisoners and on their march to

Chihuahua,—if this fource comes against them, and there is scarcely a doubt of it, what will be the consequences—'tis painful to think of it—they must all be cut to pieces, every thing seized, they march on to *us* here. I shall be torn from the dearest object to me on earth, perhaps both of us murdered, or at best he will be put into one prison, while I am sent to an other without even my bible, or my poor journal to comfort me. But though they may deprive me of *these things,* there are others that they cannot move. I have a *soul,* I have a Savior, the means of prayer are always within my reach. It has comforted me more than once—and

> Who that knows the worth of prayer,
> But wishes to be often there.

If I could but see *mi alma* easy; he is troubled, does nothing but walk the floor waiting for the next intelligence. I shall be patient and under any circumstances, I hope be resigned and collected. Christ himself warns us that we must not fear those who can kill and in any wise injure the body, and can do nothing to the *immortal* soul. But he says "rather fear Ye him who after he hath killed hath power to cast into hell."

Sunday 20th. The news today is not quite so discouraging. An other man later from the Pass says there are no regular troops there; and only some three or four hundred men—that Maj. Gilpin had not, when he left there (four days since) arrived; but he has sent back by express to Col. Donaphan, that there is *"plenty of water beyond the jornada."* This is not as discouraging as we expected yesterday to have heard. This man (a Mexican) [Senor Gonzales] is one that

escorted brother James down. He was also sent to
jail from whence he broke out, and came to the Pass,
where he was retaken and again put in confinement.
A second escape though has brought him into the
American portion of the Republic, where he deems
himself *safe*. He has been very persevering in his
efforts; if Brother James, who he says he left in prison,
could be as fortunate 'twould be a very fortunate
thing.

Monday 21st. We have heard nothing new today,
but are constantly expecting something that will
either continue us on our journey or turn us back.

Tuesday 22nd. The movements of the army as we
hear it is all I can find to write about these days. Some
Americans from the copper mines, and lately from
Chihuahua, bring the news today, that we have been
so long wishing to hear—viz: where Gen. Wool is
passing his time—he has joined Gen. Taylor, and together they have with 24,000 men marched on from
Montere [Monterey] to San Luis Potosi, there to
meet Gen. Santa Anna, and I suppose to determine
by one great battle the fate of the traders *here,* as well
as many other things resting the Republic. Our pre-
sumption is, if the American arms are successful, the
war is at an end, without farther say, if not the whole
Republic will be so elated and so confident of their
superior valour, they will be unwilling to close it till
they have been entirely beaten by the still increasing
fource of the American Army, as Congress has ordered out *60, 000* in case the present army is unable to
end the War.

Wednesday 23d. Today brings it that the troops

have passed through *el janad* [*El Jornado*—the day's journey], and are encamped just on the other side; they have sent back in haste for the artilery which is some half way on their way from Santa Fé, preparing for an engagement,—they talk of building a Fort there; and also of passing the winter instead of going on to Chihuahua.

Tuesday 29th. This is truly exciting times! I doubt if my honoured Grandmother ever saw or heard of more to excite, in the War she was in [War of 1812], than I have here. The Indians are all around us; coming into the soldiers' camp and driving off their stock, and killing the men in attendance on them.

The enemy are advancing on us as we hear today and have even had a battle with our troops only about eighty miles from us. Lieut. Lee[75] from the army passed us post-haste this morning, for the artillery, as they must have it before el Passo can be taken. . . . He says the battle was fought on Christmas-day 'twas not a severe one, only lasting about 20 or 30 minutes, and is calculated to inspire our troops with more confidence than we had expected. Just as they had gotten into camp & staked out their horses, not expecting the enemy to be any ways near, for scouts had been out in all directions, a dust was seen rising and in a few moments a fource of some five or seven hundred dragoons, and nearly as many volunteers and pressed soldiers stood before them. Of course all was in confusion; order was soon restored though, and as will long be remembered of him, Col. Donaphan's first

[75] This was Lieutenant James Lea of Doniphan's Regiment. He served as assistant quartermaster and commissary officer.

order in battle to his men was "prepare to squat," rather a ludicrous command—but a wise one as the sequel will show, as they squated the enemy fired, and of course all the bullets *passed over their heads,* killing none and wounding only five and they not seriously. It was now our turn for a round—the *first* that, perhaps, every one in our little army of six or seven hundred ever fired. Thirty of the Mexicans were shot dead, five were taken prisoners of war, the wounded we have not heard of and the remaining portion *fled,* leaving one field piece. I believe the only one they had, a good deal of ammunition, and some muskets, which of course our Col. has taken as trophies of victory,— on the whole 'twas quite a nice little skirmish.[76]

[76] The Battle of *Brazito* (Little Arm) was named after a bend in the river near the site of the conflict. This was the first battle of the army of the west, the Mexicans moving upon Doniphan while his men were engaged in pitching camp. He himself was playing cards with his staff to determine which one of the members of the advance guard should have a fine horse, which had just been captured. The horse had been abandoned in flight by some one of a party of Mexican scouts which had been surprised. Doniphan and the members of his staff were each playing for an individual in the guard. Suddenly a forked cloud of dust arose in the distance, arousing suspicion, and Doniphan ordered his men to form in line on foot. A large battle line of the enemy soon came into view, about one-half mile away. Presently a single horseman, an officer bearing a black flag with skull and crossbones on it, approached. He was met by the interpreter, Caldwell, to whom he expressed the desire of his commander for an interview with the American commander. Caldwell told him they could meet halfway between the lines. The man demanded that Doniphan come into the Mexican camp, which was refused. The Mexican then remarked that they would come and get him, and pointed to

Wednesday 30th. The express *mi alma* sent to bring news from the Pass has returned today at 3 o'clock P. M. having been absent a little more than two weeks. The intelligence is altogether in our favour. Col. D. entered and took el Passo on the 28th, the Mexican army having evacuated it the day previous. A company, of three hundred men, has been sent in pursuit of them for the purpose of taking their canon, five or six pieces. Although the number of our troops is not one-third of the enemy 'tis believed they will succeed in their undertaking. Elated with their late success, they will manifest greater courage still, whereas the other party are *flying,* and discouraged, and are expecting to be cut to pieces if overtaken. We learn that their number lost on the 25th was thirty-eight instead of 30.

Enero [January] *de 1847.*

Thursday 14th. Is it possible that two whole weeks enstranged us, my Journal? What have I been about that I have neglected you so long. Well I hope I have

his black flag which portrayed their motto: "No quarter asked or given." Caldwell said: "Come on! they are ready for you."

The battle soon began, with the American footmen kneeling and firing alternately, number two firing only when number one stopped to reload. Only seven Americans were wounded, none mortally. The Mexicans were routed and lost sixty-three killed, one hundred seventy-two wounded, including their commander, Captain Ponce de Leon, and three hundred missing.

After the battle Doniphan and his staff went back to the card game, but after they found out which member of the guard was to have the horse, they also discovered that during the battle the horse had been allowed to escape. (M. B. Edwards, "Journal of an Expedition to New Mexico," p. 132, MS.)

not been so badly occupied that I am ashamed to render an account of myself. The sick have called my time.

William has never recovered yet, and how he lingers along, with very little pain too, only weakness, with very excitable pulse, and no appetite. For three or four days *mi alma* was confined to his bed, with severe head-ache, cold, and irritation of the bladder. This was about the first of this month. Next, I had an ugly cold myself which required two or three nights' sweating, and onion poltice before I found relief. For several days past poor little Francisco has been very ill with flux, and I don't know but that it may kill him yet, though I hope and trust that the medicines given him may be blest to his recovery. I shall endeavour to do my duty, as the only benefactors of the orphan, leaving all things in the hands of the Great Giver of all things, knowing that he will never neglect. . . . People have been sending in every day for "remedias," both in the village and from a distance; sickness is great in the country now, and *mi alma* has his name up among the people of the Rio Bajo as a skillful medico, some of the medicines he has administered to the suffering having been of material service. One Snr. Pino[77] sent some few days since, a horse for him to go

[77] Don Manuel Pino belonged to one of the most influential families in New Mexico. When the news reached Santa Fé of the invasion of New Mexico by the American Army, the Pino brothers, Manuel and Nicolas, immediately responded to the call issued by Governor Armijo for volunteers, with all the means at their disposal. They at once began raising companies and procuring arms and ammunition. They were with General Armijo

some twenty miles to see his wife, sick of a fever; as this was impossible tho' he gave the servant some medicines for her, and today Snr. Pino, himself, has come down to return his grateful thanks for the good it has done, and, as no charges are made, he presented some fresh meat pork and carnaro [*carnero*—mutton]. It shows a feeling of pure gratitude which I constantly see manifested among these people for any little kindness done them. . . . Yesterday Lieut. Lee who went up for the artillery, arrived; he went back as far as Santa Fé, and there found Col. Price engaged in quelling a revolution that would have been, some of the unruly Mexicans having endeavoured to make a breakout, the heads who were put in prison are Archulette,[78] one [Tomas] Ortis, Salasar,[79] the great enemy to the Texan prisoners, that were.

at Apache Pass, and protested against the abandonment of the Mexican position at that place. When Santa Fé was taken by Kearny the Pinos refused to take the oath of allegiance. Nicolas Pino was implicated in the Mexican conspiracy to drive out the American officials from New Mexico, and was arrested by General Price on December 21, 1846. After the failure of the conspiracy at Santa Fé, neither Manuel nor his brother Nicolas Pino took any part in the later revolutionary movements, Don Nicolas Pino having taken the oath of allegiance to the United States upon his release from prison in Santa Fé. These brothers were ever after very loyal citizens of the United States.

[78] Diego Archuleta was of higher quality than most of the Mexican officials of his time. His father, Jean Andres Archuleta, was a wealthy resident of Rio Arriba, in which county of New Mexico Diego was born, at Plaza Alcalde, on March 27, 1814. The son received part of his education in the public school, and also studied under Father Antonio José Martinez. Later, while still a boy, he went to Durango, where he studied eight years in

The artillery will be on in a few days and immediately on its arrival at el Passo, we are told that Col. D will leave for Chihuahua, anxious I suppose to reap

preparation for the priesthood. After receiving several minor orders he changed his mind about this vocation, and in 1840 returned to his native county.

Not long after the return of Archuleta to New Mexico, he was appointed captain of militia by the Mexican Government, and as such took part in the capture of the Texans involved in the ill-fated Texas-Santa Fé Expedition. This distinction was followed by many others, including a deputyship in the Mexican Congress for two years from 1843. The Golden Cross of Honor was conferred upon him in recognition of distinguished service as an officer in the Mexican Army. At the time of the American advance on New Mexico he was colonel, lieutenant governor, and second in command of the army.

Diego Archuleta has been described by historians as an intense patriot, and he was the leader of a large contingent. Whatever caused him to fall victim to the influence of James Magoffin is difficult to say with any degree of positiveness. Certainly Magoffin understood his man. Armijo had fled and his troops disbanded, at least twenty-four hours before General Kearny reached Apache Pass. Threats of assassination were being made against Armijo by officers under Archuleta, and the latter certainly was determined to use his following for defense of the pass. He was given the impression, which generally prevailed, that General Kearny would leave the western part of the territory untouched, and Magoffin recommended to him that he seize that portion of the country for himself. He was perhaps tempted to make the best of a bad situation, and thought he was trading a temporary victory for a permanent establishment in the western part of New Mexico.

He agreed not to fight and lived up to his agreement. Magoffin, however, was unable to prove his own sincerity. General Kearny, much to Magoffin's surprise, had orders from Washington to take possession of the whole country and move on to California.

if possible the glory of taking it himself before Gen.
Wool's arrival. I shall be glad when we can start
again, though the chances with our sick family, are
rather against us for the present.

Archuleta naturally felt that he had been cheated and after two
unsuccessful revolts organized by him, he fled the country. In
one of these revolts Governor Charles Bent of New Mexico was
cruelly killed.

Archuleta was afterwards invited to return, and did so. He
took the oath of allegiance to the United States and filled a number of offices in and about Santa Fé. These included Indian agent
in 1857, brigadier-general, 1861, and member of the general
assembly of New Mexico for a period of fourteen years.

In 1841 Archuleta was married to Jesusita Trujillo, there
being seven children by this union. He died of heart trouble at
Santa Fé, March 21, 1884, while a member of the legislative
assembly. (Twitchell, *Military Occupation of New Mexico*, p.
238.)

[79] Salazar is treated by Davis, in his *El Gringo,* as follows:
"Toward the close of the month I chanced to meet in Santa Fé
the notorious Captain Salazar, the same who figures in not a
very enviable position in Kendall's 'Santa Fé Expedition.' He is
the man who had charge of the Texan prisoners while marching
through New Mexico, and treated them with such a savage
cruelty, cutting off their ears, and inflicting other unheard-of
barbarities upon them. He is a dark and swarthy-looking individual, and by no means prepossessing in his appearance. Upon
this occasion he had come in to see the governor, in order to claim
damages for his son, who had been killed by the Indians a few
days before, out upon the Plains, while hunting buffalo. He laid
a valuation of five thousand dollars upon his life, because, he said,
it had cost a good deal of money to rear and educate him, and
he now wished the United States to pay for his loss. But, as the
Indian Intercourse Act does not recognize such claims, the
governor declined either to make him any remuneration, or refer
his demand to the government."

Friday 15th. A gentleman from the Pass, Mr. Cauldwell,[80] has passed us today with the intelligence that Gen. Wool is still on his rout to C.[hihuahua] instead of having joined Gen. Taylor as we heard. The news is pretty strait, having come through an intercepted letter from the Gov. of Chi[huahua] (Trius)[81] himself to one of the officers that evacuated the Pass

[80] Thomas Caldwell acted as interpreter for Doniphan's command. He exhibited great coolness and daring during the battle of Brazito, and several times rode close to the enemy's line, in order to hear the orders that were there given. He remained with Colonel Doniphan until January, 1847, when he felt himself aggrieved, left the army and returned to Missouri. He reached St. Louis the following April.

[81] Don Angel Trias, governor of Chihuahua and brigadier-general commanding the Chihuahua volunteers. He owned a large estate in and around the village of Encinillas. "He was for years governor of the State of Chihuahua, a gentleman of large wealth and fine accomplishments. After receiving his education he went to Europe, where he spent eight years traveling in various parts, although he remained most of the time in England and France. He was well versed in several of the European languages, and spoke English with great correctness. With large estates, a cultivated mind, and elegant manners, General Trias naturally exercised a great influence in the State. His estate at the time of the invasion of the Americans contained many thousand head of cattle, which he gave to his government for the support of the army, and for which he has never made a claim. The sacrifices he made for his country greatly impoverished him. There is no doubt that General Trias detested the Americans as a people; yet American gentlemen and officers who stopped at Chihuahua were always treated by him with great politeness and attention. He was ardently devoted to Santa Anna and was considered to be the head of the war party in his State." (Bartlett, *Personal Narrative of Explorations and Incidents,* vol. 2, p. 426.)

on Col. Doniphan's arrival. He writes that "Gen. Wool has taken Paris [Parras] (S. E. from C.[hihuahua]) and is on his march with 2500 men to the North." Whether for Chihuahua or Durango, we know not, but 'tis more than probable 'tis the former place, as his first orders were to go there. If so, by this time he must be near the end of his march, and Chi.[huahua] they say is not in the best situation to defend herself having been unable to get assistance from below. We must hear something decisive soon!

Friday 22nd. Well at last Maj. Clark of the artillery has arrived! How long we have been expecting him; he brings a good excuse though for his delay. The outbreak at Santa Fé, or rather San Miguel and Taos the other side of it has been of more importance than we have ever heard—the conspiracy was headed by one Thos. Ortis who was to be made their Governor, and one Archulette, Lieut. Govnr. At San Miguel they even beat their drums to arms. The night of the 19th of December was set as the executing of their designs, but from some sign of discovery they deferred it till the 25th, at which time Col. Price received positive information of their designs, and ordered Maj. Clark out with his artillery to stop the disturbances. Several were apprehended, and tried. They acknowledged their intentions were to rush onto Santa Fé seize and either shoot or hang on the American flag-staff immediately the Gov. Bent, Col. Price and Maj. Clark three principals. They were then to appoint this Ortis Gov. take possession of the Fort and there to establish themselves, dealing out their laws till a larger fource could come up from the Pass, when they were to give all the Americans their choice to leave the country immediately or they would meet with no mercy. The Gov. has discharged some, others are in confinement, while the two heads Ortis and Archulette have escaped. Maj. C. says they are on the search though, and if they are taken will be made a sample of by being put to death.—Quite a bold step this has been, and but for the fortunate disclosure of it we might have been killed before this.[82]

[82] The insurgents were: Tomas Ortiz, who had been chief alcalde of Santa Fé, Juan Felipe Ortiz, the vicario, Diego Archuleta, Domingo C. de Baca, Miguel E. Pino, Nicolas Pino, Manuel Chaves, Santiago Armijo, Agustin Duran, Pablo Dominguez, José Maria Sanchez, Antonio Marie Trujillo, Santiago Martinez, Pascual Martinez, Vincente Martinez, Antonio Ortiz, Facundo Pino, Rev. Antonio José Martinez, and Fr. Leyva. These men considered themselves to be patriots, and unwilling to see their country lost without a single effective blow. Not one of them had favored the abandonment of Apache Pass by Armijo, and all were related either by blood or marriage. The plan as formed by these men was that on the appointed day those engaged in the conspiracy in Santa Fé were to gather in the parochial church and remain concealed. Meanwhile friends from the surrounding country, under the lead of Archuleta, were to be brought into the city and distributed in various houses where they would be unobserved. At midnight the church bell was to sound and then the men within the church were to come forth and all were to rendezvous immediately in the plaza, seize the cannon there, and aim them so as to command the leading points, while detachments under special orders were to attack the palace and the quarters of General Price, and make them prisoners. The people throughout the whole north had been secretly notified and were only awaiting news of the rising at Santa Fé in order to join in the revolt and make it a success. (Twitchell, *Leading Facts of New Mexican History*, vol. 2, p. 232.)

Thursday 28th. Eight miles below Bosquito [Bosquecito]. Again on the road, and with what foreboadings. For three days I have been trying to find time to write but failed. Dctr. Richardson[83] of the army arrived in haste at our house in Bosquecito, with his wagon of medicines and an escort of five men beside his waggoner. He brought news that started us from the village in haste or as soon as we could be ready, which took us till Wednesday noon.

The news is that the Taos people have risen, and murdered every American citizen in Taos including the Gov.[84] (then on a visit there). That all the troops

[83] Robert F. Richardson, born in Tennessee. He was appointed surgeon of Major Meriwether Lewis Clark's Battalion of Missouri Volunteers, July 7, 1846, and was honorably discharged June 30, 1847.

[84] Charles Bent was appointed governor of New Mexico on September 22, 1846, by General Kearny. The latter having visited some of the Pueblo Indians and assured himself that the country was tranquil, appointed the governor and a full set of territorial officials, and marched off to California. He had hardly gone, however, when evidences of a growing revolt by the Mexicans and part of the Pueblo Indian population began to appear. On December 17, following, Governor Bent arrested seven of the conspirators, and the military and civil officers were sent in pursuit of two of the prime movers in the rebellion. During the state of unrest caused by these conspiracies, of which Diego Archuleta was the prime mover, Governor Bent happened to be visiting his family at San Fernando de Taos. Very early in the morning, on January 19, 1847, a mob of drunken Indians went into the town and demanded the release of two Pueblo Indians held in prison for stealing. Sheriff Stephen L. Lee refused their demands and they murdered him, as well as the prefect of the town, a Mexican named Vigil, the latter having infuriated them by calling them

from Albaquerque (the regulars) have been ordered
to Santa Fé leaving this portion of the territory at the
mercy of the mob. It is a perfect revolution there;

all thieves. They chopped his body up into small bits. A number
of Mexicans then joined the mob and it proceeded to the house
occupied by the governor. Warned of their approach by the
noise, Governor Bent quickly dressed and armed himself.

It soon became evident to the governor that resistance would
be futile. Instead he attempted to reason with them, recalling
the many kindnesses he had done for them during his twenty
years' residence among them. But they were beyond all reason,
and only replied with wild angry yells and attacks upon the
house. They climbed upon the roof and dug a hole in it, while
the governor's wife and children plead with him to use his pistols
in defense of his life. This he refused to do, as he believed such
action would only make the mob determined to kill all the occu-
pants of the house, as well as himself. These were his three children, his wife and her sister, Mrs. Kit Carson, Mrs. Tom Boggs,
and a Mexican woman servant.

In the meantime neighbors, a French Canadian and his Mexican wife, were aiding the women in the besieged dwelling to cut
a hole through the adobe wall. This completed, the women and
children escaped into the adjoining house, but Governor Bent
held back, and was unwilling to follow. He finally yielded, but
not before being wounded, and thereafter was fired on through
the window of a room to which he had retreated. Taking paper
from his pocket and attempting to write, his strength failed him.
He was only able to speak a last word to his weeping wife and
children, and fell dead from the bullet of a Pueblo. Thus the
first American governor of New Mexico died a martyr. The
Indians broke into the house, shot him with their arrows and his
own pistols, took his scalp, stretched it on a board with brass-
headed tacks, and paraded with it all over the town.

Charles Bent was born at Charleston, Virginia, November 11,
1799, the son of Silas and Martha (Kerr) Bent. With his brother,
William, and Ceran St. Vrain, he engaged in the fur trade; later

they are mounting the cannon on the fort—the citizens have all deserted the place, and Col. Price is in readiness to subdue the rebels, and has perhaps before this time will have done some fighting.

The Dctr. was prevailed upon by *mi alma* to attach himself to our party for strength's sake, they are seven and add much to us while we protect them too, and this is absolutely necessary now. We left in much haste they are rising between us and Santa Fé now under one of the Armijos [Santiago Armijo], and in truth we are *flying* before them.—My knowledge of these people has been extended very much in one day. There are among them some of the greatest villains, smooth-faced assassins in the world and some good people too. But yesterday morning while we were packing our trunks and some bales of goods, my suspicions were highly roused though perhaps unjustly; a good many men came in, some to buy goods, others merely to talk and as I suspected to see some thing of our strength, for without doubt 'tis the intention of nearly every one of them to murder without distinction every American in the country if the least thing should turn in their favour, for which reason we are going on now to overtake the troops below us, as 'tis a time when wisdom

his brothers, George and Robert, were taken into the firm. Charles was very popular with the traders and trappers of the upper Arkansas, but he seemed to prefer the trade about Santa Fé. He took up that branch of it, and went into New Mexico in 1829, settling in the valley of the Taos. There he married Marie Ignacia Jaramillo, who belonged to one of the leading families of New Mexico. Her younger sister, Josefa, became the wife of Kit Carson. (Grinnell, *Bent's Old Fort and Its Builders,* Kansas Historical Collections, vol. 15, pp. 78-81.)

says "keep with the fource." I often observed these
men yesterday whispering slighly about the room, and
especially when *mi alma* went out of the room, always
peeping out after him to see if he was near or far off,
on which occasions they talked more and faster than
if he was only about the door. Everything was said in
whisper and of course I could hear nothing, but
whether right or wrong my suspicion made it of a very
dark nature. One of them is a brother to a chief leader
in the disturbances above—Pino, is his name, and a
man that, from his looks and whole demeanor I should
say would not hesitate to do a "deed in the dark"! An
other one made me suspicion him *from his flattering
talk of the Americans* and abuse of his own people; the
same was sly enough in gathering up some goods he
had bought, to slip in a whole piece of calico more than
belonged to him but did not succeed in carrying it off
for being discovered and the piece recovered.

The whole company of us were on the look out—
mi alma was often on the house top; William, the
Dctr. and his seven men quietly *skouted* the town, and
I kept watch within door. We remained at this camp
all this day, making preparations for a constant travel
from tomorrow, in the mean time all fire arms are being examined, shot off and reloaded to be all in readiness for an attack. And we are well prepared for it;
all the wagoners are well armed, William and the
Dctr's company, and within our little tent we have
twelve sure rounds, a double-barreled shot gun, a pair
of holster and one pair of belt pistols, with one of
Colts six barreled revolvers—a formidable core for
only two people to muster. I hope and pray none of

them may have to be used, though we have good ground to expect an attack either from these, or a party of Indians reported to be below us a little—and to paint the scene as frightful as possible—we might have both to attack us.

Friday 29th. Camp No. 2. Well our travel today of some seven or eight miles has been *safe* though over very heavy roads along the river.

How exceedingly cold it is; water froze to the thickness of an inch and a half in a cup on our table last night, and the inmates of the bed suffered though under a buffalo robe, a counterpain and three pairs of Mackenaw blankets.

February 1847.

Monday 1st. By the goodness of God we have come this far in safety. We are almost at the mouth of the *Jornada* (the long journey without water) have been traveling slowly the roads being exceedingly heavy, with two or three severe hills; one we passed this morning, about a half mile in length, and the sand so heavy all the teams doubled and were then just able to get over with resting half a dozen times. 'Tis an ugly road very, but they say 'twill be better after this; I hope so indeed, for the poor animals work so hard. One month of this year is gone and eight months since we started on this long journey. I wonder if I shall ever get home again? But 'tis all the same if I do or do not, I must learn to look farther ahead than to earthly things. Now that a conviction has been awakened within my dark and sinful soul, how greater is my sin if I suffer it to die away without seeking my Savior's pardon for multiplied transgressions against his infinite goodness and forbearance. I am sinful my flesh is prone to do evil, and if I remain in this state what says the Apostle is my doom—*"Indignation, wrath, tribulation and anguish* upon every soul of man that doeth evil. But glory, honour and peace to every man that worketh good." The two great rewards are laid before me, with the command to choose the "evil or the good." What must I do? I am conscious of my great polution, my unworthyness of God's mercies and shall I stop at this? No, there is certain ruin if I do. If pardon is offered the penitent, "I will arise and go unto my Father and say unto Him Father I have sinned against Heaven and in thy sight and am not worthy to be called thy child, make me as one of thy hired servants."

Tuesday 2nd. Fray Cristobal. Well we have arrived at the last point on the *River* before taking the Jornaday. Fray Cristoval is a celebrated place, not from the beauty or number of its houses, but from its being a regular camping-ground never passed without the traveler stops a day or two or at the least the half of a day to rest his animals for the *Jornada.* One would think that as long as they have been passing towns all down the River, that this must be one too, or at least a settlement; but no, there is not even the dusky walls of an adobe house to cheer its lonely solitude. Like Valverde it is only a regular camping place with a name. At present I can say nothing of its beauties— the bleak hill sides look lovely enough and feel cold enough. In the summer season though I suspect it is quite attractive; the River bottom is then green; the cottonwoods are leaved; the stream, though at all times dark and ugly, is more brisk and lively in its flow and these now unattractive sand-hills serve as a variation in the scene; with all I guess it is not so disagreeable.

Three men from El Passo, passed us today; the news they bring is little and of little importance. Nothing has been heard of Gen. Wool, they are preparing at Chihuahua to *receive* Col. Donavan [Doniphan], who will march to *accept of their kindness,* immediately on the arrival of the artillery at El Passo today or tomorrow.

Wednesday 3rd. Three miles from Fray Cristoval tonight, ready to take the jornada[85] tomorrow evening. No one has passed us today, at one time this P. M. though we thought to have had some news; soon after we started from F. C. we observed a wagon far off to our right, standing near a little woods, and several oxen feeding a short distance from it. *Mi alma* and Gabriel immediately started off, but soon returned reporting the wagon as empty and the animals (which we take by the way) as broken down. They gave out I suppose and their owner was obliged to leave his wagon for the want of a team to pull it.

Three of the Dctr's men have gone on tonight as

[85] *Jornada del muerto* (the day's journey of the dead man) was along a detour of the highway for a distance of about eighty miles, made necessary by the obstruction of a mountain at the river's edge. In dry seasons there was no water supply along this journey, and a Mexican who tried to make it in a day, without supplies, perished on the road. Hence the name. It was a dangerous pass and cost the lives of many travelers.

express to give Col. D.[oniphan] intelligence of the insurrection above. It is a dangerous journey for only three men to undertake, but I hope and pray they may be protected safely thro' it.

Friday 5th. A la leguna del muerto.[86] 2 O'k last evening we started into the *jornada*, traveled till 5 o'k and stoped two hours to rest the animals and get a little supper. The wind blew high all the evening and the dust considerable. A short time after we stoped or when the fire was made the scene reminded me of one described by Mr. Gregg, in his Prairie scenes the grass caught fire near to our baggage wagon and but for the great activity of the servants and wagoners all of whom collected around, we should have been now with out the wagon or any thing in it and perhaps worse off than that, the consequent explosion of two powder keggs in it might have caused [cost] the life of some of us. They beat it out with blankets, sticks, wagon-whips & in short every thing within their reach, half-dozen of the men pushed the wagon off as fast as the fire advanced towards them, till 'twas entirely extinguished. It is singular how rapidly it will spread in the dry grass—before the alarm could be given yesterday it spread several yards.

About 7 o'clock we again resumed our travel for the

[86] *Laguna del Muerto,* or Dead Man's Lake. Depended upon to water thirsty animals. In dry seasons it was a mere depression in the plains, and to get water the drivers would have to go five or six miles into a narrow gorge to Ojo del Muerto (Dead Man's Spring). Here many of them were killed by Apache Indians, who frequented the neighborhood. (Gregg, *Commerce of the Prairies,* 1844 ed., vol. 2, p. 73.)

night. The ox teams in front, myself and train next, while the mules brought up the rear. *La luna* made her appearance about 10—and afforded us a beautiful light to travel by; the road is hard and level and we made fine progress, arriving at this place about 25 miles by 2 o'k this morning—and here I am now to describe this place—"The dead man's lake," *"Laguna del muerto"* is some six ms. from where we are camped on the road. Travellers generally stop here and send off their animals to water at this spring quite a long distance too, but tis quite necessary as we shall not find water again till we strike the River forty miles ahead. The exact circumstances of the derivation of the name of "laguna del muerto" I do not recollect, but tis from a traveller once in attempting to find a road to the south more practicable than the River course, started through here alone, and was after found dead at the spring. How the appearance of the country is immediately about there I know not, but to judge from the appearances here the regular camping ground, I should fully say the name it bears is not too solitary for it. The country is quite level immediately around us, with dark hills in the distance. The grass is short and dry, the soil sandy, the little Prairie dogs have spread their habitation far and wide around and the whole puts on a gloomy aspect.

Monday 8th. Neither yesterday or the day before have I written. Friday night we travelled all night by a fine moon, till daylight, when we stoped and took a rest of a few hours. During the night we met a company of new Mexicans returning from the Pass, and with them an American gentleman named White[87] for whom *mi alma* wrote for him to come up to take some charge of his business as he is in want of such an one as he is—a persevering, hard working and confidential man—and *mi alma* has now sent him back to buy corn and to "look out" to hear all the sly news, to endeavour to procure if possible some protection from Col. Donaphan, as we do not like the idea of being left entirely behind & alone too—I am not an advocate though for night travelling when I have to be shut up in the carriage in a road I know nothing of, and the driver nodding all the time, and letting the reins drop from his hands to the entire will of the mules. I was kept in a *fever* the whole night, though every one complained bitterly of cold. Saturday morning early we were off

[87] James White was a merchant of Independence and Santa Fé. In October, 1849, while traveling with his wife and young daughter to Santa Fé, along with the caravan of another trader (F. X. Aubrey), they were attacked by Apache Indians. At the time they were at a place supposed to be past the danger from Indian attack, and were driving some distance in advance of the caravan, accompanied by only eight men. The men were all killed by the Indians, and the woman and child taken captive. The murder was discovered and reported by an American merchant named Spencer, and Major Grier, with Kit Carson and Joachim Leroux as guides, was detailed for their rescue. The guides found the Indians, but in spite of Carson's advice Major Grier stopped for a parley with them, thinking it a sure way to rescue the captives. The momentary delay gave the Indians a chance to escape. Mrs. White ran toward her rescuers, but was mortally wounded by the Indians, and the child was never found. Although the War Department furnished Isaac Dunn, Mrs. White's brother, an escort to search for the child, he failed to find her.

again, travelled till 3 o'clock P. M. when we again stoped to rest our fatigued animals; the grass is fine, and though they are doing with out water and pulling long and hard they are not suffering in this point— the grama-grass is what they are fond of from its being very sweet and slightly green near the roots, it grows in bunches all over the Mountains, has a jointed stem with curling blades & growing out from each joint. It grows to the height of two feet, though in general not more than six or eight inches. At all seasons the taller portion has a white and harvest-like appearance, large fields of it are like hay. Saturday evening we again started and travelled till 12, when we reached the River, camped on a high bluff about two miles from the water, and sent the stock down to it. All day Sunday we remained at this place to re-cruit a little, and sent Mr. White on ahead to purchase corn at Don Ana or *Don Llana* [Doña Ana]. Not-withstanding the many reports of Indians stealing animals and murdering people about here, I have been bold enough to climb up and down these beautiful and rugged cliffs both yesterday and today, but I shall be more careful hereafter, as it is really dangerous. We are in the heart of the Apache range and *mi alma* thinks I am wrong to go two hundred yards from the camp, we are now putting our little *house mui cirquita de los carros* [within the corral of wagons].

Wednesday 10th. Don Llana [Doña Ana]. Last evening we arrived here after a long day's travel— Nooned in on the River about four miles back, and came up this P. M. to the only settlement between the jornada and El Passo, owing to the destructive disposition of the Apaches, a few nights since they came into this town and drove off twenty yoke of oxen belonging to government. For the protection of the inhabitants against them for the future, Col. Donaphan has left them a canon, and by the way we came near getting ourselves into a fine scrape last night by the wild impudence of some of the waggoners. They went into the village, "got on a spree" and ran off with the canon, brought it to the camp and persisted in taking it as being *unfit for Mexicans.* As 'twas done without provocation, and with seeming hostile intentions, the Alcalde told us this morning, that if *mi alma* had not then sent him an apology then —by Gabriel that the men were drunk and he would have it returned in the morning, he intended raising a fource, and immediately sending an express off to the governor in the Pass informing him of the hostile move made against him, and this morning the old gentleman is in a gib of trouble, for the men on finding they were not allowed to retain their trophy, spiked the touch-hole so that it will not fire, and if the Indians were to come they would be without protection. *Mi alma* could only apologize, take the Alcalde's part, by agreeing with him that an express must be sent to the governor in el Passo, and at the same time has set down in his own private book the names of the two gentleman who committed the depredations.

Camp 10 miles from Don Llana [Doña Ana]. Mr. White came up with us this evening; has been twenty miles below El Passo to see Col. Donaphan. The troops have all left the pass—and Col. D. has taken with him five or six of the most influential citizens as hostages for the good behavior of those remaining, to ourselves and all the traders, it is quite a propper step. Many of *mi alma's* friends in the Pass send him word to come on without fear, that they have always been friendly to him and still are, their houses are open to receive us when we arrive. On the whole we could look for nothing better.

Friday 12th. We have come over some dark looking ground today. This morning the whole road lay through musquite thickets, which made me rather careful in walking out. The Indian is a wily man, and one cannot be too precausious when in his territory. Yesterday we passed over the spot where a few years since a party of the Apaches attacked Gen. Armijo as he returned from the Pass with a party of troops, and killed some fourteen of his men, the graves of whom, marked by a rude cross, are now seen, he himself received a wound in his leg, from which he will always be lame. This morning we passed the spot were they attacked brother James' little party of a dozen men, this summer, and [de]spoiled them of all their goods. And today we nooned it at *Brasito,* the battle-field long to be remembered by Col. Donaphan and his little band of seven hundred volunteers. I rode over the battle ground, (a perfect plain) and brought off as trophies two cartridges one Mexican the other Amer.

This P. M. we were overtaken by an express mail from Col. Price at Santa Fé to Col. Doniphan, and with orders for the Pass only, as he has left there, and there is no one to receive it in that place. Dctr. Richardson, now with us, as concerned with the army has taken charge of it to send it on tomorrow; he opened it tonight, and we have all the news contained in the newspapers up to the 27th Nov. from the U. S. and to the 4th do. from Taylor's army, then just leaving Monterey for San Louis Potosi, via, Satilla [Saltillo] and Tampico. Gen. Wool with part of his army is to join him, while the other part is sent on to Chihuahua. I hope and trust they may go and moreover be successful with Col. Doniphan, otherwise we can have no hope of safety farther. The friends of those prisoners taken from the Pass can of course have no very friendly feeling towards us, and if they once get the advantage of us what must the consequences be? I heartily wish we were back at Santa Fé in Fort Marcy, and we would be soon too if our animals were in a condition to carry us. They bring me two letters from Lex.[ington, Kentucky] in which I find news of the death of Aunt McDowell,[88] and Uncle Dick Hart; the marriage of several acquaintances; many wishes for my return, and sorrow that I ever left home at all. I almost wish so myself, since we have been detained so long, and if we get back at all I shall call it God's blessing.

Saturday 13th. Today we have come about ten miles. Our camp is not on the River, but five or six miles from it, in a real Indian country. The place is called *La Laguna,* simply a saltwater pond, half grown over with reeds; gloomy looking mountains rear their heads in our rear and sides; the grass has

[88] Sarah Shelby, daughter of Governor Isaac Shelby, born 1785, married, in 1802, Dr. Ephraim McDowell, the most distinguished surgeon of his time. She was always called by her family "Aunt McDowell."

been all *camped* off, and all together it is a gloomy place. The musquite thicket all around us, look the very abodes of the savage red man, and *fear* has at length determined me to remain within my quiet little tent in place of roaming about in search of any little curiosity I might chance to find. Our stay at Bosquesito during the fall months has prevented me from preserving many wild flower seeds as I intended, the birds and wind have well-nigh gathered all.

Sunday 14th. Three miles we are from the crossing, today the country improves a little from yesterday. El Rio winds its way through the mountains, and if the naked cottonwood trees and willow bushes scattered along its banks, were only covered with green leaves I know 'twould be pretty. I am beginning to long for a church to attend, *el camino* [the road] has ceased to engage my attention as much as formerly and especially on the Sabbath, but as it is there is no preventative now; I came out on this travel regardless of the Sabbath, not bearing in mind the Lord's command "Remember the Sabbath-day to keep it holy; in it thou shalt not do any work" &c. But God in his infinite mercy has come near unto me, when I was far off, and called me when I sought not after him. My sins and transgressions are heavy on my head, and but for the great and precious promises to the sinner penitent, every where to be met with in the Holy scripture, I should at once and forever despair of peace and pardon in this world or hereafter. There is no excuse for me now, for "the word is very nigh unto me, in my mouth, and in my heart, that I may do it." Though I am now in darkness, the Lord has said "Awake thou that sleepest, and arise from the dead, and Christ shall give thee light."

Monday 15th. En casa de Don Agapita [In the house of Don Agapita]. Leaving the wagons this morning we crossed the River and came into town to the house of *mi alma's* old friend Don Agapita an old Gauchupine [a Mexican name for a native-born Spaniard]. The house is kept by the old gentleman's single daughter Doña Josefita, a very interesting and lady-like girl of twenty two years, she is affible, perfectly easy in her manners, and I think if some of the foreigners who have come into this country, and judged of the whole population from what they have seen—on the frontiers, would, to see her a little time, be entirely satisfied of his error in regard to the refinement of the people, although I have not judged so rashly as most persons, I confess I am surprised a little—and Don Agapita is a man ever to be beloved, for his hospitable feelings extended to all classes of people. He has sympathy for those in distress or trouble and shows it by endeavouring to serve them; he is a man of learning, experience and good sound sense, and more than all he has a sincere heart. When we arrived he met us at the door with a hearty welcome to his old friend and his wife (I hope though he will like me for myself by and by) threw open his house to us with a request for us to take it as our own. I should like to spend *muncho tiempo* [*mucho*—much time] with them, but tomorrow we shall remove to *el Senor Cura's,* as we are invited and the house has been especially prepared for us.

But a little in regard to the house of our host and

hostess and its management &c. &c. *La casa* is not very large but of ordinary size; the sala fronts the street, and is nearly the whole length of the house, the walls instead of papering are painted in flowers, vases, &c and at first had a very antique and singular, but now that a few hours' sight have made it accustomed to my visage, I think it equally as pretty as our papering. From the sala opens a door into our chamber, a pretty, nice little room with one window and a snug fire place, a bed in one corner, a lounge in an other. Outside in the patio are flour-pots, bird-cages, cats playing and pigeons eating, and such a quantity of the latter I have not seen for a long time. A back door opens into a *garden,* where fruit trees and grape vines grow in abundance, with here and there a rose bush, a lilly bed, or some thing of the kind; as it is winter time now of course there are no bright blossoms to cheer the scene, but the weather is so mild the trees are leaving, and in a little time more there will be fruit. Next comes the table in propper routine; we take coffee about 7½ o'clock, breakfast at 10, and dinner at 5— with fruit between meals. Our dishes are all Mexican, but good ones, some are delightful; one great importance they are well cooked; their meats are all boiled, the healthiest way of preparing them, and are in most instances cooked with vegetables, which are onions, cabbage, and tomatoes; with the addition of apples and grapes; the courses for dinner are four, one dish at a time; for breakfast two, ending always with beans. Brandy and wine are regularly put on at each meal, and never go off with out being honoured with the salutations of all the company.

Tuesday 16th. The more I see of this family the more I like them, they are so kind and attentive, so desirous to make us easy, so anxious for our welfare in the disturbances of the country. I can't help loving them. The old gentleman remarked at breakfast this morning, that he sympathized—for the experience of many years has taught him that sympathy is a soothing balm—much with me in the troubles, dangers, and difficulties I have been in, those I am now in, and those that I may be in, but with all he says I am learning a lesson that not one could have taught me but experience, the ways of the world. Tis true as he says; I have seen and read of Ky. till I know it all by heart, but who could by telling me, make me sensible of what I have seen and felt since I left home to travel. His arguments are quite phylosophical, and in fine he is a man not met with every day in any part of the world.

Wednesday 17th. En casa del Senor Cura [The house of the Curate]. Agreeable to our arrangements we moved our boarding last evening to this the residence of the Priest,[89] who is now a prisoner in the hands of Col. Doniphan, though I hope for no bad

[89] Reverend Ramon Ortiz was curate òf El Paso del Norte. He was a shrewd, intelligent, and generous man. Kendall speaks of him in very complimentary terms, as treating with much kindness the Texan prisoners who were brought to El Paso by the notorious Salazar. He not only fed and clothed the men, but also gave them money. During the Mexican War he was suspected of sending information to Chihuahua. For this reason Colonel Doniphan, on his march to Chihuahua, took him, Senor Pino, and several other influential men as hostages. Later when the soldiers were suffering from thirst, and while he was still a prisoner, he

end. So far I find the family exceedingly kind and attentive. The affairs are in the hands of his two sisters Doña Anna Maria, a widow lady, and Doña Rosalita, Doña Anna's daughter, Doña Josafa, with her three children compose the family. Doña Anna Maria is a second Mrs. Ross in her person, age, conversation and manners. She is good & kind and seems to have rather the principal management, bears the name of a favorite in the village, she is a *mui Senora* in my estimation. How much I am struck with their manner of rearing children. The little daughter of Doña Josafita, only six years of age, carries with her the dignity of our girls of eighteen. It attracted my attention particularly the evening I came, with the same ease of a lady much accustomed to society, she entered the room, with a polite bow and *"Bonus tardes"* [*Buenas tardes*—good evening], shook hands with me and seated herself.—The eldest daughter of 17 years is sick with *sarampion* [measles].

Thursday 18th. I am altogether pleased with our boarding house—the inmates are exceedingly kind and exert themselves so much to make me enjoy myself, 'twould be cruel if I did not attend to their solicitations. We have chocolate every morning on rising, breakfast about 10 o'k. dinner at two, chocolate again at dark, and supper at 9 o'clock, all are attentive, indeed we are so free and easy, 'tis almost a hotel, meals are served in our own room, one of the ladies always being in attendance to see and know if we are propperly attended to; the dishes are often changed, and well

arranged to have water brought from the Del Norte for their use. At this time he was a man of about thirty years of age.

prepared. I shall have to make me a recipe book, to take home, the cooking in every thing is entirely different from ours, and some, indeed all of their dishes are so fine 'twould be a shame not to let my friends have a taste of them too.

Don José Ygnacio Rouquia, his Senora and three little daughters called this P. M.; and la Senora Garcia and daughter. My book is drawing so near to a close, and I have so much to write each day, I shall only take a few notes on each hereafter.

Friday 19th. We are all getting quite familiar and friendly in our dealings; as our acquaintance extends it is more agreeable, and to me more improving; as I am quite inquisitive, for I see so many new and strange ways of making every thing, I always ask something about it, and in return I give my way. I shall make me a recipe book.

Sunday 21st. This morning I have been to mass—not led by idle curiosity, not by a blind faith, a belief in the creed there practiced, but because tis the house of God, and whether Christian or pagan, I can worship there within myself, as well as in a protestant church, or my own private chamber. If I have sinned in going there in this belief, I pray for pardon for 'twas done in ignorance. I am not an advocate for the Catholic faith. It is not for me to judge; whether it be right or wrong; judgement alone belongs to God. If they are wrong we (if alone in the right way) are not to rail at them, but in brotherly love to use our little influence to guide them into the straight path. One thing among them they are sincere in what they do. I speak of the people; of the Priests and leaders I know nothing. I am told to "judge no man but to bear the burden of my brother." As for myself I must first remove the beam from mine own eye, and then shall I see clearly to pull out the moat out of my brother's eye. In my weakness I will endeavour to walk according to God's laws, as my own understanding points them out to me; and at all times I have a help both in the light and in darkness. . . . The Sabbath is not enough observed, it is a day for visiting; and entirely contrary to my feelings and wishes, I have been obliged today to see several ladies that called; there is far more pleasure to me in my Bible, prayer book, and retirement, and if I could I would have it so; here we have but one room, and persons come in and out, to see me as they are in the habit of visiting other inmates of the house. . . . I wish *mi alma* would observe the Sabbath more than he does, and, though 'tis the custom of the country to do otherwise, shut his store up. It hurts me more than I can tell; that he does not find six days of the week sufficient to gain the goods of this poor world, but is also constrained to devote the day that God himself has appointed us to keep holy, to the same business. And I too am to be a partaker of the gain of this day! Oh, I hope and pray that the Lord will make us better, will create within our sinful breasts feelings holy and pious, loving his laws and commands more than we do, and desires to walk continually in the humble foot-steps of him who has offered himself as a guide and a light to those who walk in darkness.

Monday 22nd—Tuesday 23rd. Both yesterday and today I have been returning my calls. Of all the houses

and families I have visited that of Don Ygnacio Rouquia pleases me most, to say nothing to disparage the
others. Mrs. Rouquia is a lady easy in her own house,
commanding respect from her servants, and respect-
ful affection from her children, and exerting herself
to entertain her visitors agreeably. Her house is large,
though as yet unfurnished, and the placita quite
pretty, for she takes pride in rearing choice fruit trees,
as oranges, figs, apricots, almonds &c., all of which are
tastefully arranged, while in the center of the patio she
has a raised bed of earth some four feet, for flowers;
she bears the name of an industrious housewife, and to
me shows far better at home than abroad; her children
are studying English and French, and their parents
are very anxious to have them proficient in them.

Don Ygnacio is a second George Washington in his
appearance, and is altogether a great admirer of the
man whose name is ever dear to the hearts of the
American; he says the course Mr. Polk is persuing in
regard to this war, is entirely against the principals of
Washington, which were to remain at home, encour-
age all home improvements, to defend our rights *there*
against the incroachments of others, and never to invade the territory of an other nation. . . . Doña Refu-
jio, wife of Senor Belumdis, now a prisoner by Col.
Doniphan, lives opposite to Don. Y. She is a lady much
given to talking, though perhaps means no harm by
it; but to one not accustomed to such tis rather strange
I must confess. Along with many like questions she
asked me if I was never jealous of my husband, and
when I could not understand what "zeloso" [jealous]
meant she was quite particular to explain to me that

at that moment he might be off with his other *Senorita.*
Oh, how I was shocked, I could have cried my eyes out
for any one else to suppose such a thing let alone myself! And how twould hurt him too if I should tell him,
when my own heart tells me he is a husband as true
as the world *ever* contained. I generally tell him every
thing that happens in my visiting, but *this,* I couldn't
try his feelings so much, but you my poor journal
must hear all whether good or bad, whether in praise
or disparagement.

Wednesday 3rd March 1847. Oh, the ups and
downs of this world! One day we are in greatest life
the next affairs bring different faces. A whole week
has passed away since I wrote in my journal, and for
why, as my friends tell me I am so *triste* [sad]; and
no wonder, when nothing but the dark bear walls of
a Mexican prison are staring me in the face—in pros-
pective only though. I'll see though if I can remember
a few incidents since my last insercion; all last Wednesday I was half deranged with headache, (this is no
good news) but notwithstanding, most of the day was
spent I hope in doing good, making a chemise for
"Maria *la tonta*" [the stupid], this needs an explanation however. Maria is a deranged woman entirely dependent on the charities of the citizens, and to do them
justice, I must say they are both liberal and attentive
to her as well as the other poor. The first Sabbath I
attended mass here, she discovered me in the church—
an object of curiosity of course, at once signalized me
by the name of *"Nana"* [aunt], and since that day she
has been a constant visitor at my room. I am *"Nana,"*
Doña Josefa *"Mama,"* mi alma *"tata* [tato—

brother], and Doña Rufujio "Mana Juga" [Mama Fuja—a burlesque on the name Doña Refujio], so we all have our respective names. She is truely singular in her conversation, causing mirth at every word she says, while she herself appears more delighted if we laugh at her expressions than when we remain silent. She grew very angry with me this P. M. when she found I did not finish her garment, which on acct. of my head I was unable to do. A little coaxing, persuading, fruit and money, reconciled her at the last and she bid me good bye till tomorrow. Don Sista, his wife Doña Francisca, and her sister Doña Josafita Albo made us a call this P. M. The ladies requested to see some *modas Americanas,* for dresses, so accordingly I opened four or five dresses, all of which seemed to strike their different tastes, tomorrow, with my permission, they will take two or three of them as patterns for a few days till they can cut or make themselves some.

Friday 26th. This afternoon with Doñas Josafa y Rifujio, I called at Doña Agapita's, sat with them an hour or so, and returned home to hear nothing but bad news, viz: Gen. Taylor has been defeated in a great battle at San Luis Potosi, and taken prisoner with the whole of his army; that Gen. Wool is blockaded in Monterey; that a large fource is coming up from Durango to assist the Chihuahuans, who of themselves number they say 8000 now in arms, in capturing Col. Doniphan's little army of 1000. Saturday has been a day of great suspense and further confirmation of the *noticias de ayer* [news of yesterday]. Sunday morning I attended mass with the family, not for a show, but to worship God.

Monday the first of March comes with a wind, and such news as makes at least two hearts sad, my heart aches to the very core for my husband's sufferings of mind, and more too, when I sit down by him and he looks on me with sorrow and says he never in his life, though he has encountered many severe troubles, till now been troubled by his misfortunes; "in all others I have been *alone,* and could endure them patiently, but to think of you now, that you are compelled to endure so much it is too heart rending." Eight men have arrived today from Chihuahua, still confirming the last news, with additions that Santa Anna is preparing to invade Texas; and that a large fource is leaving Chi. to encounter Col. D. who has but six pieces of artillery, while the others have thirty-four pieces; that the enemy Mexican fources are commanded by Trius, Jinedia, and Martinus, three good generals, that as soon as they have fixed Doniphan, which they look upon as fixed already, they will march on here to take New Mexico; that Brother James has been sent off to Durango, perhaps to Mexico [City], and who knows what will become of him, and is not all this enough to make our hearts sick? There is under these circumstances no fate before us but to be taken by a band of lawless soldiers, every thing we have in the world seized and divided among themselves as pay for their services, while we are dragged off to prison, separated and may be *forever.* Oh, my dear husband would that *I* could relieve you of the anguish of mind you are labouring under! But alas, alas! I myself am no better off. It behooves me though to put on more fortitude than this. I must be his comfort and not his trouble. I can console him a little, and that little in such times as these is a great deal. I can do all that's in my power, and when that is done I can pray for him, for God ever liveth to "send help from the sanctuary, and strength out of Zion."

Tuesday the same as before; tonight a *friend* sends for *mi alma* and tells him in secret to be on his guard, that a mob is about to rise in the town and rob his waggons. And *friends* (for we have a few here) tell him every day that not only his wagons are observed but, that as soon as the least news favourable to the Mexican arms below, neither himself or his wife will be spared, we may be seized and murdered in a moment for we are Americans, and though disposed to be peaceable, are here entirely against our own will, judgement and inclination, still we must suffer notwithstanding the efforts that this family, to whom we are and shall always be indebted for their unceasing kindness to us, say they would make to save us. A reckless mob is an awful thing to peaceful citizens.

But to speak one word in regard to this interesting family—our situations are truly singular; we have a brother prisoner in Chi.[huahua], while they have one *el Senor Cura* [the priest] held as hostage by our army for his safety, and we are here in the same house and as I trust, friends. I know on the part of ourselves we are sincere, and I have no right to doubt the sincerity of the others. I shall regret deeply when we have to leave them; twould be injustice to say that I like one more than an other for I love them all. *Mi alma* has

215

offered his services, and would either write or go himself if he could be of any service to el *Senor Cura* as regards his liberation, but they are looking for him in a few days as liberated by his own countrymen.*

Wednesday 3rd. Oh, such suspense we have been in this day! the citizens have been confidently expecting a courier bearing news fatal to us—but heartfelt thanks to the giver of all good, the prayers of a wicked servant have been heard and the evil so far as been withheld from us. Never could I wish harm to or exult over the other party, if I were able I would have all peace. Tonight a man has arrived a courier to us he says from brother James, with intelligence that he is still in Chi.[huahua] that the Mexican army consists of only 3000 men with nine pieces of cannon, and that they are now in a treaty in regard to their prisoners and will have no battle. We know not how to believe a word of it tho' for he brings no letter or paper, and talks himself in such an insane way it all must be false, notwithstanding, true or false, it has raised our drooping spirits a little. I hope they will not fight. . . . Our wagons have been brought in today and placed in the square, under the protection of the civil authorities, to keep them from the mob.

Friday 5th. Can we ever be too thankful for the mercy shown us by our Heavenly Father? Can we ever repay the debt we owe him for the preservation of our lives in all the danger that has surrounded us? But a day since, we were in hourly expectation of being

* While at this house and in the critical situation we were in I never wrote all I might have done, for fear of my journal being seized had things gone with us differently.

either murdered or sent off to prison, as a lawless set of robbers or spies, and now the scene is changed. We were struck with consternation about 12 o'clock today while quietly talking with our friend, Mr. White, Don Ygnacio Rouquia suddenly steped in at the door, with hair somewhat on ends and features ghastly. At once our minds were filled with apprehensions lest the dread sentence had been passed. Without seating himself, and scarcely saying good morning, he took Mr. Magoffin by the hand and led him out of the room in haste, and with tears in his eyes told him that "he was a Mexican, and it pained him to the heart to know that the American army had gained the battle[90] and taken pos-

[90] The battle of Sacramento River "not only gave increased reputation to our arms, but was one of the most important which occurred during the war in its results and effects. It was the means of keeping down the disturbances which had broken out in New Mexico a short time previous, and secured peace in our newly acquired possessions in that quarter. It made the Indian tribes look upon us as a race far superior to the Mexicans, and overawed them. It prevented a large amount of property in the hands of the traders from falling into their hands; property which was sufficient to have supported the whole Mexican Army for several months, and at that particular time would have been of the utmost value to Santa Anna and the government. We captured the *Black Flag* which cut such a conspicuous figure at Brazito, but the bearer of it made his escape, and it was well he did, for our men would have made mincemeat of him. We found in a trunk three thousand dollars in copper coin which appeared to be their military chest, but the men made large acquisitions of silver and one I understand got one hundred doubloons." (Gibson, "Diary of the Mexican War," MS.) This "Black Flag" now hangs in the museum of the Missouri Historical Society at St. Louis.

This battle was fought February 28, 1847, and lasted three

session of Chi.[huahua]." No particulars as yet are
known, save that 'twas a severe battle, fought on Sunday last, and we will have official accounts in a few
days. I would not for the world exult or say one word
to hurt the feelings of this family, but 'tis a natural
consequence that I am delighted with the news. They
were condoling with me the other day, and now 'tis
in my power perhaps to offer them in return a little
consolation in regard to *el Senor Cura,* who, this
courier to Don Ygnacio says, is safe, and during the
action remained with the other prisoners with the
traders at their camp. He asserts the news we heard in
regard to Gen. Taylor as false and that more American forces are disembarking at Vera Cruz. With this
I feel rather in better spirits than the other evening,
when every moment almost I expected to hear news
that would have made my heart sick, such as would
have robbed me of the dearest thing, to me, on Earth,
for a time, and may be forever.

Sunday 7th. Attended mass this morning as usual,
and passed the day after it, in reading; no visits much
to my satisfaction. It is exceedingly windy these last
few days, more so I believe than in Ky. this month;
there is so much dust one cannot even stand at the

and a half hours, with losses to the American forces of Major
Owens killed, one mortally wounded, and seven others who
recovered. The Mexican casualties were about three hundred
killed and about the same number wounded, many of whom died
later, and about forty prisoners. There were 924 effective Americans (at least one hundred of whom were engaged in holding
horses and driving teams) opposed to almost four thousand
Mexicans.

door or window without having their eyes nearly put out, much less going into the street, where nothing scarcely can be seen but flying sand. Things in regard to the news of Friday continue quiet.

Monday 8th. No curreo todo dia [No courier all day], but contradictions of the news of the 5th. Last night or evening about twilight the whole village was thrown into commotion by the reported arrival of two Pueblo Indians, sent on from the last settlement below, by the *alcalde* [mayor] of that place, Sorocco, who they say arrived there yesterday, fainting from a wound received in the battle of the 28th ultimo. The news is, they fought all day Sunday, and commenced again on Mon. that a great many have been killed, and among the number El Senor Cura and Don Sibastien. As he left on Sunday he cannot tell the final termination of the battle, but gives this as his opinion, that though American arms gained the first day, the Mexicans will have the last for they were receiving recruits from below. Tues. this news was proven false, for the wisdom of the place got together, made search for the bearers of this, and they could never be found, *as they had not arrived in the city.* But this did not stop the movements of Doña Ana Maria, interest for her brother is first, and lest the news might be true she dispatched a servant to Socorro, to see if the reported arrival of the Senor Ruis were true, and to learn from his own mouth the particulars. The servant returned this morning about day-break with the expression, (very common now adays) *"todo es mentira"* [the whole thing is a falsehood], then of one burden we are freed. This morning a letter was brought to the

wife of Don Sibastien written by Ruis, from Chi.
[huahua] or very near there, in which he says the
Americans have gained the action, and not to be uneasy for the prisoners, that they have been treated by
the American troops as officers and either have or are
soon to have their liberty, I forget which.

Tuesday 9th. An other man arrives this A. M. but
still no official express. He says the Americans have
entered Chi.; the Mexican forces left it for Durango;
el Senor Cura is at liberty and will be here in a day or
two; brother James has been sent off some place he
does not know where; and that our friend Col. Owens[91]

[91] Samuel C. Owens emigrated to Missouri when he was very
young, and became prominent among the early settlers. He was
a native of Kentucky, the son of Nathaniel Owens, one of the
wealthiest and most influential men of Green County, Kentucky.
The famous Mary Owens, courted by Abraham Lincoln during her
sojourn at New Salem, Illinois, and who afterwards became Mrs.
Jesse Vineyard of Weston, Missouri, was half-sister to Samuel
Owens. Colonel Owens, as he was popularly known, was the first
clerk of Jackson County, Missouri, and served also as clerk of the
county court, recorder of deeds, and representative in the state
legislature. He operated large caravans along the trail, was one
of the principal wholesalers connected with the Mexican trade,
and had also a general store on the southeast corner of the Square
at Independence, Missouri. Many of his purchases were made in
Philadelphia, being brought by the Ohio, Mississippi, and Missouri rivers from Pittsburgh.

During the Mexican War, Owens was with other traders on
the Santa Fé trail. In obedience to the orders of General Kearny,
all traders and caravans were required to accompany Colonel
Doniphan's command. This was to keep their large stores from
falling into the hands of the enemy and thus supplying him for
his military campaign. Shortly before the battle of Sacramento,

was killed in the battle by a rifle ball shot at him, *a league and a half off;* it is a great rifle that, equal to the report of the first arrival of the American canon.

Doniphan impressed these traders and most of their teamsters into military service, forming an extra battalion of one hundred and fifty men under the command of Owens as their major, and Messrs. Skillman and Glasgow as their captains. These took part in the battle of Sacramento. It may be noted here that the United States Government never paid these men and never allowed them pensions, the reason given being that Colonel Doniphan had no legal authority to create new companies of troops.

During the battle of Sacramento a charge was made by four of the companies upon one of the twenty-eight Mexican redoubts which had proved especially troublesome. The charge of these companies was not made simultaneously, and through some confusion of orders they paused in a dangerous position. Captain Reid, of one of the companies, dashed ahead, accompanied by only a few men, including Major Owens, who had joined them voluntarily. Upon nearing the enemy Captain Reid and the others turned to the left and ran along the Mexican front past several redoubts, drawing the fire of the entire Mexican line. This circumstance made it necessary for the Mexicans to reload their flintlock guns and the delay incident thereto permitted the whole American line to get over the redoubts and rout the Mexican Army. Major Owens, instead of turning with the others, who escaped unhurt, charged single-handed upon the Mexican redoubt, and both he and his horse were killed.

There have been various comments upon this spectacular bravery of Major Owens. Colonel Doniphan said in a letter to a mutual friend: "He lost his life by excessive bravery, or rather rashness. He rode up to the redoubt, filled with armed men, and continued to fire his pistols into it until himself and horse fell, pierced with balls, upon its very brink."

Major Owens had recently suffered a very sad domestic tragedy, and there were many who thought he welcomed death. One account says that he went into battle dressed in white and

We, viz: Doñas Josefita and Rafujio went out from town about a league this P. M. to return the call of Doña Guadalupe Herques or Heques, an old lady who has honoured us in her visit. She is, now I should think, upwards of sixty and perhaps quite 70 years of age; her hair is perfectly gray and of its self calls respect, she has her home affairs carried on with out any bustle or confusion, she is exceedingly active and attends to it herself in person, carrying about her bunch of keys large and heavy enough to fatigue any common woman. Her whole family of children and grand children big and little came in and saluted us; and in half an hour or less after our arrival chocolate was brought. She questioned me a great deal about the U. S., my own family &c. and as she is a lady of no

mounted upon a white horse, so as to be an easy target for the enemy. One of his men is reported as saying that before the battle he shaved and dressed himself with care because "he did not know what might happen and knew of no more honorable or desirable end than to die in battle."

After the arrival of the troops at Chihuahua, Major Owens, who was a Catholic, was buried with great pomp. The ceremonies were conducted by Mexican priests. In the church there was a procession of priests, singing as they marched, with music from different and strange kinds of instruments, and about three hundred lighted candles set around the place where the corpse lay. The body was interred with both Masonic and military honors.

The death of Major Owens was a great loss to the traders; they could better have spared almost any other man. His influence was great and his judgment sound. He was an "outfitter" who would trust them for wagons, teams, provisions, and everything necessary for a trip, and he counseled them as if they were his children.

trifling mind I gave her the best information I had on all subjects; finally she concluded with sympathies for Mama in regard to my being so far from her, and hoped that God would permit me again to return to her in health and happiness.

All day Thursday we have remained without news! What happens?

Friday 10th. Well joy to this family, *el Senor Cura* has at last returned; arrived this morning about 10 o'clock. The news is as we have heard all along. Doniphan is in possession of Chi.[huahua]; the battle was not a severe one lasting only about 30 minutes, and not more than seven to fourteen killed on either side; but it is true in regard to our friend Owens, who was appointed Lieut. Col. of a company formed of the wagoners, and was in the front of the battle; he was shot with two rifle balls one through the head the other through the breast, each of them mortal wounds, and a canon ball broke both legs about the knees; he was interred with military honours in Chi.[huahua] and has left a name behind not soon to fade from the annals of our country; but what does that name profit him now? has it brought him a crown in Heaven, has it won him a seat at his Savior's feet? if not, it may be that name has ruined him.

Sunday 14th. Succorro [Socorro]. We left El Passo this A. M., about 11 o'ck. and after a ride of six hours, jolting over saquias [*acequias*—ditches] till I scarcely knew myself, and stoping under a big tree to lunch, we arrived at this little village south of the Pass, here we remain tonight.

Wednesday 17th. Once more at camp, after remain-

ing two days at the Presidio where we went to from
Succorro on Monday, at the house of Montiz, the
agent or superintendent to the business of our friend
Don Ygnacio Rouquia. I can't like very much this
plan of stoping at houses while we are travelling
through the settlements. I am better satisfied in my
tent; there is more ease, more comfort, more independence, tho' our host and hostess exerted themselves
no doubt to the fullest extent of their power, and we
were contented with all, still the luxuries of this little
home surpass the whole. I was sick from the time we
got there till we left and for my part, had the cooking
been ever so exquisite all would have been alike to me;
but my poor *querido* [darling], I am sure he gained
no more flesh from eating onions, dried meat, cold
beans, and tortillas. I often thought of some of the
nicely prepared dishes we had at the Cura's.

Thursday 18th. We have made a long drive today,
and crossed a branch of the River, quite a bold little
stream, camped tonight on the bank of it, first burning off the tall grass, as this windy March weather in-
sures no safety in case of a fire, and tho' the Rio is near
twould take a N. Y. fire co. to save us from being
burned to death.

Monday 22. Ojo [Spring]. We are just through an
other *jornada.* Saturday evening we started into it,
travelled all that night nearly; stoped near daylight,
rested some two hours, took a little sleep, and started
again, travelled till noon, stoped a few hours, and
then drove on till mid-night, rested till day—and
started again, and now at noon we have made the first
water, a mean little spring out in the level plain; the

water is *black,* and standing, the animals are sent off
some three miles to a *laguna* where they get fresh
water. Here we shall remain tonight, and I hope I
shall have something more to do in the sleeping line,
than I've had these last two nights past. . . . I wonder
where Don Santiago (the Frenchman) is, that he is
not up with us today. I fear he with his three little
wagons one [may] have gotten into some difficulty,
yesterday when our wagons stoped in the road a few
minutes and detained him that long, as he was behind,
he concluded "he travel well, he go ahead wid his
teams"; since he does not "go ahead" I fear for him.

Tuesday 23rd. This morning we have passed a perfect curiosity, a *spring in the top of a hill;* which occupies I think an acre of ground; the spring itself is some
six feet wide, the water clear, rather warm and runs
off down the side of the hill loosing itself in the sand
at its foot. And again this P. M. we visited a warm
spring on an other elevation; the sand boils in it all
over bursting in one place and then an other, and re-
quiring I should think immense fource; as yet no bottom has been found to it; the water is perfectly clear
some eighteen inches in depth, when the sand is met
with, it is in constant motion below as far as the clear
water will admit of a sight. Of the two springs this
to me is the most curious; one is a cold spring *in the
top of a high sand-hill,* the other a *boiling spring,* both
of them curiosities to any one.

Wednesday 24th. Carazal. Or rather on the sequia
[*acequia*—canal] of Carazal, some three quarters of
a mile from the village; the water is perfectly *clear
lime-stone water,* the first I have seen since we left

Santa Fé, *six months,* and in truth, its pure, sweet taste so astonished me on tasting it, I really stoped to see if I were drinking water, or something else.—I have often heard and read of odd curiosities met with in travels and of curiosities in the form of men composing companies, but there can be none more curious than a few individuals in ours. First on the list I believe stands John the Dutchman—or as he is called by his companions in service *"Dutch";* his *length* and *bredth* are as near the same as some writers describe as being *equal,* i.e. he is about five feet five inches in height, with shoulders something more than two feet, he suits well for an ox driver with his gees and "wo dares"; he is generally silent, but when he does speak, it is all the most perfectly earnest, dry and in *Dutch English.*—Patrick the Irishman is quaint enough, making one laugh at all his witty sayings which by the way are not a few. He loves his *"drap"* now and then much to the annoyance of his employer the Dctr.; these two with Don Santiago, who by the way is quite angry with "Mr. *Uite,* because he swap me two bad hoxen for my good hox, one of de hoxen he give me I have to leave him in de road and dat is charging me $18. for my good hoxen. I will remember Mr. Uite."

Thursday 25. Ojo Caliente [Hot spring]. Left Caresel this A. M. about 10 o'clock arrived here (twelve miles) by 3 o'k P. M., here we shall visit a day or two, prior to starting into the *last jornada.*

The *"Ojo Caliente"* is a pretty place; the water bursts out at the foot of a hill making a beautiful pool, which is some four or five feet deep, perfectly clear, and warm; it runs off into a beautiful and long stream;

it is the regular and last camping spot before entering an other *jornada* of 50 miles.

Monday 29th. Guyllego spring. A most beautiful spot indeed, well may one rejoice at passing that last long *jornada,* for they not only leave it behind them forever perhaps—but they exchange it for one of nature's "beauty spots." The spring which takes its name from a place in old Spain, (whether a spring or cave I know not) is at the foot of an exceeding high mountain, so steep and rocky it looks wholly impassable for man; on either side are similar ones, steep, rugged and perpendicular; the spring resembles a cave, though a very small one, the water is rather warm, runs off in a brisk little branch, forming a small pool one hundred yards from the spring; from this first pool it runs off some 100 and twenty to fifty yards, forming two others rather larger than the first; for a quarter of a mile before reaching the spring, are green trees and bushes, all of which are new to me; one resembles the box elder of the U. S., and one the ash, of which they must be species.

Wednesday 31. Salt Lake. We made our travel for today, last night leaving the Guyllego spring at 2 o'clock yesterday P. M. we made this water twenty five or thirty miles, at two drives, by 1 o'clock last night. Here we find *Don Santiago* who came ahead of us on Monday. I suppose he still think he go very well, as he *believe* he go ahead in de morning. We are getting into the neighborhood of Chihuahua, having passed some two or three ranchos. The lake we are encamped on is some ten miles in length, situated on the right side of the road. Well the *Dctr. has left us,* gone on to report himself not yet *dead or lost,* but only remaining behind till all the battles are fought. I shant say for what—I suppose he himself knows.

Thursday 1st April 1847. Today we are encamped on a little stream seperating us from the little village of Ynsenias [Encinillas], the place where Mr. Gregg had his little difficulty with Gov. Trius [Trias], in regard to beef cattle he unceremoniously took, here a similar occurrance has taken place with us, without any law suits however; two beeves were shot down yesterday by our half-starved camp, while they were at work skining &c. the owner made his appearance and demanded his pay, which was promptly done—$12. in goods each, and he disappeared rather better satisfied than his excellency the Governor is represented to have been. Our travels now are made altogether after night on account of the heat. Though it is not very agreeable to me, as my head and stomach are somewhat delicate of late. I came to travel and therefore take it patiently, as a custom of the road.

Saltillo May 23rd 1847. I have been so negligent of late I scarcely know how to begin my journal again. Since the 1st of April has been a long time, many things have transpired, and we have travelled a long distance. I cannot now go into full detail but will merely give a brief sketch. We arrived at Chihuahua on the 4th April; here we found Col. Doniphan's command occupying the city, and a beautiful sight they have made of it in some respects. Instead of seeing it in its original beauty as I thought to have done twelve months since, I saw it filled with Missouri volunteers who though good to fight are not careful at all

how much they soil the property of a friend much
less an enemy. The good citizens of Chi. had never
dreamed I dare say that their loved homes would be
turned into quarters for common soldiers, their fine
houses many of them turned into stables, the rooves
made kitchens of, their public *pila* [drinking foun-
tain] used as a bathing trough, the fine trees of their
beautiful *alamador* [*alameda*—public walk] barked
and forever spoiled, and a hundred other deprivations
equal to any of these, but yet all has been done; Chihuahua was quite an indifferent looking place when
I saw it. We took a comfortable house a square off
from the plaza, as none could be had in it, and spent
three weeks in it as pleasantly as we could under the
circumstances; the families all had left, so I of course
saw none of them. I only made the acquaintance of
two gentlemen only, Don José Cordero and Don
Pedro Olivares, two of the first in the place and friends
of my husband's. The latter is a very affable man, intelligent, has visited the U. S. and speaks some English; we often had hearty laughs, he and I. He always
spoke to me in English and I to him in Spanish and
I think I learned quite as much in the few conversa-
tions I had with him, as I have with any one person in
a much longer time. The family of Mr. Potts[92] an

[92] John Potts, an Englishman, was acting English consul at
Chihuahua, and president of the Mining Company and Mint.
When Colonel David D. Mitchell arrived in Chihuahua he was
directed to make search of all the principal houses for contraband
of war. On March 4, 1847, he reached the residence of Governor
Trias, who had deserted the city. Finding it locked he called for
the key. Mr. Potts came forward and stated that the governor

Englishman, and owner of the mint, I visited several times, dined with them once, supped twice, and rode with the Ladies, i.e. Mrs. P. and her sister Miss Meadows to see their summer retreat. They are quite lively, play on the harp and piano, and make the time of their visitors pass agreeably.

After a short stay, and on a very short notice, the troops having been ordered to join Gen. Taylor, or to return by this route home, we left there on the 28th April.[93]

And now for our travel down; I must first say I

had left the house and its contents in his charge, and that neither Colonel Mitchell nor anyone else should enter it. He contended that it was under the British flag, and any violation would be reported to his government. Colonel Mitchell replied that he must go in; and that he had a key which would open the door. He sent his sergeant for two howitzers, which he had referred to as the key, lit a match and was advancing, when the Englishman begged him not to fire, as his brother was in the house. He then surrendered the key to Colonel Mitchell. An examination of the house was made and nothing but private property was found, which was respected.

[93] On March 1, 1847, the Americans entered Chihuahua. Doniphan issued a proclamation based upon those previously issued by General Kearny, in which he announced that the United States by virtue of its conquest laid claim to the state of Chihuahua. General Wool not having coöperated with him, Doniphan was at a loss to know what to do. He sent a small body of men to General Wool asking to be allowed to join Taylor's army. On April 22 this detachment returned and shortly afterwards Doniphan with his whole force abandoned Chihuahua and started towards Saltillo. They reported to General Wool on May 22 and were reviewed by him near the field of Buena Vista. In his general orders General Wool highly complimented these Missourians. On May

trust fortune will never compell me to make the same
again. I thought I had done some very hard travelling
before and in truth I had, but, this has surpassed all.
We travelled regularly 20, 25, 30 and 35 miles a day,
for three successive weeks, resting but two days of
the time, and over the worst roads I ever saw in my
life. Many nights I have layed down not to sleep for
my bones ached too much for that, even had I had
the time, but to rest an hour or two prior to traveling
the remainder and greater portion of the night to get
a little ahead of the command; some times I slept not
above two hours out of the twenty-four. The dust
every day was almost suffocating; if we went a head
of all, we had no satisfaction in any thing, if we stoped
to rest a few moments, they crowded on too.

Saltillo, Mexico June 20th 1847. An alarm this
morning of the approach of the enemy, one or two
piquets cut off. Gen. Wool has ordered the citizens to
form a company, to assemble on the hill above the city,
at the fireing of a cannon, for its defense; he himself
has taken severel pieces of cannon from the fortification, to his encampment, there to act from circumstances, to be governed by the movements of the foe.
Our fources are small not more than 2000 and probably only 1,500, while those of the enemy are reported
14,000, nine to one. I've heard of wars and rumours of
wars and have been as I thought almost in them, but
this is nearer than ever—I presume long ere this an

27 they reported to General Taylor at Monterey. From there they
proceeded by way of Matamoras and New Orleans to St. Louis,
reaching home about the first of July, 1847, after an absence of
thirteen months.

express has been despatched to Gen Taylor at Monteray, and in a little time reinfourcements must be here. 'twill take a day to go there, and one and a half to come, so we ought to have assistance by Tuesday morning. The enemy are on what is called Pelomas road from San Luis Potosi.

6 o'clock P. M. Cpt Howard[94] has just stoped a minute at the street window and gives us the latest. One of the piquets reported to have been taken has returned, the other not yet heard of. Dr. Johnson the Gen's interpretor out from town some five or six miles was attacked by a small party of he thinks regular cavalry and wounded in the arm, and a book in his cap only saved his skull from being cleaved the cap and one back of the book having been cut in its place. Scouting parties have been sent out in all directions, well mounted and prepared to retreat if necessary. Cpt H is just starting himself with a few dragoons to learn something of the enemy . . . Maj. Washington[95] I see is active in moving some of the artillery

[94] John Eager Howard was born in Maryland. He was commissioned captain of a company of infantry February 23, 1847, and brevetted major September 13, 1847, for gallant and meritorious conduct in the battle of Chapultepec, Mexico. Major Howard was honorably discharged August 25, 1848. He died in 1862.

[95] John M. Washington was a native of Virginia and a graduate of West Point. He was appointed October 24, 1814, and assigned to artillery July 17, 1817; served in Florida War 1836-1838, and with General Wool's column in war with Mexico, as major. Washington commanded a battery at Buena Vista and was promoted for gallantry in that engagement. He was acting governor of Saltillo, Mexico, June 24 to December 14, 1847;

to a more advantageous situation than he has probably
occupied. . . . I am really tired—we have counted
and baled up all the money in the house, ready to send
it to a safer place in case of necessity. All the pistols
and guns have been cleaned and loaded. I shall say I
had a hand in this too. Dr. [James] Hewitson has
been down and very kindly invited us to go to his
house in the plaza, which perhaps not more safe than
our own, will be rather more cheerful if there can be
anything cheerful in such times. I've thrown a few
things into my trunk in case of a retreat.

9 o'clock—still nothing positive, the streets are
quiet, a strong patrol is moving thro' all parts of the
city, some three or four hundred of the N. C. volunteers from Monterey will be in by 11 o'clock as the
express to meet them reports them but a little distance
off, and marching. I think I'll now retire, to rest an
attack is expected by some, tho' all is quiet now, to
morrows sun may tell another story for Saltillo.

Monday 21st. The sun rises as bright as ever this
morning, and brings us no news of troops being very
near; this after all, I believe is going to be what Cpt.
Donaldson calls a stampede, I hope so. *Mi querido*
[my darling], since he sees no danger yet, has ventured to tell me what I did not know last night. An at-

chief of artillery of General Wool's division March 12 to December 9, 1847, and of the army of occupation December 9 to
May 30, 1848. Was civil and military governor of New Mexico
October, 1848, to October, 1849. On December 24, 1853, he was
washed overboard during a violent storm and drowned, with a
number of the troops, while traveling to California. Of one
hundred and eighty soldiers and four officers only two survived.

tack was certainly expected, he had made the arrangements with Cpt. Donaldson[96] to attach himself to his
company after having taken me to the safest point
nearest the redoubt on the hill, he was too sad all last
evening to speak scarcely and no wonder, when all
dear to him in the world might be ere long left in a
stranger land with out a protector and heart broken.
The reflection that the next day might put an end to
his existance and this must then be the consequence,
or even if he should survive to be left penniless with
more than himself to feel its effects, (tho' God knows
this would have been cheerfully bourn by me) either
were enough to dround even the feeling of any one
more especially of one who has the soul to feel as he
has. I was alarmed and sad enough to think of the
danger we must be in in any house, that Wm who
attached himself to the company of citizens might
be killed, that numbers of my countrymen must perish
and perhaps all of us cut off by the over whelming
number of the enemy, tis well I knew nothing of my
husbands thoughts or designs. I am only thankful
now that none of the latter were fourced into execu-
tion, and that we are still safe; as we hear from San
Luis potosi direct this morning and no one from there

[96] James Lowry Donaldson was appointed to the United States
Military Academy from Maryland, his native state, on September
1, 1832. He was sent from there into the 3d Artillery July 1,
1836, and after successive promotions was made major, February
23, 1847, for gallantry in battle of Buena Vista. On March 13,
1865, he was made a major-general, on account of meritorious
service in war between the states. He resigned January 1, 1874,
and died November 4, 1885.

is coming. Tis said that a letter has been intercepted by Gen Taylor's spies, from Gen Urea[97] to the wealthy Sanchez of this place telling him to be ready on the 20th (yesterday) with his rancheros, that he himself would be here that day with 6000 men to sack the city. Those seen yesterday & the day before might have been his spies but he knowing of his failure in his express has kept himself at a propper distance.

Friday 25th A company of Virginians has just past out to Buena Vista. Tis sad to see them really, and my heart ached as I looked on so many manly forms and fearless faces, who have left homes and friends many of them destined never to return; all looked determined and eager. I particularly marked one of them a youth of apparently eighteen years; his face was pale, young and innocent; he moved with a step worthy of riper years; his musket was bourn on his right side clasped firmly by his left hand, on the finger of which I observed a ring, placed there perhaps by a fond and only sister—or it may be the pledge of the maiden of his youthful heart, whose love

[97] General José Urrea distinguished himself in the Texan-Mexican War by capturing a small force of Texans under the command of Captain King, March 11, 1835. Two days later General Urrea captured the entire force of Colonel Ward, a Texan, consisting of 112 men; he also captured Colonel Fannin, another Texan, and all his men. In 1839 Urrea headed a revolution against President Anastacio Bustamante, and had the audacity to undertake, surreptitiously, the capture and apprehension of Bustamante by surprising the guard at the presidential mansion and entering the president's sleeping apartment. Bustamante was attacked and arrested before he could realize what was happening. (Benjamin M. Read, of Santa Fé, New Mexico.)

he now wishes to make himself more worthy of by some brave deed—

Friday, July 2nd Wrote a long letter to Mama this evening. I do wish I could have a letter from home; how lonely it is, week after week & month after month, and I hear nothing more than if I never belonged to their numbers. 'twould indeed give new energy to my being to hear from them, quite a new creature I should feel but as it is I am perfectly isolated.

Sunday, July 4th The second one passed from home and out of the U. S. tho' in quite a different way from the last, and in a much more agreeable one. I wish they (the officers) had defered the celebration til the 5th, they would have shown more stamina of character in observing the Sabbath religiously, and establishing the customs of the U. S. here, instead of following the example of this people in making it a feasting day.

Gen Kearny I am sure would have defered it, and by his own example have taught others the propriety of remembering the Sabbath to keep it holy. Gen. Wool had a grand review of his command at Buena Vista in the morning. To avoid complying with an invitation to dine with the officers we accepted one to dine at Dctr Hewitsons with his family only. We had a variety of dishes all served in Mexican style, vegetable, beef, fowl, a nicely stuffed and roasted *cabrita* [kid]—and a good dessert, the recipes for making which I must get of Mrs. H. after dinner which lasted an hour, in true Mexican *modo* we were shewn into a nice bed-room with an invite to a siesta; at 5 oclock we came home, with a promise to return after tea to see

the rockets to be thrown up in the public square—
Here we met with several gentlemen—one Cpt Webster[98] who tells us that Maj. Hunter[99] the quartermaster at Monterey has written to him when we intend leaving for the U. S. that he wishes to place Mrs.
H, who was bold enough to follow her husband to the
wars, under the Magoffins protection, she has seen

[98] Lucian B. Webster was born in the state of Vermont and
appointed to United States Military Academy, August 28, 1819.
From there he went into the artillery, and after several promotions became captain of the 1st Artillery September 30, 1836. He
was engaged in the battles of Monterey and Buena Vista. Brevetted major September 23, 1846, for gallant and meritorious
conduct in the several conflicts at Monterey, and lieutenant-
colonel February 23, 1847, for gallant conduct in the battle of
Buena Vista. He was made major of the 4th Artillery August 3,
1852, and on November 4, 1853, died at Fort Brown, Texas, aged
fifty-two years.

[99] David Hunter was appointed to West Point, September 14,
1818, from the District of Columbia, where he was born. From
there he went into the infantry July 1, 1822. He served on the
frontier from 1823 to 1835 and resigned July 4, 1836. On March
14, 1842, he was reappointed with rank of major on the staff of
the paymaster. He was chief paymaster of General Wool's
column on his march through Mexico in 1846, and of the army of
occupation 1847-1848; was colonel of 6th Cavalry May 14, 1861,
and was wounded in the battle of Bull Run, Virginia, on July
21, 1861; soon afterwards was made major-general of volunteers.
Brevetted major-general in the regular army March 13, 1865,
for gallant service in war between the states. He served on the
military commission for trial of alleged conspirators in the
assassination of President Lincoln, May 9 to July 6, 1865. He
retired July 31, 1866, being over sixty-two years of age, and
died February 2, 1886.

quite enough of the elephant,[100] and is now anxious to
return to the U. S. The Cpt speaks of her as a lady
with whom I can enjoy myself. dear knows I am glad
to hear of a *lady* again, an American, with whom I
can sit & converse freely, and about things that each
of us are acquainted with. An other individual at the
dctrs, was an Irishman named I cant say what, for
I cant recollect it—but he is worthy of a remark, having as he says been in every place, is one day a British
subject, the next a Louisiana Irishman, and many
other changes, he is as gray as ever man can be, and
tho' he says himself that he is only 45, I'll venture to
say he'll never see sixty again. he is an incessant talker,
and tells of his leaving Erin when a mere boy, of his
having lived many years in Kingston Jamaica, a long
time & dozens of other places, and is climated every-
where. his age tho' is the worst point with him as he
wishes to get married, and as he must know too well
that his looks speak nothing in favour of his youth, he
makes his tongue do the business, and broaches it on
all occasions he is not a little tormented either by his
countryman the Dctr who invariable gives him a rub.

Friday 9th Cpt Prentice[101] called with Cpt. or

[100] "I've seen the elephant." When a man is disappointed in
anything he undertakes, when he has seen enough, when he gets
sick and tired of any job he may have set himself about, he has
"seen the elephant." (Kendall, vol. 1, p. 109.)

[101] James H. Prentiss was born in Massachusetts, and appointed to the United States Military Academy July 1, 1826,
from the state of Indiana. He served in the Florida war against
the Seminole Indians as first lieutenant and aide-de-camp to
General Eustis, being in the skirmish of Okihumphy Swamp
March 30, 1836. During the Mexican War he was assistant ad-

Lieut. Rucker,[102] to hear our final decision in regard to leaving for Monterey, as the only hinderance (the wagons) was made known to him, they may possibly be disposed of thro' his instrumentality to government. I long to see the day when they are sold, now for the last fourteen months I've seen and heard more of wagons than in all my life before.

Friday 16th This P. M. with Mrs Hewitson in my carriage with myself, the *Dctr* and *mi alma* on horse back, we rode to the cotton factory of the former gent. situated six miles South of Saltillo; the road some times rough but pleasant and tis many days since I enjoyed a ride so much, after being shut up in town

jutant-general under General Wool on the march through Chihuahua, September 12 to December, 1846, and later in command of a battery of heavy artillery. After the war Lieutenant Prentiss was on frontier duty at Fort Polk, Texas, where he died September 22, 1848, aged thirty-nine years.

[102] Daniel Henry Rucker was born in Belleville, New Jersey, April 28, 1812. He entered the army from Michigan as second lieutenant of 1st Dragoons October, 1837, served in Michigan and against the Indians in the West and Southwest, and was promoted to captain February 7, 1847. In the war with Mexico he commanded a squadron at the battle of Buena Vista, and was brevetted major February 23, 1847, for gallant and meritorious conduct in that battle. He was commissioned major quartermaster August 3, 1861, and by further promotions reached the grade of brigadier-general of volunteers May 23, 1863. He was mustered out of volunteer service, and afterwards, July 18, 1866, was commissioned colonel and assistant quartermaster-general of the regular army, and brigadier-general February 13, 1882, retiring February 23, 1882. For diligent and meritorious service during the Civil War he was brevetted major-general of the United States Army and United States Volunteers.

for so long a time, the pure country air was truely delightful, and made me wish to be again travelling. Well we went through the Dctrs factory from the lowest to the uppermost room; tis by no means on a small scale. From this we proceeded to the village church, which like all others in the country, is adorned with a goodly number of saints, both figures and paintings all of which are time worn and indifferent looking; the alter is entirely gilded and has rather a glittering appearance; we found it dressed over with fresh flowers, the patron saint of the place is represented by a small wax figure inclosed within a glass door above the alter, around the sides of which are hung many small paintings, emblematic of our Saviors and the apostles lives. After visiting these places we went to see Mrs Bently an American woman, and wife of the mayor domo of the establishment, a plain good woman, from New Jersey. She gave us a cup of coffee with some nice light-bread and butter truely American, after a hearty repast we returned to town, arriving sometime after 7 o'clock.

Saturday 17th There is some talk of an other stampede report says that Cpt Rucker's company of dragoon scouts has been cut off by 3000 Mex., and a picket guard comes in in haste to the General saying they had seen some 3000 Mexicanos, but all except a few were without arms. I think they must have seen a flock of goats. a Mexican reports himself to gov. Washington, saying tis the intention of his countrymen here to rise and cut off the Americans, but I since the last stampede have grown too incredulous to any of the reports I hear.

Wednesday 21st Dctr and *Mrs* Hewitson came around about 4 o'clock this P. M. to take us, according to a promise, to see the church, which is pronounced a facsimile of all the churches of Mexico. The interior is truely magnificent and to describe it minutely requires the pen of a Kendall[103] or a Prentiss.[104] The form is a sala with two wings as it were each of which has in it an altar to different saints; over one of them is hung a large oil painting some eighteen or twenty ft square; it represents purgatory, and the Virgin Mary descending from Heaven attended by

[103] George Wilkins Kendall, journalist, was born in Amherst (now Mount Vernon), New Hampshire, August 22, 1809; died in Oak Spring, near Bowie, Texas, October 22, 1867. He went to New Orleans in 1835 and two years later established there, with Francis A. Lumsden, the *Picayune.* In 1841, partly from love of adventure and partly for his health, he joined an ill-fated Santa Fé trading expedition, was taken prisoner and carried to the city of Mexico, but was released after seven months of captivity. During the war with Mexico he accompanied the United States forces under General Taylor, and later under General Scott, and by means of pony expresses and steamers supplied his paper with the latest news. He published *Narrative of the Texan Santa Fé Expedition* and *The War between the United States and Mexico.* On his tombstone are the words: "Poet, journalist, author, farmer—eminent in all; clear head, stout heart, a man of many friends, best beloved by those who knew him best."

[104] George Denison Prentice, journalist, author, and humorist, was born in Preston, Connecticut, December 18, 1802; died at Louisville, Kentucky, January 22, 1870. He was editor of *Connecticut Mirror* in 1825, and in 1828 became editor of *New England Weekly Review,* in which he published many of his poems. Two years later he was editor of the *Louisville Journal.* Mr. Prentice wrote a campaign biography of Henry Clay.

many angels, with the infant Jesus in her arms, and calling the saints through him to asscend from their transient abode to a home of happiness.—The principal altar is truely magnificent, reaching almost to the ceiling which is some   in height; it is four immense pillows [pillars] against the wall, two of them on either side of the throne of the patron saint of the church, which is inclosed in a glass case decked with artificial flowers; on each side of the saint and between the pillows are some half doz statues representing different saints, the altar is a solid mass of gilt which glitters by daylight, and with the church lit up with those immense candles, it must be a dazzling sight.—To describe all the altars in the church would be too much, so I'll leave off with these two and say a few words in regard to the chapel adjoining the church and from whense a door opens to it, solely for the worship of Christ. The chapel is not large neither is the altar so much ornamented save with flowers, as the large one in the church, it is magnificent tho' and if anything richer than the other. The center of it is covered with a curtain and on sight contrasts strangely with the rich trimming of the altar, it was raised (by our attendant—a little boy) in a moment by means of a pully, and opened to our view an image of Christ crucified as large as life, made of a highly polished wood, and inclosed in a large glass case gilted and decked with flowers, it looks so like a human figure I shuddered as I looked upon it: his accusation is written above on a plate of solid gold, some ten or twelve inches by six. When we had looked at it for some time, the little boy lowered the curtain with deep respect—shutting the sacred image from our view.

From the Church we went to the convent now occupied as an arsenal by our troops; the officers took us through the different apartments and pointed out all the ammunition stores, cannon balls, grape, canister, &c, showed us their guns; then took us to see the church of Saint Antonio; it resembles the large church in the square, tho' not on so large a scale. In the meantime the evening parade in the convent yard commenced, we left the church to see it, and at its close retired to the *Dctrs* where we rested ourself after a long and to me very fatiguing walk, refreshed ourselves with a cup of Doña Josefa's nice chocolate and returned home at 7¾ oclock.

Friday 23rd Took Doña Josefa out riding this P. M. in my carriage, the Dctr and Mr. M. on horseback, rode through the *alameda,* the Pueblo, and other precinct of the city called ———— Twas a cool and refreshing ride, the trees loaded with fruit at the Pueblo contrasted well with the tall shady poplars of the *alameda.*

Monday 26th This world is filled with trials and woes. God sends all tho', and dare we murmer even if they are hard? worse ones may come upon us. We receive intelligence this evening of the assassination of brother James, it comes so straight we can scarcely doubt its truth. An English gentleman just arrived from Guanajuata brings it, as received by a Spaniard of his acquaintance at Aguas Calientes, in a letter from Chi.[huahua] where our brother arrived from Durango about the 20th ult., the statement is that he

was murdered in his own house by some person who
had a previous difficulty with him. *Mi almi* is incon-
solable, nothing I believe could affect him more. He
heard the rumor at 9½ O'clock A. M. and tho' it
made him feel miserable enough, the severest blow was
not yet given; late this evening I heard the straited
account. After a long hesitation I summoned courage
to tell him, and may the like task never devolve upon
me again. At the words "I fear there's no hope," his
pent up feeling burst forth in one groan, followed by
tears. How my heart aches to write it, but it aches far
more to see the agony of *mi alma*. Dctr. Hewitson has
been down and offered all the consolation he could;
he can feel for him for he knows well the attachment
that years of a life together in a foreign land has
wrought between the two brothers: though he endeavoured to cheer him with the probability of its
falsity as being the news of Mexicans mostly, he told
me at the door that from what Mr. Meeds tells him it
comes too straight to hope. Oh, that I could see one
little ray, one beam to cling to. *Mi alma's* grief poured
forth in deepest sighs will undo me; tonight is one of
misery to him.

Tuesday 27th. How hard it is to deceive my husband
but the Dctr. charges me by the love I bear him, to
tell him nothing of the news of tonight, at least a part
of it, the better half he knows, and his drooping spirits
raised a little. A Mr. Chapman from Parras, to which
place all news flies quickly, has heard nothing of it;
this the doctor told my dear, and I hope he feels something easier in mind, that is a relief to me, though I am
intrusted with the secret of its confirmation by an

Irishman in Mr. Meed's employ who talked with the express man from Chi. and hears from his own lip that *he had seen my brother's body,* that he was murdered in his own bedroom just before daylight, but on what day Mr. Kelly did not ask him.

To tell him I cannot, the Dctr. warns me not, and yet I know he must hear it ere long. But I'll wait; the news must come and the way may be easier than I can contrive.

August 1847.

Sunday 1st. My gratification is better conceived than written, at receiving a letter this A. M. from sister Letty after a silence so long that I had concluded myself no longer thought of by the dearest of friends, and to hear too that all are well, no deaths save that of Aunts McDowell and Taylor each of whom we have every reason to believe has made the brightest exchange, that of sickness, earthly sufferings temptations &c. for peace and never ending happiness, we can better envy than bewail them. The marriage of several cousins and births of a few more children, among the no. sister Anna has an *Isaac Shelby*—mean thing for taking the name from me, she might have waited a few months longer. I do think a woman *em beraso* [*embarazada*—pregnant] has a hard time of it, some sickness all the time, heart-burn, head-ache, cramp etc. after all this thing of marrying is not what it is cracked up to be.

Sunday 8th. A letter from Papa today all well, and since Letty's, answered it immediately.

Friday 14th. We had quite a fright last night from

I suppose intended house breakers, as we are left entirely to suspicion, and this morning tells us that some gents. of the same calling were caught a few doors from ours while complimenting the family. About 12 O'clock we were aroused by foot steps on the roof of our room, *mi alma* sprang to the window and I of course after him, and called out "who is that" both in English and Spanish, when the parties immediately ran to the front of the house answering in the latter tongue most confusedly "munchos Mexicano" [*muchos Mexicanos*—many Mexicans]' *"munchos ladrones"* [many robbers], and when called to for explanation no one knows what they said, 'twas so mysteriously confused, at the same time the light of a lantern was thrown into the patio. *Mi alma* now called to the sentinel at the quartermaster's door in front if he could see any one, and he responded two men. At this the rogues ran down the roof to the coral and disappeared, when we retired again.

Sunday 15th. No news from Chi.[huahua] till to-day when Mr. Spyres[105] received a letter, say[ing]

[105] Albert Speyers, whose name was spelled with many variations, was a merchant trader, for many years transporting goods by caravans to Santa Fé and other places in Mexico. He was a Prussian Jew and always carried with him both British and Prussian passports.

On the occasion previously mentioned, Speyers was carrying two wagon-loads of arms and ammunition for delivery in Mexico. This was denied by him and others, but subsequent events have proved conclusively that such was the fact. General Kearny got information on June 5, 1846, from George T. Howard, government agent and then on the Santa Fé Trail, that Speyers in partnership with Governor Armijo was carrying a large quantity

all has gone on well except the murder of Mr. Aull—
nothing is said of bro. James so we infer the news we
heard to be false. A few days must bring us some news.

Friday 20th. Received marching orders, for Monterey tomorrow 2 O'clock P. M., today at 12 O'clock
scarcely giving me time to turn around. Gen. Cushing[106] is going down and as it is probably the strongest

of arms and ammunition, and that two companies of Mexican
dragoons were marching from Santa Fé to meet and escort the
ammunition in safety. He also got word from Captain Waldo that
Armijo was getting a large shipment of goods into Mexico.
Kearny therefore ordered Captain Benjamin Moore with a
squadron of dragoons to pursue Speyers and detain him. Captain
Moore was unable to overtake him. Speyers was traveling forty-
five miles per day, but he afterwards claimed that his haste was
not due to the fact that he carried ammunition. He said he wanted
to get a certificate from the custom house at Santa Fé before the
United States should take possession of it.

Speyers was dispossessed, forcibly, of most or all of the arms
and ammunition by the Mexicans. He went to Chihuahua and
made complaint to Governor Trias, saying to him that he had
come to present "a claim on the Government of Mexico for arms
forcibly seized, in payment of which I only have a bond."
Speyers left Independence in the middle of May and arrived at
Chihuahua in September, shortly after Kearny took possession
of Santa Fé. He proceeded from there into the interior without
molestation from the authorities and sold his goods at a handsome profit.

On March 21, 1848, Speyers arrived at New Orleans and
proceeded from there to Europe to purchase goods for the
Mexican market. He finally quit the Mexican trade, probably
sojourning for awhile in Kansas City, Missouri, and then went
to New York. There he became involved in a Wall Street crash
and committed suicide.

[106] General Caleb Cushing, born in Salisbury, Massachusetts,

escort for some time, we embrace it, bidding farewell to Saltillo with few regrets on my part, for tho' not going immediately home my situation not admiting of a sea voyage for three or four months yet, we shall be

January 17, 1800, was educated at Harvard University and graduated with honors in 1817. Later he studied law and practiced in his native town until 1825, when he was elected representative in the lower house of Massachusetts as a Whig. He was elected again in 1833, and in 1834 was elected to the United States Congress, continuing in that office until 1843, when President Tyler sent him to China. There he made the first treaty between that country and the United States. Returning to the United States he was elected again to Congress. In January, 1847, he raised a regiment of volunteers, equipped them at his own expense, and was commissioned colonel. Subsequently he was promoted to brigadier-general. He joined General Taylor during the summer, but was afterwards ordered to Vera Cruz. He was honorably discharged July 20, 1848.

Soon after his discharge from the army General Cushing was nominated by the Democratic party of his state for governor, but failed in the election. From 1850 to 1852 he was again a member of the legislature of his state, and at the expiration of his term appointed associate justice of the Supreme Court of Massachusetts. In 1853 President Pierce appointed him United States attorney-general. At the close of 1860 he was sent to Charleston by President Buchanan as confidential commissioner to the Secessionists of South Carolina, and in 1866 he was appointed one of three commissioners to revise and codify the laws of Congress. In 1873 he was nominated for office of chief justice of the United States, but the nomination was subsequently withdrawn. A year later he was appointed minister to Spain. General Cushing wrote a number of books, among which was a life of President William H. Harrison. He died at Newburyport, Massachusetts, January 2, 1879. (Appleton's *Cyclopædia of American Biography,* vol. 2, p. 38.)

so much nearer, letters can be received twice as often. I shall meet at Monterey a female companion in Mrs. Hunter wife of Maj. H. paymaster there, she is spoken of by officers here, as a fine companion and 'twill be a feast to see one of my countrywomen again. I've done all the packing this P. M. and no little is it, and tonight I am sick and weary. Mrs. Hewitson called to bid me good bye—gave her a little hair pin as a memorial of me, and she this afternoon sent me a beautifully worked napkin, along with some delicacy for the road.

Wrote to Mama Magoffin this morning, but shall have to carry the letter myself till I meet with a mail, whether at Monterey or Matamoras, to which place we shall probably go immediately.

Wrote a long letter to brother James, who we now know positively to be safe in Chi. a letter from Mr. Belden[107] of Durango to Mr. Chapman of Parras giving us the wished for intelligence, he, Mr. B. having received a letter from him some ten days since in which he speaks of our supposed departure for the U. S. as his reason for not having written.

Monterey August 23rd. Arrived here last night after two days of the roughest ride I ever had. Yesterday in particular was almost insupportably rough for a carriage yet notwithstanding through necessity

[107] John Belden went to Mexico from the city of New York. He was successful in business and had accumulated a large fortune. Either to please himself, or the Mexicans, he often wore costly diamond jewels, and hence he was called the "Prince of Diamonds." (Gilliam, *Travels in Mexico during the Years 1843 and 1844,* p. 215.)

as William was riding my horse, I stood it out nearly the entire day, having my husband to hold me as steady as could be under the circumstances, or otherwise I could not have reached here without some accident. But dear me what a dreadfully warm place this is. Saltillo certainly has the advantage in climate. Cloaths are almost insupportable.

Mrs. Hunter called soon after breakfast, being quite as anxious to see a "white woman" as I am. She is tall, good looking about thirty years of age, and affable in her manners. We are to spend this evening with her, and as we are beginning quite well, I think we'll be sociable. *Mi alma,* with Cpt. Thompson[108] who came down with us called on Gen. Taylor at his encampment "Walnut Grove" near town.

Tuesday 24th. Mrs. Hunter called tonight, (I have been unable to fulfill an engagement to ride this P. M. from great soreness) sat some time. We dine with her tomorrow. Gen. Cushing and Cpt. Thompson called.

[108] Philip R. Thompson was born in Georgia, and appointed from that state to the United States Military Academy July 1, 1830. By successive promotions he reached the rank of captain of the 1st Dragoons, June 30, 1846. He was engaged in the battles of Brazito and Sacramento, and was acting inspector-general of General Wool's column on its march through Chihuahua, May to October, 1847; brevetted major February 26, 1847, for gallant and meritorious conduct in the battle of Sacramento. Major Thompson served in New Mexico and Indian campaigns 1851-1855. He was cashiered September 4, 1855, for disrespect to a court-martial, and after his dismissal became adjutant-general with the rank of captain of a filibustering expedition to Nicaragua, February 11, 1856, to May 1, 1857. He died June 24, 1857, in the Gulf of Mexico, aged forty-five years. (Cullum, *Biographical Register,* vol. 1, p. 481.)

Wednesday 25th. Well we've lost no time today. I can well say that two women meeting after an entire sepperation of twelve months from female society, are certainly a curiosity. We talked *all* the morning till dinner, and after eating, on account of the great heat, in part, and *to be alone* leaving the gents, one Cpt. Ramsey[109] beside our husbands, to take care of themselves, we undressed ourselves and layed down for a couple of hours, loosing not a minute of the time for our tongues were as incessantly in motion as the bell clappers in Mexico, telling of our adventures in travel, anxiety to reach home, the wishes of our friends &c &c. We stayed to tea, and came home after 9 O'clock, having made an engagement to ride out to the General's tomorrow evening.

By the way I had almost forgotten to say that the wonder of all present wonders, the American Lyon or "emphant" has called on me today In the old general I am agreeably disappointed; from the cognomen

[109] George Douglas Ramsey was born in Dumfries, Virginia, February 21, 1802; entered the United States Military Academy from the District of Columbia, August 20, 1816; served in the artillery, topographical and ordnance departments, from 1820 to 1835. During the military occupation of Texas, 1845-1846, was ordnance officer at Corpus Christi and Point Isabel. Took part in the battle of Monterey, September 21-23, 1846, and was brevetted major for gallantry in that battle. He was chief of ordnance of the army commanded by General Taylor; major of ordnance April 22, 1860; lieutenant-colonel August 3, 1861, and brigadier-general and chief of ordnance of the United States Army September 15, 1863. Retired from active service September 12, 1864. Brevetted major-general March 13, 1865, for long and faithful services. Died in Washington, D. C., May 23, 1882.

he has received—"rough and ready,"[110] I had not thought to find him possessed of so mild manners, such apparent high regard for female character; he is very talkative, agreeable and quite polite, tho' plain and entirely unassuming.

He wore his uniform which I am told is *no common custom* with him, and I should think so from the number of wrinkles in it, the work of many weeks packing. I am told the honour is worth remembering. His aid-de-camp Maj. Bliss[111] called with him, a placid coun-

[110] Mrs. Magoffin's comment on General Taylor's personal appearance suggests the reason for his sobriquet. Because of indifference to his personal appearance, and his blunt readiness for meeting any emergency, his troops in the Mexican War dubbed General Taylor "Rough and Ready."

Much against his judgment and inclination, he became a candidate on the Whig ticket for president. In protesting against his nomination, the general remarked that he was a plain, simple soldier, bred to the profession of arms, knowing nothing of the intricacies of statecraft, and he distrusted his fitness for high civic position. He was elected in 1848, and, notwithstanding his modest depreciation of himself, his administration began well, and with the promise of successful continuation. General Taylor served as president of the United States for only sixteen months, dying in the White House July 9, 1850.

[111] William Wallace Smith Bliss was born in August, 1815, at Whitehall, New York. He was graduated from the United States Military Academy in 1833, and served in the campaign against the Cherokees in 1834. He was a professor at the Academy for six years, chief of staff in the Florida War, and served against the western Indians. During the Mexican War he was conspicuous for gallant conduct in the battles of Palo Alto, Resaca de la Palma, and Buena Vista. He acted as adjutant to General Taylor during his campaign in Mexico. After General Taylor was inaugurated president, Colonel Bliss became his private secretary.

tenance he has, talks little, forehead very high or rather bald.

Thursday 26th Returned the General's call this afternoon: he has a beautiful camping spot four miles from town on the Matamoras road, in a thick grove of trees. The old gentleman was very glad to see us, talked a great deal, handed cake and champagne, and proved himself exceedingly hospitable. His tent is caracteristic of the man, very plain and small his sleeping apartments, but just in front a little seperated from it is a large awning affording a pleasant shade and is termed the *"drawing-room."* The general was dressed in his famed old gray sack coat, striped cotton trowsers blue calico neck-kerchief. With all this I am most agreeably disappointed in him. Most of the wild stories I've heard of him I now believe false and instead of the uncouth back-woodsman I expected to have seen I find him polite, affable and altogether agreeable.

Friday 27th. This evening we road out to see the famous "black-fort."[112] It has been thoroughly re-

After the death of the President he became adjutant-general of the western division of the army, with headquarters at New Orleans. On December 5, 1848, he married Miss Mary Elizabeth, daughter of General Zachary Taylor. Colonel Bliss died in East Pascagoula, Mississippi, August 5, 1853. He was affectionately nicknamed "Perfect Bliss."

[112] Was called "Black Fort" because the Mexican Black Flag floated over the fort during the battle of Monterey. It was a large rectangular fortress, known as the citadel, and covered nearly three acres of ground, with four bastion fronts, surrounded by a work of solid masonry and supplied with heavy guns. At the time of General Taylor's attack it was not finished. After-

paired by the Americans and I consequently see it to best advantage. Within the parripet wall 2000 men may be stationed, the castle stands in the center, and within this is the magazine built entirely by the Americans. Around the outside wall is a deep and wide trench making it impossible for the enemy to scale the wall if but a small force be within it. The whole is in fine order for a siege, with wells of water, abundance of amunition, and the provisions that can be taken there from the store-houses in town, they will be well fixed. . . . We also drove to Aristas garden at the out-skirts of town the south side, a celebrated place tho' not half as much improved as the *gardens* in the U. S., that have been but one year in making. In two large, deep baths, one on either side, it has a luxury resembling the more antique nations.

Saturday 28th Road around to see the fortifications of the Mexicans in the siege of this place. Many of them remain perfect, tho' most have been removed. A number of houses on the W. side of the city where all the hard fighting was done, are perforated with cannon balls, while the walls outside are covered with marks of smaller arms. The spots where Col. Mitchell[113] and Majr Barbour[114] were killed were

wards it was completed by the General's order and rendered almost impregnable. When Monterey surrendered, after three days of desperate fighting and the loss of many Americans, the Black Fort was evacuated by the Mexicans. This occurred September 25, 1846.

[113] Alexander M. Mitchell, born in North Carolina, was appointed a cadet to the United States Military Academy July 1, 1830. After his graduation he served in the garrisons at Baton Rouge and New Orleans, and took part in the Florida war

pointed out to me. The bishops Palace, which was
taken by Gen. Worth[115] is distinctly visible on a high

against the Seminole Indians. He resigned from the army March
25, 1837; was civil engineer in the service of the United States
1837-1838; chief engineer of Milwaukee and Rock River Canal
1838, and of the territory of Wisconsin 1839-1840. Served in
the war with Mexico as colonel of the 1st Ohio Volunteers. In
the battle of Monterey he was severely wounded. Recovering from
his wounds he served as military governor of Monterey from
April to June, 1847. After the war he practiced law for a time at
Cincinnati, Ohio, and in 1849 was appointed United States
marshal of the Territory of Minnesota. He died at St. Joseph,
Missouri, February 28, 1861. (Cullum, *Biographical Register of
U. S. Military Academy*, vol. 1, p. 480.)

[114] Philip Nordbourne Barbour was born near Bardstown,
Kentucky, April 14, 1813, the son of Colonel Philip Barbour.
He was graduated at West Point in June, 1834, and from that
time on until his death, he was engaged in constant and dangerous
service. He was killed September 21, 1846, in one of the streets
of Monterey while leading his company on to battle in the very
thickest of the fight. Major Barbour was brevetted captain for
active and highly meritorious service in the war against the
Florida Indians; and major, May 9, 1846, for gallant and distinguished service in the battles of Palo Alto and Resaca de la
Palma.

[115] General William Jenkins Worth, born in Hudson, New
York, March 1, 1794, died in San Antonio, Texas, May 17, 1849.
He was of Quaker ancestry and of a family that produced many
well-known men. After receiving only a common school education he went to work in a store until he was eighteen. On the
opening of the second war with Great Britain he applied for a
commission in the army, and was appointed first lieutenant. He
was aide to General Winfield Scott, and distinguished himself in
battle, rising to the rank of major. At the close of the war he was
appointed superintendent of the United States Military Academy.
In 1838 he became colonel of the 8th Infantry, and was active in

hill to the South. It resembles an old delapidated church for which I took it.

Sunday 29th Remained at home all day. At night Cptns Thompson, Lynard,[116] and Ramsey called, the latter I've met several times at Maj. Hunters, and he has also called here before. Cpt. T. is an old Chi.[huahua] acquaintance, but Cptn Lynard of the topographical engineers I've not met before.

Tuesday 31st The Gen. invited us out today to see his light artillery under Maj. Bragg[117] reviewed. I

the Florida War. He was second in command to General Taylor at the beginning of the war with Mexico, and subsequently joined General Scott. He was a handsome, manly fellow of generous nature; a good horseman and possessed of many talents. A monument was erected to his memory by the city of New York at the junction of Broadway and Fifth Avenue.

[116] Thomas B. Linnard was appointed from Pennsylvania, his native state, to United States Military Academy on July 1, 1825; assigned to artillery July 1, 1830. He was engaged in the Florida war against the Seminole Indians. He was promoted for gallantry September 30, 1836, marched through Chihuahua 1846-1847, and took part in the battle of Buena Vista, February 22-23, 1847. He was brevetted major for gallantry in this battle. Later, 1849-1851, he took part in the construction of iron lighthouses on Carysfort Reef and Sand Key, Florida. He died at the age of forty in Philadelphia, April 24, 1851.

[117] Braxton Bragg, born in Warren County, North Carolina, March 22, 1817, entered United States Military Academy July 1, 1833, and served in the Seminole War. On May 9, 1846, he was brevetted captain for gallant and distinguished conduct in the defense of Fort Brown, Texas; and major, September 23, 1846, for gallant and meritorious conduct in the battle of Buena Vista. After the battle of Buena Vista two attempts were made to assassinate Major Bragg. He resigned from the army January 3, 1856, and became an extensive planter in Louisiana. On the

was pleased with their manueverings which are both expeditious and beautiful. The Maj. is called a great disiplinarian drilling his men twice a day much to their dissatisfaction, they a few nights since placed a shell with a slow match, intending to kill him, but fortunately tho' it exploded about 11 O'clock shattering the roof of his tent, his trunk, part of his cott and even piercing the bed-cloathing, *he was unhurt*. Tonight I'm in the packing business again. We leave tomorrow for Matamoras. Col. Wright[118] in command of 500 Mass volunteers for Gen. Scotts column is our escort.

Wednesday, Seaptr 1st 1847. The hour for starting was set for 6 O'clock this morning, but as is too often in the first days start no attention was payed to orders,

secession of Louisiana, he was made a brigadier-general in the Confederate Army, and was the first commander of the military forces of Louisiana. He commanded the right wing of the Army of the Mississippi at Shiloh, and was made general after the death of Albert Sidney Johnston. He succeeded General Beauregard as commander of the Army of the Tenneseee. Later he was given control of the Confederate Army's military operations at Richmond. After the war he was state engineer of Alabama, and died in Galveston, Texas, September 27, 1876.

[118] George Wright was born in Vermont in the year 1803, and as a cadet from that state graduated from the United States Military Academy. He served in the 3d Infantry, and as captain thereof took part in the war against the Florida Indians. For meritorious conduct in that war he was brevetted major March 15, 1842. He took part in the war with Mexico, and in the battle of Molino del Rey was wounded while leading a storming party. For gallant conduct in this battle he was brevetted colonel. He served in California and Washington from 1852 to 1860, and was appointed to command the Department of Oregon July 5, 1860. From September 28, 1861, to July 1, 1864, he was in command

and the troop did not leave town till noon; we sent our baggage-wagon with them to the first night's camp four miles from town. We ourselves lunched at home, and went to Maj. Hunter's about 3½ o'clock P. M. and sat with them an hour and more. They rode out with us (she in the carriage with me) as far as Gen. Taylor's camp and there bid us good bye. I am disappointed that she does not go on with us; but still I hope to see her in Matamoras before Nov. next.

The General with his blue twill trousers, old brown coat, and broad brimed sombrero Mexicano came out to meet us, and twould be wrong to doubt the sincerity of his hearty welcome. He called his horse and conducted us through his entire encampment to ours near by. There he dismounted and sat half an hour with us before our tent door; talked about Grandpapa who was his intimate friend and of Uncles James and Thomas[119] whom he knows; he bade us good bye each with hearty shake of the hand and wished for our safe arrival at home.

Sunday 5th Cirelvo [Cerralvo]. Till now I've done

of the Department of the Pacific, with the rank of brigadier-general, United States Volunteers. On July 30, 1865, at the age of sixty-two years, he was drowned, in the wreck of the steamer *Jonathan,* while on his way to take charge of the Department of the Columbia. (Appleton, *Cyclopædia of American Biography,* vol. 6, p. 622.)

[119] James Shelby, son of Governor Isaac Shelby, born 1784, married Mary Pindell. He was a major in the War of 1812, and later brigadier-general of the Kentucky State Militia. He died in 1848.

Thomas Hart Shelby, also a son of Governor Shelby, born May 27, 1789, died February 14, 1869.

nothing but travel, every morning up by 1 o'clock and on the road by 3 o'clock jolting over stumps, stones and ditches, half asleep, expecting an attack from Mexicans constantly. In one place we passed the *bones* of murdered countrymen, remains of burned wagons, all destroyed by Mexicans. The second night out we found none but brackish water, and sent off some three miles to the burned town of Marine for a barrel of well water. At this place I made a *comadre* of an old woman witch, who brought eggs and bread down to the encampment to sell; she stoped at our tent door, she looked up at me, and said, "take me with you to your country," "why," said I. *"le guerro V. los Americans"* [You are at war with the Americans]? She neither answered yes or no, but gave me a sharp pinch on my cheek, I suppose to see if the flesh and colour of it were natural—and said *"na guerro este"* [there is no war]. The pinch did not feel very comfortable, but I could but laugh at her cunning reply.

Mier, Wednesday 8th. Such a place this is! The seat of so many country-men's wrongs, the most miserable hole imaginable; impossible to get a house we are stowed away in a room with a family of men, women and children. The town is in confusion. Last night a band of robbers entered, shot down a sentinel, rode through the plaza, hitched up and drove off five wagons loaded with merchandise belonging to a Frenchman who says "he go and publish one reward." A runner comes in this evening from the party of forty dragoons sent in pursuit of them by Col. Belknap[120]

[120] William Goldsmith Belknap, a native of Newburgh, New York, entered the army as third lieutenant of 23d Infantry, April

saying that they have come upon the thieves, some hundred in number *dividing out the spoils and only twelve or fifteen miles from town,* have had a fight, killed fifteen of the enemy, retaken the goods with all the Mexican equipage, guns, blankets, saddles, &c., and all without any loss on our side; they are returning to town . . . Col. Belknap, the commanding officer here has been very kind to send us dinner and supper, for the sleeping we must ourselves provide, and we have done so, our bed is here on the sala floor, two or three beds in the room are filled with the inmates, our trunks piled up serving as a screen between us and they. William and Capt. Thompson have their bed along with the servants and some visitors or boarders, in the San Juan or the *front passage to this room,* there is no door shut between us, and it is all as *common as one room,* and if I ever have the pleasure of seeing Mrs. Thompson that may be, I shall make her laugh with the scenes of this night.—We have said good bye to land travel and tomorrow shall take a steamboat for Comargo [Camargo].

5, 1813, and served throughout the War of 1812. Remaining in the army he was promoted to captain of 3d Infantry, February 1, 1822. Brevetted major February 1, 1832, for ten years' faithful service in one grade; lieutenant-colonel, March 15, 1842, for general good conduct in the war against Florida Indians; colonel, May 9, 1846, for gallant and distinguished services at the battles of Palo Alto and Resaca de la Palma, Texas, and brigadier-general, February 23, 1847, for gallant and meritorious conduct in the battle of Buena Vista, Mexico. General Belknap died November 10, 1851.

APPENDIX

APPENDIX

WAR DEPARTMENT,

Washington, June 18, 1846.

Sir:—

AT the request of the President I commend to your favorable consideration the bearer hereof, Colonel James W. Magoffin. Mr. M. is now and has been for some years a resident of Chihuahua and extensively engaged in trade in that and other settlements of Mexico. He is well acquainted with the people of Chihuahua, Santa Fe and intermediate country. He was introduced to the President by Col. Benton as a gentleman of intelligence and most respectable character. The President has had several interviews with him and is favorably impressed with his character, intelligence and disposition to the cause of the United States. His knowledge of the country and the people is such as induces the President to believe he may render important services to you in regard to your military movements in New Mexico. He will leave here for Santa Fe immediately and will probably overtake you before you arrive at that place. Considering his intelligence, his credit with the people and his business capacity, it is believed he will give important information and make arrangements to furnish your troops with abundant supplies in New Mexico. Should you apprehend difficulties of this nature it is recommended to you to avail yourself in this respect and others of his services for which he will as a matter of course be entitled to a fair consideration.

Very respectfully,

Your obt. serv.

(*Signed*) W. L. MARCY,
SECRETARY OF WAR.

Colonel S. W. Kearny.

Philadelphia, February 21, 1849.

To J. W. MAGOFFIN, ESQ.,

Dear Sir:

IF the following statement of such of your important services as came to my personal knowledge during the invasion of New Mexico can serve to elucidate your sacrifices and risks during the war, it gives me pleasure to make it.

I shall not easily forget the pleasure which your company gave me when I preceded the army with a flag, from Bent's Fort to Santa Fe, nor the advantages of your knowledge of the country and its language.

I am strongly impressed with the skill you exhibited not to compromise your old influence over the Mexican General, by an *appearance* of your real connexion with myself (even furnishing an interpreter, rather than appear on the official occasion). At night, however, you accompanied Genl. Armijo to my quarters when, by your aid, we had a secret conference. I then understood the Mexican Governor's real disinclination to actual resistance, to which, I believe, according to your instructions, you gave important encouragement particularly in neutralizing the contrary influence of the young Colonel Archuletta, by suggesting to his ambition the part *of* bringing about a pronunciamento of Western New Mexico in favor of *annexation;* (Genl. Kearny's first proclamation claiming only to the Rio Grande).

I had personal knowledge of the high opinion which the General [Kearny] entertained of your discretion and services; and, that it may well be considered a piece of good fortune, that at the expense of a large bribe, you were suffered to destroy the General's own statement of them only shows how narrowly you escaped with your life, in your further efforts to serve our Government in Chihuahua.

> With high respect, sir, I remain,
>
> Your ob. Servant,
>
> > (*Signed*) P. St. George Cooke,
> > Major 2 Drags.

BIBLIOGRAPHY

BIBLIOGRAPHY

MANUSCRIPTS, BOOKS AND NEWSPAPERS CONSULTED IN THE PREPARATION OF THIS VOLUME

MANUSCRIPTS

BROADHEAD COLLECTION: Santa Fé Papers.

DONIPHAN, ALEXANDER W.: Collection of Letters and Papers.

DRESCHER, WILLIAM B.: Mexican War Recollections.

EDWARDS, MARCELLIN B.: Journal of an Expedition to New Mexico and the Southern Provinces, conducted first by Gen. S. W. Kearny, afterwards by Col. A. W. Doniphan in 1846-1847.

FERGUSON, PHILIP C.: Diary of a Soldier in the Mexican War.

KEARNY, STEPHEN WATTS: Letterbook of the Mexican War.

KRIBBEN, CHRISTIAN: Letters of . . . on the Mexican War.

MILLER, ROBERT: Papers of . . . relating to the Mexican War.

WALDO, DR. DAVID: Letters and papers of Dr. Waldo and the Waldo Family.

All of the above manuscript collections in the Missouri Historical Society, St. Louis, Missouri.

BOOKS AND PERIODICALS

ABERT, J. W.: Journal of Lieutenant J. W. Abert from Bent's Fort to St. Louis in 1845. [Washington, 1846.] 29th Cong. 1st Sess. Senate Doc. 438.

Report of Lieut. J. W. Abert of his examination of New Mexico, in the Years 1846-1847. 30th Cong. 1st Sess. House Ex. Doc. 41.

ALCARUS, RAMON: The Other Side or Notes from the History of the War between Mexico and the United States. (Albert C. Ramsey ed.) N. Y., 1850.

Appleton's Cyclopedia of American Biography. 6 vols. N. Y., 1888.

BIBLIOGRAPHY

AUBRY, FELIX X.: Aubry's Journey from California to New Mexico. In *Western Journal and Civilian*, St. Louis, 1853, v. 11: 84.

BANCROFT, HUBERT HOWE: History of the Life of William Gilpin. San Francisco, 1889.

History of Arizona and New Mexico. San Francisco, 1888.

History of Mexico. 6 vols. San Francisco, 1884.

North Mexican States and Texas. 2 vols. San Francisco, 1889.

BENTON, THOMAS HART: Thirty Years' View. 2 vols. N. Y., 1854.

BIEBER, RALPH P.: Papers of James J. Webb, Santa Fe Merchant 1844-1861. In *Washington University Studies*, Humanistic Series, v. 11: 255-305.

Some Aspects of the Santa Fe Trail. In *Chronicles of Oklahoma*, v. 2: 1-8.

BLEDSOE, A. J.: Indian Wars of the Northwest. A California Sketch. San Francisco, 1885.

BRADLEY, GLENN D.: The Story of the Santa Fe. Boston, 1920.

Winning the Southwest; a Story of Conquest. Chicago, 1912.

BROOKS, NATHAN COVINGTON: a Complete History of the Mexican War. Phila., 1849.

BROWNE, JOHN ROSS: Adventures in the Apache Country. N. Y., 1869.

BRYANT, EDWIN: What I Saw in California. N. Y., 1848.

BUSHNELL, DAVID I., JR.: John Mix Stanley, artist-explorer. In *Smithsonian Report* for 1924. Washington, 1925.

CAMPION, J. S.: On the Frontier. London, 1878.

CARPENTER, WILLIAM W.: Travels and Adventures in Mexico. N. Y., 1851.

CHITTENDEN, HIRAM M.: The American Fur Trade of the Far West. 3 vols. N. Y., 1902.

CONARD, HOWARD L.: "Uncle Dick" Wootton, The Pioneer Frontiersman of the Rocky Mountain Region. Chicago, 1890.

CONNELLEY, WILLIAM E.: Doniphan's Expedition and the Conquest of New Mexico and California. Topeka, 1907.

Standard History of Kansas and Kansans. 5 vols. Chicago, 1918.

BIBLIOGRAPHY

COOKE, PHILIP ST. GEORGE: Conquest of New Mexico and California. N. Y., 1878.
Scenes and Adventures in the Army. Phila., 1857.

CULLUM, GEORGE W.: Biographical Register of the Officers and Graduates of the United States Military Academy at West Point. 3 vols. N. Y., 1868.

CUTTS, JAMES MADISON: The Conquest of California and New Mexico. Phila., 1847.

DAUGHTERS OF THE AMERICAN REVOLUTION. Kansas City Chapter: The Old Santa Fe Trail, the story of a great highway. [Kansas City, 1909.]

DAVIS, W. W. H.: El Gringo; or New Mexico and her people. N. Y., 1857.

DRANNAN, WILLIAM F.: Thirty-one years on the Plains and in the Mountains. Chicago, 1906.

EDWARDS, FRANK S.: A Campaign in New Mexico with Col. Doniphan. Phila., 1847.

EMORY, WILLIAM H.: Notes of a Military Reconnoissance from Fort Leavenworth in Missouri to San Diego in California. Washington, 1848.

FALCONER, THOMAS: Expedition to Santa Fe. An account of its Journey from Texas through Mexico. New Orleans, 1842.

FRÉMONT, JOHN C.: Report of the Exploring Expedition to the Rocky Mountains in the year 1842, and to Oregon and North California in the years 1843-1844. Washington, 1845.

GERRARD, LEWIS H.: Wah-To-Yah, and the Taos Trail. Cincinnati, 1850.

GILLIAM, ALBERT M.: Travels in Mexico during the years 1843 and 1844. Aberdeen, 1847.

GREGG, JOSIAH: Commerce of the Prairies. 2 vols. N. Y., 1844.

GREEN, THOMAS J.: Journal of the Texian Expedition against Mier. N. Y., 1845.

GREEN, CHARLES R.: . . . Along the Santa Fe Trail. Olathe, Kansas, 1912.

GREENE, JEREMIAH E.: The Santa Fe Trade: its route and character. Worcester, 1893.

271

BIBLIOGRAPHY

GRINNELL, GEORGE B.: Bent's Old Fort and its Builders. In *Kansas State Historical Society Collections*, v. 15: 28.

HAINES, HELEN: History of New Mexico. N. Y., 1891.

HARVEY, CHARLES M.: Story of the Santa Fe Trail. In *Atlantic Monthly*, v. CIV: 774.

HAYES, A. A.: New Colorado and the Santa Fe Trail. N. Y., 1880.

HEITMAN, FRANCIS: Historical Register and Dictionary of the United States Army. Washington, 1903.

HIGGINS, CHARLES A.: To California over the Santa Fe Trail. Chicago, 1902.

History of Caldwell and Livingston County, Missouri. St. Louis, 1886.

History of Clay and Platte Counties, Missouri. St. Louis, 1885.

History of Howard and Cooper Counties, Missouri. St. Louis, 1883.

History of Jackson County, Missouri. Kansas City, 1881.

HOBBS, JAMES: Wild Life in the Far West; Personal Adventures of a Border Mountain Man. Hartford, 1873.

HODGE, FREDERICK W.: Handbook of American Indians North of Mexico. 2 vols. 1907. Washington, 1907.

HUGHES, JOHN TAYLOR: Doniphan's Expedition. Cincinnati, 1848.

INMAN, HENRY: The Old Santa Fe Trail. N. Y., 1898.

The Great Salt Lake Trail. London, 1898.

JAMES, THOMAS: Three Years among the Indians and Mexicans (Walter B. Douglas edition). St. Louis, 1916.

JAY, WILLIAM: Review of the Causes and Consequences of the Mexican War. N. Y., 1849.

JOHNSTON, A. R.: Journal of . . . Santa Fe to California, 1846. 30th Cong. 1st Sess. Ex. Doc. 41.

KEARNY, STEPHEN W.: Report of a summer campaign to the Rocky Mountains, in 1845. 29th Cong. 1st Sess. Sen. Ex. Doc. 1.

KENDALL, GEORGE W.: Narrative of the Texan Santa Fe Expedition. 2 vols. N. Y., 1844.

LITTLE, J. A.: What I saw on the Old Santa Fe Trail. Indianapolis, [1904].

BIBLIOGRAPHY

LOWE, PERCIVAL GREEN: Five Years a Dragoon, and other Adventures on the Great Plains. Kansas City, 1906.

McELROY, ROBERT McN.: Winning of the Far West. N. Y., 1914.

MANSFIELD, EDWARD D.: The Mexican War. N. Y., 1848.

MANNING, WILLIAM R.: Early Diplomatic Relations between the United States and Mexico. Baltimore, 1906.

MARMADUKE, M. M.: Journal of the Santa Fe Trail. In *Missouri Historical Review*, v. 6: 1-10.

MARCY, RANDOLPH B.: Prairie Traveler. N. Y., 1859.

Thirty Years of Army Life on the Border. N. Y., 1866.

MELINE, JAMES F.: Two thousand miles on horseback. N. Y., 1872.

MILLS, W. W.: Forty years at El Paso, 1858-1898. [El Paso, 1901.]

Missouri-Santa Fe Trade. Republished from *Missouri Intelligencer*, September 3, 1822, and April 22, 1823. In *Missouri Historical Society Collections*, v. 2, part 10: 55-67.

MOREHOUSE, GEORGE P.: Santa Fe Trail; brief summary of the Santa Fe Trail through Kansas. [Topeka, 1912.]

NAPTON, W. N.: Over the Santa Fe Trail, 1857. Kansas City, 1905.

PAXTON, WILLIAM McC.: Annals of Platte County, Missouri. Kansas City, 1897.

POLK, JAMES K.: The Diary of James K. Polk during his presidency 1845 to 1849. Edited by Milo Milton Quaife. 4 vols. Chicago, 1910.

PORTER, VALENTINE M.: History of Battery "A" of St. Louis. In *Missouri Historical Society Collections*, v. 2, no. 4.

PRINCE, BRADFORD: A Concise History of New Mexico. Cedar Rapids, 1912.

Old Fort Marcy. Santa Fe, 1912.

QUISENBERRY, ANDERSON C.: History by illustration. General Taylor and the Mexican War. Frankfort, 1911.

READ, BENJAMIN M.: Illustrated History of New Mexico. Santa Fe, 1912.

REID, SAMUEL C.: Scouting Expeditions of McCulloch's Texas Rangers. Phila., 1847.

BIBLIOGRAPHY

RITCH, WILLIAM C.: Aztlan. Historical Resources and Attractions of New Mexico. Boston, 1885.

RIVES, GEORGE L.: The United States and Mexico, 1821-1848. 2 vols. N. Y., 1913.

ROBINSON, JACOB S.: Sketches of the Great West. A Journal of the Santa Fe Expedition under Doniphan. Portsmouth, 1848.

ROOT, FRANK A., and WILLIAM E. CONNELLEY: Overland Stage to California. Topeka, 1901.

RUXTON, GEORGE F.: Adventures in Mexico and the Rocky Mountains. N. Y., 1848.

Life in the Far West. Edinburgh, 1851.

RYUS, WILLIAM H.: The Second William Penn; a true account of Incidents that Happened along the Old Santa Fe Trail in the Sixties. Kansas City, 1913.

SABIN, EDWIN L.: Kit Carson Days, 1809-1868. Chicago, 1914.

SAGE, RUFUS B.: Scenes in the Rocky Mountains and in Oregon, California, New Mexico, Texas and the Grand Prairies. Phila., 1846.

Santa Fe and the Far West. In *Niles' Register,* December 4, 1841. v. 61: 209.

SCHARF, JOHN T.: History of St. Louis City and County. 2 vols. Phila., 1883.

SIBLEY, GEORGE C.: Route to Santa Fe, Council Grove, etc. In *Western Journal,* December, 1852, v. 5: 178.

SIMPSON, JAMES H.: Journal of a Military Reconnaissance from Santa Fe, New Mexico, to the Navajo Country, made with the Troops under Command of Brevet Lt. Col. John M. Washington. Phila., 1852.

SMITH, JUSTIN H.: The War with Mexico. 2 vols. N. Y., 1919.

SPALDING, CHARLES C.: Annals of the City of Kansas; embracing full Details of Trade and Commerce of the Great Western Plains. Kansas City, 1858.

STEPHENS, F. F.: Missouri and the Santa Fe Trade. In *Missouri Historical Review,* v. 10: 233; 11: 289.

STEVENS, WALTER B.: Centennial History of Missouri. 4 vols. St. Louis, 1921.

TAYLOR, ZACHARY: Letters of . . . from the battle-fields of the

BIBLIOGRAPHY

Mexican War. Reprinted from the Originals in the Collection of Mr. William K. Bixby. Rochester, 1908.

TWITCHELL, RALPH E.: Historical Sketch and Diary of Governor William Carr Lane. In *Historical Society of New Mexico,* Publication 4.

The History of the Military Occupation of New Mexico 1846-1851 by the Government of the United States. Denver, 1909.

The Leading Facts of New Mexican History. 2 vols. Cedar Rapids, 1911.

VERNON, J. S.: Along the Old Trail. Larned, Kansas, 1910.

WALDO, WILLIAM: Recollections of a septuagenarian. In *Missouri Historical Society Publications,* vol. 1, nos. 2 and 3.

[Westport Improvement Association.] Westport, 1812-1912. Commemorating the centennial of the Santa Fe Trail. Kansas City, 1912.

WETMORE, ALPHONSO: Diary of . . . In *Missouri Historical Review,* v. 8: 177.

WISLIZENUS, ADOLPHUS: Memoir of a Tour to New Mexico 1846 and 1847. Washington, 1848.

YOAKUM, HENDERSON: History of Texas. 2 vols. N. Y., 1856.

NEWSPAPERS

Boonville (Missouri) *Boonville Commercial Bulletin,* 1846-1848.

Brunswick (Mo.) *Brunswicker,* 1847-1849.

Fayette (Mo.) *Missouri Democrat,* 1846-1849.

Franklin (Mo.) *Missouri Intelligencer,* 1822-1824.

Glasgow (Mo.) *Glasgow News,* 1845-1847.

Independence (Mo.) *Independence Journal,* September 12-October 31, 1844.

Platte City (Mo.) *Platte Argus,* 1848-1849.

St. Charles (Mo.) *Missouri Patriot,* May 6, 1846-October 21, 1847.

St. Louis *Daily Missouri Republican,* 1845-1850.

St. Louis *Weekly Reveille,* 1845-1849.

Santa Fe (New Mexico) *Santa Fe Republican,* September 10, 1847, to April 2, 1848.

BIBLIOGRAPHY

Springfield (Mo.) *Springfield Advertiser,* July 11, 1848-1849.

Warsaw (Mo.) *Saturday Morning Visitor,* June 10, 1848-May, 1849.

Weston (Mo.) *Weston Journal* (continuation of *Independence Journal*), January 4 to April 19, 1845.

INDEX

ABREU, Santiago, Governor of New Mexico, 62 n.

Abreu, Doña Solidad, wife of Eugene Leitensdorfer, 62 n.

Agapita, Don, house of, 205.

Aguas Calientes, Mexico, 243.

Aguardiente, process of making, 89 n.

Albuquerque, N. M., 152.

Albo, Doña Josefita, 213.

Allen and Hickman, partners at Fayette and Boonville, Mo., 58 n.

Ampudia, Gen. Pedro, sketch of, 170 n.

Apache Indians, rob James Magoffin, 151; murder James White and party, 199 n; drive off cattle, 201.

Apache Pass, the approach to Santa Fé, 184 n, 188, 189 n.

Appleton's *Cyclopedia of American Biography,* quoted, 83 n, 248, 258.

"Arcadia," birthplace of Susan Shelby Magoffin, xxi.

Archuleta, Col. Diego, influenced by Magoffin, xiii; organizes revolt, xiii; intended to defend Santa Fé, xv; heads revolution, 184; sketch of, 184 n; arrest and escape of, 189.

Archuleta, Jean Andres, father of Col. Archuleta, 184 n.

Arkansas River, camp on, 37, 39.

Armijo, A. J., Santa Fé trader, 5 n.

Armijo, J. C., Santa Fé trader, 5 n.

Armijo, Gen. Manuel, influenced by Magoffin, xii; strength of troops, xiii; Mexicans unfriendly to, xiv; abandons defense of Santa Fé, xv; James Magoffin negotiates with, 84, 264; flees to Chihuahua, 96; sketch of, 96 n; called a coward, 109; mentioned, 115, 159; threats against, 185 n; wounded by Apache, 202; partner of Albert Speyers, 246 n.

Armijo, Rafael, Santa Fé trader, 5 n; store of, 152.

Armijo, Santiago, leader of revolution, 192.

Arapaho Indians, visit Fort Bent, 67.

Arrow Rock Creek, 36.

Ash Creek, accident at, 41; referred to, 86.

Atkinson, Chilton, acknowledgment to, xxv.

Aubrey, F. X., attacked by Apache Indians, 199 n.

takes citizens as hostages, 207; report capture of, 213; impresses traders, 221 n; comment on Col. Owen's death, 221 n; in possession of Chihuahua, 223, 228; seeks to join Taylor, 230 n.

Doniphan, Joseph, father of Col. Doniphan, 122 n.

Dunn, Isaac, furnished escort by War Department, 199 n.

Durango, Mexican forces reported leaving, 220; James Magoffin removed to prison at, 214.

EDWARDS, Gov. John C., of Missouri, 121 n.

Edwards, Marcellus, quoted, 182 n.

El Paso Public Library, acknowledgment to, xxv.

El Paso del Norte, Mexico, taken by Doniphan, 182; artillery arrives at, 185.

El Paso, Texas, James Magoffin pioneer of, xix.

Emory, Lieut. William H., 136 n; locates site of Fort Marcy, 139 n.

Encinillas, Mexico, 228.

FISHBACK, Rev. James, husband of Susanna Shelby, 167 n.

Fitzhugh, ——, mentioned, 5.

Fort Bent, see Bent's Fort.

Fort Bliss, Texas, location of, xx.

Fort Marcy, described, 139 n.

Fort McKenzie, built by Col. Mitchell, 174 n.

Fort William, known as Bent's Fort, 59 n.

Fray Cristobal, New Mexico, 195.

Frémont, Col. Charles, court-martial of, 125 n, 144 n; appointed governor of California, 155 n.

Frijoles, popular Mexican dish, 157 n.

GAMACHE, Euphrosine, mother of Leitensdorfer brothers, 62 n.

Garcia, Señora, calls on Mrs. Magoffin, 209.

Gespar, Don, mentioned, 137.

Gibson, George R., diary quoted, 217 n.

Gilliam, Albert M., quoted, 249 n.

Gilmer, Lieut. Jeremy Francis, designs Fort Marcy, 139 n; sketch of, 141 n; attends ball at Santa Fé, 144.

Gilpin, Maj. William, sketch of, 175 n; his command reported imprisoned, 177; not at the Pass, 178.

Glasgow, Edward J., 50; sketch of, 51 n; partner of Dr. Connelly, 105 n; calls

INDEX

THE YALE PAPERBOUNDS

Printed in the United States
3802